Clinical Faces of Childhood

VOLUME ONE

The Oppositional Child
The Inhibited Child
The Depressed Child

Edited by
E. James Anthony, M.D.
and
Doris C. Gilpin, M.D.

JASON ARONSON INC.
Northvale, New Jersey
London

THE MASTER WORK SERIES

First softcover edition 1994

Library of Congress Cataloging-in-Publication Data

ISBN: 1-56821-334-4
Library of Congress Catalog Card Number: 94-72350

Manufactured in the United States of America. Jason Aronson Inc. offers books and cassettes. For information and catalog write to Jason Aronson Inc., 230 Livingston Street, Northvale, New Jersey 07647.

To Meg,

My Newest Love

Contributors

E. JAMES ANTHONY, M.D.
Blanche F. Ittleson Professor
of Child Psychiatry
Director, William Greenleaf Eliot Division of Child Psychiatry
Director, Edison Child Development
Research Center
Washington University School of Medicine
St. Louis, Missouri

JAMES P. COMER, M.D.
Department of Psychiatry
Yale University School of Medicine
New Haven, Connecticut

DORIS C. GILPIN, M.D.
Division of Child Psychiatry
Child Guidance Clinic
Washington University School of Medicine
St. Louis, Missouri

CARL P. MALMQUIST, M.D.
Departments of Law and Criminal
Justice and Child Development
University of Minnesota
Minneapolis, Minnesota

PAMELA FINEMAN MALTZ, M.S.W.
South Shore Mental Health Clinic
Boston, Massachusetts

ARTHUR MANDELBAUM, M.S.W.
Discipline of Social Work
Menninger School of Psychiatry
Topeka, Kansas

PETER B. NEUBAUER, M.D.
Director, Child Development Center
Department of Child Psychoanalysis
Downstate Medical Center
New York

FRITZ REDL, M.D.
Department of Behavioral Sciences
Wayne State University
Detroit, Michigan

JUDITH SCHECHTMAN, M.S.W., A.C.S.W.
Child Guidance Clinic
Division of Child Psychiatry
Washington University School of Medicine
St. Louis, Missouri

ALBERT J. SOLNIT, M.D.
Departments of Pediatrics and Psychiatry
Director, Child Study Center
Yale University School of Medicine
New Haven, Connecticut

JULIEN WORLAND, Ph.D.
Child Guidance Clinic
Department of Medical Psychology
Washington University School of Medicine
St. Louis, Missouri

Preface

At the Washington University Child Guidance Clinic in St. Louis, a weekly exploratory seminar has been held for a year on each of the three topics considered in this volume. The format of these seminars remained fairly constant: they involved a variety of disciplines, each addings its quota to the growth of knowledge, a search through the literature for relevant references, a study of past clinic cases, and a sharing of experiences. We are deeply indebted to all the participants for their contributions to these meetings.

Once a year, during these three years, the Clinic has organized a two-day workshop (with emphasis very much on work in small groups) devoted to one of the main topics investigated during the year: oppositional behavior, inhibition, and depression. Distinguished guest speakers from different parts of the country who had specialized in the particular subjects were invited to present their views and respond to questions raised in the workshop groups. The workshops proved so successful that, at the enthusiastic request of those who attended, it was decided to publish the proceedings as a contribution to clinical practice.

We wish to acknowledge, with gratitude, the considerable help that we have received with the preparation of the manuscript. Dr. Jay Worland assisted with the analysis of the data, Miss Darcy Gilpin with the preparation of the graphs and Miss Carol Cordes, Mrs. Margot Thiebauth, and Mrs. Sally Clayburgh with the typing and retyping of the manuscript.

E. JAMES ANTHONY, M.D.
DORIS C GILPIN, M.D.

Contents

PART III: *THE DEPRESSED CHILD*

PART I: *The Oppositional Child*

CHAPTER 1

The Genesis of Oppositional Behavior

E. JAMES ANTHONY, M.D.

A little rebellion now and then is a good thing.

Thomas Jefferson, 1787.

From the outset, it should be stated that oppositional attitudes and behavior are distributed normally through the general population and occur at all stages of the life cycle. Under certain conditions and with certain provocations, they may reach abnormal or clinical proportions. It is therefore important, when discussing the phenomenon of opposition to define the term carefully and not to infer pathology whenever it makes its appearance. There is a need to say "no" when the development of individuation demands it and a need to say "no" when the occasion requires it. The same can be said of "yes" when a similar lesson must be learned.

In certain individuals, during the toddler phase of life, there is a growing wish owing to circumstances not only to say "no" but to say it more loudly, emphatically, aggressively and, at times, even tempestuously. Prior to the work of several developmental psychologists, it was assumed that children were born stiff-necked from the womb and this may indeed be so since neonates already seem to be in possession of given characteristics that differentiate them from one another and lay the groundwork of their future personalities, but the contributions from the human environment have also to be considered. To obtain some balance in perspective, both innate and transactional factors must be taken into account. When this is done, the act of opposition emerges as the very quintessence of life itself and as present from the beginning.

In his monumental work, Spitz came to the conclusion that "no" behavior was "beyond a doubt the most spectacular intellectual and semantic achievement in early childhood" and tremendous gain in autonomy. As a result of this first negativism, the child became gradually aware of the separateness of his self from the rest of the world. Spitz pointed out that the capacity to say "no" antedates the capacity to say "yes" by several months so that developmentally opposition preceded acquiescence. According to Spitz, these basic responses were built into the neurophysiological system in which rotation of the neck was achieved before flexion. The motor aspect of "no" originated in the earliest nursing situation when the head was turned away from the nipple to avoid drinking. From nine to twelve months, the child acquired his first understanding of prohibitions expressed by the adult verbally and gesturally and between fifteen and eighteen months, he made use of a head-shaking type of refusal. In all these situations, not only did the child imitate the adult but the adult enforced the mechanisms by imitating the child. In the second year of life, the child passed from the "no" gesture to the "no" word after a transitional period when he would say "no" and shake his head as well while, at the same time, reaching for offered objects. Also in this second year, the child begins to use "no" towards himself in playing the role of the mother in mother-child situations.

It is easy to observe that the utterance of "no" has a far greater impact on the child's early environment than has "yes" which is altogether less intrusive and less of a problem for the caretaker. Because it develops earlier and apparently has more of an influence, "no" has been credited with having a greater influence on personality development. In developmental studies, a well defined phase of negativism in the toddler has long been recognized but there is no equivalent "yes" phase. The child apparently needs acquiescence far less to affirm his autonomy.

This balance of "yes" and "no" represents a very delicate equilibrium between pleasure and reality, independence and conformity, and omnipotence and impotence and allows for the emergence of the self as a self-reliant, self-confident and self-controlled entity.

During latency, "yes" and "no" decisions are for the most part shelved or go underground and the child at this stage is inclined to accept, quite uncritically, the image of himself and of the world around him projected by adults. The built-in humiliation of being a child, as Erikson puts it, makes him see himself as small, unreliable, incompetent and ignorant. He is quite unable to believe that his "yes" and "no" carry any weight upon the universe. At adolescence, however, he once again meets the world head-on as he challenges the adult in a reactivation of the toddler's negativism.[1] Even then, the disturbance of balance is not usually of clinical intensity.

However, the equilibrium can be seriously upset so that opposition is either absent or predominant. In the first case, the consequences for the child's development may be grave and he may develop autism, pathological passivity, identity confusion or an "as-if" personality. When the growth of opposition is hypertrophied, the clinical outcome may take the form of passive-aggression, rebelliousness, antisocial behavior and delinquency.

The Power Struggle

When the imbalance reaches a pathological level, a fierce power struggle emerges in both overt and covert forms. The opposition may be even greater when passively expressed than when active. The conflict may become intense and disruptive. The areas of opposition are often chosen uncannily by the child in relation to the weaknesses and sensitivities of the adults who seek to control him and he tests them out constantly through a wide strategy of manipulations. The parents may not even recognize the fact that they are being manipulated, so artfully is the oppositional child able to work. The parents in turn oppose the child for righteous reasons: they want him to become someone who conforms to the codes of society and lives his life within the social and emotional range permitted in the family. They see it as their God-given right to curb the child's omnipotence and unlimited need for gratification and bring him into line with the expectations of the environment. In the hands of normal parents, the institution of control can be tactfully managed but with authoritarian personalities where power is a lust in itself, the susceptabilities of the smaller personalities can be frequently overlooked.

As a matter of everyday experience, it takes two to produce oppositional behavior and this is particularily true of the clinical situation, where in association with the oppositional child there is invariably an oppositional parent and beyond him an oppositional society to back up the oppositional parent. These three protagonists—child, parent, and society as represented by school or juvenile court—may work together to set up a vicious cycle of opposition that increasingly consolidates the oppositional behavior of the child and makes it more intractable. Here the phenomenon is an aspect of an authoritarian system that holds sway at all levels of home, family, school, community and society. To relieve the situation and to reduce its potential for pathology, one requires the services of an "incorruptable intervener," that is, who is not easily seduced by power. He enters the system as counselor, psychiatrist, clergyman or physician and helps to generate a new type of undemanding, uncompelling mode of interaction.

Looking at the individual again, the oppositional tendency may show itself at one time as undue rebelliousness and at another as abject conformity, which are two sides of the same coin. The following variations on the oppositional theme may make their appearance:

1. Rebelliousness or passive aggression
2. Opposition restricted to a single phase of development or multiphasic
3. Opposition confined to some focal issue or diffusely characterological in form
4. The child's opposition within the family to parental patterns of dominance and submission

The child guidance clinical subculture is strikingly matriarchal with power and control, at least as seen from the child's point of view, being located mainly in the mother. The identification of the oppositional child is with this more powerful parent since she is the figure to be reckoned with in the nursery. The clinic father is generally passive, peripheral and impotent, again as seen from the child's viewpoint. Identification with the aggressor is frequently the mechanism at work in the difficult child who may be passive-aggressive within the maternal orbit but fiercely oppositional elsewhere. There is a popular European notion that American children, in comparison with obedient European ones, are obnoxiously negativistic and defiant and treat adults as peers. Europeans feel that American parents have allowed democracy to invade the nursery where, according to them, it should have no place. With parental authority being thus abrogated, the children become unmanageable. It is believed, furthermore, that American parents are actually afraid of the oppositional monsters that they create and are preoccupied with pacifying them, indulging them or abandoning them to baby-sitters whenever possible. It is not therefore surprising that on the other side of the Atlantic ocean, oppositionalism is looked upon as a peculiarly American disease and consequently not at all surprising that it took Americans to discover and describe it. These notions are, of course, mythical because although behavior has large cultural components, rebelliousness and negativism are by no means confined to these shores. However, the great concessions to self-expression accorded to American children may have helped in making it more manifest.

The name of David Levy will be repeated frequently in the context of the oppositional syndromes since he almost invented this new psychopathology of childhood.[4] in his pioneering effort, Levy took the first clinical look at the compulsion to oppose as it occurred normally and abnormally during different periods of psychological development, and linked it to several other phenomena encountered by clinicians, such as obstinacy, procrastination, negativism, temper tantrums, refusal to eat and mutism. He noted the appearance of opposition from infancy onward in the baby's refusal to suck, in the eight-month-old's "stranger reaction," in the battle of the spoon at ten or eleven months (when the child, as the anxious mother sees it, seems almost to go on hunger strike), in the toddler's refusal to accept help of any kind or to stay at stated intervals in his crib, and in the momentous conflict that sometimes arises over bowel and bladder training. All these developmental battles represent a clash of wills between the oppositional child and his oppositional parent and the child's autonomy is the major stake in the play. In extreme cases, both are equally determined not to give ground or let the other get the better of him or her.

In this developmental perspective, therefore, opposition is manifested as a normative curve peaking in the *first oppositional phase* between the ages of eighteen months and two years and later, during the *second oppositional phase* occurring in early adolescence.

According to Levy, normal opposition is the logical outcome to the process of "domestication" in which the child's instinctual life is trained to conform to the demands of his psychosocial environment. The opposition was a necessary reaction to this. The toddler's "no" stage marked the beginning of his autonomy and the first emanations of the self. The second bout of opposition arose in conjunction with the second phase of individuation following puberty and terminated at the end of adolescence in normal conformity to the rules and regulations of society.

The fact that opposition is normal does not however mean that the phenomenon does not make its mark on the household. It is true that some parents may welcome it as an expression of "rugged individualism" but the average parent is less impressed by the wonder of this negativism and tends understandably to become at times a little exasperated. As one remarked, "I really don't mind his saying 'no' sometimes because that is his privilege, but does he have to make a career out of it?"

Some mothers become adept at developing varying techniques of out-witting the oppositional child and take advantage of the fact that they are cognitively some steps ahead of him. A special kind of double talk is not unusual in many households. For example, to the child who will not come when he is told to come, the mother says, "Please don't come when I call you: I don't want you to come." The junior toddler, as yet unsubtle and unsophisticated in the ways of human mothers, usually falls for this and comes. The senior toddler, on the other hand, has begun dimly to puzzle out the notion that there is something crooked about the whole maneuver. In the dark recesses of his infantile mind, he begins to understand that when his mother says that she does not want him to come, she really means that she wants me to come, and that if I do come, then I will be doing what she really wants me to do. However, if I do what she says she wants me to do, I will be doing what she does not want me to do. By this time, the toddler has become confused and may decide to come but slowly. If his mother is smart enough, she will conceal her triumph at out-maneuvering her child so that his sense of growing autonomy is left undisturbed. Once the first period of independence (sometimes called the first puberty) has been established and a reasonably satisfying sense of independence obtained, a period of remission sets in and follows the course of latency until the second struggle for independence appears. The quiescence, according to Erikson is the interlude between the struggles for autonomy and identity,[3] and, according to Blos the interlude separates the first from the second phase of individuation.[2] There is no doubt that a similarity exists between the psychologies of nursery child and adolescent. They both seem to be fighting the same kind of battles over and over again and often in remarkably the same way. If adolescence does indeed recapitulate the earliest phase of life, then there is good reason to speak of first and second oppositional phases and link them together dynamic-ally: if the first is difficult the expectation would be that the second phase will also be extremely difficult.

In addition to the developmental continuum, it is also possible to look at oppositional behavior along a spectrum of normality and pathology, ranging from crises of opposition during normal development to various degrees of neurotic, psychopathic and psychotic negativism, and from focal opposition as expressed in a single symptom (a refusal to sleep, eat or excrete according to the rules) to a generalized oppositional character disorder. With respect to this, Levy has suggested that it is more appro-priate to speak of oppositional "syndromes" since this does not commit the clinician to a definite psychiatric diagnosis. The oppositional syndrome is then described as a cluster of oppositional attitudes and behavior that can be described phenomenologically in terms of frequency, duration and intensity and in terms of the functional areas involved and the people concerned. Since the oppositional child is so often interlocked with an oppositional parent who has also been an oppositional child in relation to an oppositional parent, some form of psychological, if not genetic, transmission must be involved. This means that the area of opposition is chosen not only by the child but also by his parent who may be hypersensitive and compulsively concerned with certain aspects of child rearing. The oppositional mother is presumably refighting ancient battles from her own nursery days, while the child is fighting the battle for his adult life, his adult self and his adult sense of autonomy and identity. If he fails in this, he is doomed to a life of conformity, submissiveness and deference. The more he succeeds, the more he will be self-reliant, self-assertive and self-confident. If the battle reaches clinical intensity, then the condition that started as an adaptive mechanism may end in a rigidly fixed character response of passive-aggression or in a schizophrenic catatonia.

There are also secondary reactions to opposition because it stirs up a great deal of frustration and hostility on the part of the parent and this, in turn, evokes a variety of fears relating to the possible loss of love with anxiety and depression, possible loss of self-esteem with feelings of shame and embarrassment, and possible retaliation coupled with feelings of guilt. How then is one symptomatic expression elected over another: why does the child elect to become negativistic rather than openly aggressive and defiant? Negativism is probably a safer course of action. It probably creates less apprehension to be unpunctual or a little messy than to be physically or verbally abusive.

Normal developmental opposition may be activated into clinical negativism by certain precipitating experiences that hurt, frighten, or overwhelm the child during his development. Levy compares this to an almost physiological mechanism of withdrawing from the noxious environment and thus resisting its influence until better equipped to do so. This is very reminiscent of Engel's theory of conservation—withdrawl with regard to the genesis of depression. The capacity to resist the environment is crucial to the development of inner controls; this is where the emergence of oppositional behavior links up with the development of conscience and superego formation.

That oppositionality is two-sided is vividly illustrated by the behavior of poultry. The chicks that gradually separate from the mother hen, first by inches and then transiently out of sight, still at this early stage respond to her alarm cry. At the next stage, they begin to show independent behavior that in humans would be regarded as oppositional, disobedient and self-willed. The mother hen may cluck desperately without result and may spend a lot of time searching for her chicks who may wander off and not return till sundown. Oddly enough, when they do come back, she pecks them away as if the process of emancipation was related not only to their wish to leave her but also to her need to expel them. When they finally leave her, the young ones frequently stay together for a while as if the sibling situation were a necessary phase on the way to full independence. This oppositional behavior seen in the poultry yard is not unlike the oppositional behavior that occurs at the very heart of the separation-individuation process in the human situation, without which the child would remain encapsulated in the symbiosis with the mother and possibly permanently fixed at the level of infantile dependency. This is not to make a virtue out of opposition but to remind us that without its presence progress would not be possible.

References

1. Anthony, E.J. (1974). Between "yes" and "no." *Psychosocial Process*. 3:2, 23-46.
2. Blos, P. (1967). The Second Individuation Process of Adolescence. In *The Psychoanalytic Study of the Child*, Vol. 22. New York:International Universities Press.
3. Erikson, E.H. (1950). *Childhood and Society*. New York:Norton.
4. Levy, D.M. (1955). Oppositional Syndromes and Oppositional Behavior. In Hoch, P. and J. Zubin eds., *Psychopathology of Childhood*. New York:Grune and Stratton.
5. Spitz, R. (1965). *No and Yes*. New York:International Universities Press.

CHAPTER 2

The Oppositional Child: Is the Black Child at a Greater Risk?

JAMES P. COMER, M.D.

The oppositional child or person is one who displays negative and stubborn behavior, usually in relation to those in authority. The pattern of response reflects a refusal to conform to ordinary requirements of obedience and convention. It is perceived as a willful contrariness that derives its satisfaction from the antagonism it provokes in pitting his will against others, in opposing the laws of society, in flaunting his disrespect for the usual amenities of society. Persons in authority often view the behavior as an attack on their prestige, their sense of power and importance, and a challenge to their validity.

Oppositionalism as a Developmental Concept

Levy, who first developed the concept, stated that initially the behavior was not personal but a defense against a disturbance of a state of being and served useful developmental purposes. He felt that the oppositional stance enabled the child to overcome his infantile dependency and facilitated his process of separation and the development of autonomy. Through resisting external influences a degree of inner control with self-motivation and

9

direction could develop. Thus, opposition propelled the child towards greater self-realization, self-reliance and perseverance in the face of obstacles. All these proclivities were of inestimable value in the service of ego development.

In addition, Levy felt that the oppositional tendencies also operated to protect the individual against submissive tendencies, and could therefore be regarded either as a defense against or as an adaptive response to the danger of being taken over, ruled by, or rendered dependent on others. It was in many ways the safest form of antagonism or aggression available to those who cannot fight back, and he referred to it as the method of choice in many situations of danger.

Anger and hostility were not components of oppositional behavior in the beginning but very soon became directed at the limit-setting, frustrating or intruding authority figure, usually parents or parent surrogates. When these were reasonable and loving, the resentment remained mild and contained, but when they were unconditionally authoritarian, a persistant rage could develop. Through the mechanisms of identification with the unloving authority figures or aggressors, the child's hostility was directed back against himself with adverse effects on the formation of his self-concept. Oppositional and resistant tendencies then combined with anger, self-doubt and self-hatred to produce severe personality problems.

The Black Stereotype

Are Black children at greater risk with regard to the development of extreme oppositional tendencies? To pursue this question one needs first to examine some past and present stereotypes of Blacks. A stereotype invariably contains a kernel of truth within the image used to degrade the individual or group being typed. That there are certain stereotypes indicate also that there are certain tendencies prevalent enough in a group to be recognized. From this point of view, there does appear to be an above average prevalence of oppositional and related tendencies in some Blacks.

The slave literature describes a "sambo" type who is dishonest, lazy, slow, stupid, unreliable, careless, unable to work alone, and so on. The "Uncle Tom" type, on the other hand, is seen as dependable, subservient, nonaggressive and essentially passive. Recently, the Black comedian Flip Wilson has given prominence to the "Geraldine" type, an assertive, aggressive Black woman who is hostile to the point of being rude and crude. Her male counterpart has not yet been characterized in the popular media, but the "crazy nigger"—aggressive, violent, hostile, sullen and dangerous—is a well-described folk type.

"Sambo" was a product of resistance and submission to control, disguised anger and hostility, self-doubt and self-hatred. His behavior was passive, but frustrating and controlling of the slave master. "Uncle Tom" represented a failure of the defenses against submissive tendencies. In this case, the slave conditions promoting dependency and subservience (controling forces) scored a victory. Because it was always safer for Black women to be more assertive than Black men in America, the "Geraldine" type emerged and symbolized an effort at self-reliance, a reaction to control . . . ("Don't you touch me!" we hear Flip Wilson say as he characterizes Geraldine.)

Because the "crazy nigger" behavior was extreme and inappropriate it was dysfunctional, and, when the violence was directed toward Whites, had to be crushed. As a result, the Black man learned to displace the direct expression of aggression on to less dangerous targets, such as himself, his family or group members as powerless as himself. In contrast, the Black militant of today is more able to turn the same hostility and assertiveness against what he perceives as the strict and unloving authority figures of White America. However, because this is still quite a dangerous position to take, the target of his aggression continues to include himself and other Blacks.

What does all of this have to do with the Black child? Let us examine some comments which I have heard expressed in reference to some Black children. From a Black teacher, "When she doesn't want to do something I ask her to do she glares and rolls her eyes at me"; a White nursery school teacher, "He wouldn't even let me put my hands on him and I was just trying to be friendly"; a White fifth grade teacher in reference to Black students bussed into the school district and in her class, "The Black children appear to have a chip on their shoulders"; a Black nurse instructing low-income students on a work-study project, "I asked them all to move back so that the one taking the blood pressure wouldn't be so anxious. But a couple of students just stood there with their mouths poked out. They wouldn't move back until I spoke to them several times."

On one occasion I was called to the emergency room to see an eleven-year-old Black youngster who had not spoken a word for two days, it was believed that he was becoming catatonic. The fact that he rolled his eyes at me when I appeared suggested otherwise. As it turned out, for the previous few days he had been pressuring his family for a bicycle, with threats to run away and other inappropriate behavior. The history revealed that he was from a strict, demanding family, straining to make ends meet economically. Both parents held two jobs, and, as a result, were unintentionally neglecting the needs of this youngster. He felt himself to be unloved. He had established the denial of a gift of a bicycle as evidence that he was either loved or unloved. Apparently denied, he was mad, evil, angry to the point of withholding even speech.

All of these behaviors reflect stubborn, negative or oppositional behavior to authority figures who were thought to be strict, unloving, or antagonistic. For example, the students bussed into the White school area assumed their White teachers to be hostile and unloving—and in some cases it was the truth. The Black nurse was new to the on-going student group and they did not know her feelings toward them.

Authority figures, as Levy described, often respond in a way to complicate the matter. A group of young Black militants confronted a city council meeting in 1968 in a loud and antagonistic way. The council president shouted, "Take off those dark glasses, take off your hats and respect this chamber." The leader said, casually, with exaggerated control, "Shut up mother-fucker." The militants roared in amusement as he described the embarrassment, confusion and sense of helplessness the council president reflected at that moment. He clearly felt an attack on his prestige and sense of power. His response was to call in the police and have them thrown out. That response intensified the conflict.

Oppositionalism as Expectable in the Black Culture

What I have described is to be expected in disproportionate amounts among Black youth, if in fact the oppositional stance serves to permit internal control, to propel a child towards self-realization against external control. Slavery was a system of forced dependency. Authority figures in the society since slavery have supported widespread exclusion and intense antagonisms toward Blacks, relenting a little only in the past decade. Thus, efforts to reverse dependency and control—some adaptive and helpful, and some maladaptive and harmful—are to be expected. But it is less what society does directly as what it does indirectly that eventually creates a disproportionate number of Black youngsters and adults manifesting dysfunctional oppositional behavior.

Black parents attempt to function in a society in which many authority figures—the employer, policemen, banker, and even the President—sometimes reveal themselves as limiting, frustrating and antagonistic toward them. There is little they can do about this. In a manner similar to low status whites, such parents, without good defensive and adaptive mechanisms, displace their anger and hostility onto their children, and because children are dependent and powerless, their safest response is an oppositional stance. Parents fight back and an interaction pattern of aggression and counter-aggression is gradually established.

Low status parents, unable to identify with the power structure of the society, obviously have more to lose from a perceived threat to their power, importance or validity within the family. Therefore, the aggressive effort to maintain their status is more frequent in low status parents. The strict, often harsh, authority stance of some Black fathers, is related to this set of circumstances. A White social worker raised questions about the way one Black father treated his son—about his harsh, punitive way. After the therapy session the mother cornered the social worker and told her that she did not understand, "That's the Black male's way." She implied that it was necessary and important because of the Black male's low position relative to the total power structure in the society.

Displacement is not the only contributing factor. During slavery and the period of extreme oppression, many Black parents had an important need to crush the aggressive spark out of their children. This was necessary because aggressive Blacks, particularly aggressive Black males, were in danger if they displayed this stance in relationships with Whites. Crushing out aggression began with a response to the assertive and aggressive behavior of a child during his efforts at achieving autonomy. In fact, the parent's suppressiveness produced as much or more counter-aggression, negativism and oppositional behavior as it did passivity, but the need to crush appeared necessary.

As a result, a disproportionate number of Blacks established harsh, controlling, child rearing practices. For many these practices are no longer related to the true level of oppression Blacks experience in the society but the attitudes have been established and will not change without conscious efforts to reverse them.

> Recently I had an opportunity to talk with a group of Black medical students. I mentioned a situation in which a Black youngster from North Carolina was brought up north and sent the next day to school with little preparation. His aunt just dropped him off on her way to work. He was in a new town, with unfamiliar relatives, in a strange, new school and in a strange new classroom. He was scared to death. He walked in, looked around, kicked the teacher in the shins and ran out. I said of that incident that that was a relatively healthy response. The students "jumped all over my back" for viewing that kind of response as indicative of health. One stated, "I would have knocked that kid down. He would have known not to kick the next time. The

teacher is the boss." One would have expected that from medical
students, as people with a fair degree of privilege within the society,
that there would have been a less punitive attitude. It does demonstrate the tenacity with which an established cultural attitude is maintained and its relative unresponsiveness to real social conditions.

The Anti-Oppositional Influence of the Black Church

Now the question is: if the circle of displaced aggression, reactive
opposition and retaliatory aggression of Black parents was set off by
antagonism towards the Blacks, why were not more Blacks affected?
Why are all Blacks not oppositional and hostile to a dysfunctional point?
At least a part of the answer lies in the fact that Blacks have had a major
adaptive mechanism, still not fully recognized, in the Black church used as
a substitute society. The Black church was an important place for self-
expression, a place where a great deal of value was placed on loving relationships, and a place where the authority figures—God, the ministers,
deacons and so on—were acting on behalf of the membership and not
against it. It was a place where a rejected people could experience a sense
of belonging. And it was because of this central experience that a large
number of Blacks were able and are still able to avoid becoming automatically hostile and oppositional in an abusing, derogating society that did
everything to provoke such behavior.

Some Implications and Conclusions

The implications for learning and relating in this society are massive.
So called deficit studies, emphasizing differences in testable intelligence
and achievement between Blacks and Whites will tell us nothing until the
effect of this crushing behavior is more fully understood and the oppositional behavior that follows inevitably in response. We need as well to
understand what happens to curiosity, motivation, internal controls and
direction as a result of this bulldozing process. All this and more must be
accounted for before comparisons between Black and White intelligence
and achievement scores can be considered a valid procedure. There is
good evidence to suggest that dysfunctional oppositional behavior limits
self-directed, self-motivated, creative and productive behavior. The struggle
with the authority figure becomes an all-engaging end in itself. One must
therefore look at the dynamics of the relationships of Blacks to the overall
societal authority system in order to get some insights into Black opposi-

tional activity. If this is true, then it follows that the intervention designed to reduce dysfunctional oppositional behavior will be most effective at the societal level. People (Black or White) need to feel that society works for them. It is tremendously important for Black parents to be able to identify with the authority figures in the society so that their position is not always one of opposition to the society; if this occurs fewer Black parents will displace their anger and frustration onto their children. The intervention must also be at the level of the family. Child rearing practices that "crush" initiative and assertiveness and promote opposition followed by parental retaliation must be reduced. This is not a problem across the entire Black community, nor is it a problem limited to Blacks; but it is a problem among a disproportionate number of Blacks as a consequence of their very difficult social circumstances in this country.

CHAPTER 3

Oppositional Behavior in Everyday Life

FRITZ REDL, PH.D.

To talk about oppositional behavior in everyday life is a wide assignment that ranges from the young toddlers who seem to have so much trouble saying "yes" unequivocally to their parents to the political stubbornness with which nations deal with one another on international issues. Therefore, I thought I would limit my discussion to nailing down a few rather clearly defined concepts rather than trying to cover the whole spectrum. In David Levy's material he approached these problems on oppositional and compliant behavior in groups of poultry and I in groups of children. He learned more about hens than I did about children but then admittedly children are more complicated. In my early attempts I tried to look at the group as such no matter who was in it, but today I am more aware of the inordinate complexity of the Black-White and Black-Black problem among kids and the histories and experiences that they bring with them into the group. For the moment, let us simply acknowledge that these huge discordant forces are constantly at work and are often therapeutically counter-productive.

An appropriate introduction to this theme is the following:

On one occasion we set off for camp by bus with a load of very aggressive and disturbed youngsters. The group included a little girl who looked like a little angel. She may have been little, but she was not an angel! Her mother came to send her off and informed her in a loud voice, "Be sure to be a good girl, and mind everything that these nice people tell you." Then, *sotto voce,* leaning down to the child, she said, "But remember you are my daughter and don't you take no shit from nobody!" And I can assure you, she didn't take no shit from nobody including me! The child was oppositional from the word go.

The Concept of Oppositionality

The concept of opposition has to be carefully defined because some of the elements included in it are more than oppositional. We need to decide whether to discuss the oppositional child or oppositional behavior, and in our own clinical work we switch constantly from the more global concept of oppositionality as a characteristic or trait to oppositionality as a behavior with which adults have trouble. One does not have to be an oppositional child to sometimes behave oppositionally. Often what we have in front of us is a normal and healthy child who can, thank goodness, defend himself against the nonsense we are dishing out to him. However, he could as well be a child who opposes every suggestion made to him out of sheer "bloody-mindedness." At a step further, we encounter abnormal children who happen to be oppositional although they are mainly disturbed. Opposition is therefore an index of behavior that points to many different syndromes. it may be difficult at any given moment to know just what sort of oppositionality we are dealing with and what the basic underlying pathology is. It may alter from time to time: The same child at 9:00 in the morning may be normally oppositional and at 4:00 in the afternoon, he may have a tantrum that verges on the psychotic. The child is the same; the label is the same, but the two phenomena may be radically different.

Age also exerts its influence. What is accepted opposition in a toddler may appear quite obnoxious in the teenager behaving like a toddler. The psychological toddler at the age of 12 also wants his own way and brooks no opposition. He has the same amount of negativism, the same degree of omnipotence, and the same refusal to consider the matter sensibly and objectively. As a result he has as much difficulty adjusting to a peer group and for about the same reasons.

What does oppositional behavior look like clinically? It has a protean number of forms and may even vary with the same child; he can be antagonistic by thought, word or deed—he can become mute, stare at the adult defiantly, throw a fit, smash the furniture or lash out at whoever is available or within distance. The main battle has to do with *not* doing what he is supposed to do, and it is the quality of his resistance that varies. At times it looks as if the child is trying desperately to survive and at other times it seems more as if the child is having a field day and it is the adult who is attempting to survive.

The Meaning of Oppositionality

First, as with any symptom we must ask ourselves what it means and what the patients get out of it. What is there in it for them? There is, again, no one answer; the same behavior can have different meanings, different motives. different histories and different justifications. At the risk of oversimplifying the phenomenon, let me enumerate (and illustrate) the fifteen most frequent meanings of oppositional behavior in terms of the actual situation without considering the variables introduced by the past, by the clinician, by the child's motives, or by the nature of his reactions.

1. For some children, oppositionality is *a face saving gesture* in terms of their developmental phase. Dr. Anthony has covered this in Chapter 1 and there is no need to say any more about it. He mentioned two oppositional phases at early childhood and at adolescence; I would like to add a third oppositional phase to be observed in this country in precocious children of the 6th and 7th grades who skip prematurely into adolescence and immigrate into a group that is at least three years ahead of them, at least nine degrees more antagonistic than their own parents would ever allow them to be in their own basements. That is the group cult into which they immigrate. Many are not even legitimately adolescent and yet they attempt to assimilate the cult. They have to prove that they belong to the group and not to the family; they have to prove that they belong to the next developmental phase and not the one they are in. And in order to prove themselves they have to be oppositional. It has a face saving aspect: "I'm not a child anymore. I'm already an adolescent. You may not recognize it because my sex glands are not functioning fully and so my voice is still squeaky and I still cannot shave. But just look at my behavior and you'll be convinced." There are times when he does not mean this. The next phase is tougher than he thought, given his inadequate equipment and he is only too ready to be rescued from a traumatic exposure to it. Thus we receive a double message from these children: they want to remain children but they want to pretend to be adolescents. We too send out a double message to them: we want them to remain little for our sentimental satisfactions but at the same time we want them to grow up, be more mature, more dependable and less of nuisances.

Sometimes oppositional behavior is primarily meant to establish the right and the prestige of the given phase a youngster is in. "I'm not a baby anymore and I am not yet an adolescent but somewhere I'm in the line, and you don't notice it." If the children waited until the adults noticed their developmental status, they might have grey beards. It is only by their opposition that they can make the adults finally conscious of what is going on under their noses.

2. The second type of oppositional behavior is aimed at providing evidence that one is autonomous and accountable for one's own actions. "Unless I first behave oppositionally how would you know that I am not simply surrendering." (See Chapter 1.) It is obvious that in order for the child to know that he is doing what he wants to do, he has to say "no." By saying "yes" he no longer has the feeling of being in charge, of being master of his own fate. If he says "no" first and then complies, this is different. He has made his point; his "I'ness" has received recognition. Saying "no" means "I" am talking for "me" and not just as a small part of the whole family.

3. The third type of gratification to be obtained out of opposition is the "pure" pleasure of protest for its own sake. He objects simply on the basis of the compulsion entailed. It is no longer: I protest, therefore I am, but I protest for the sake of protest. It is the next refinement. I have become a Protestant in the grand manner. It is not just survival but a chosen way of life. "I may be sleepy and want to go to bed, and I wish you would get me off the hook and "shoo" me off, but your command becomes my protest. I would gladly have gone to bed if you hadn't been so tactless as to mention it, especially with the addition, "you're too young to stay up." It is simply a question of diplomacy about which most young parents are ill-educated. Diplomacy is the art of allowing people to think that they are doing what they want to do. (And please be careful not to rub in the sore question of age. One of the songs of rebellious adolescents says "Everybody thinks we're too young for it" and they want to prove otherwise, whether it is sex, drugs, alcohol, pregnancy, running away from home, or V.D.) In general, if the child is being sent to bed at bedtime, this should occur without the Gettysburg Address. The child is often protesting not against the command but against the style, its flagrant, inconsiderate authoritarianism—a fine but often narrow distinction.

4. The fourth gratification from oppositional behavior has to do with the need for self-assurance around the group role. It means, for instance,

"What would the other kids think of me if they saw me succumbing so easily right now." This reaction belongs to what Freud called "the older psychology," and the infiltration of personal privacies by the herd response. The group is the prime influence on adolescent behavior and what the group does today, the group thinks tomorrow. I do not think, incidentally, that individual and group psychologies can be kept separate within different textbooks practiced by different therapists. Today's therapist must constantly remember the child in his group and the group in the child. If the child is oppositional, one must be prepared to track down this reaction to his gang, and deal with it there.

A brief vignette will illustrate this:* I had one of those oppositional children in my office at the camp. The loot is hanging out of his pocket. He knows that I know and I know that he knows that I know. And the first thing he says is, "Honest to God, Fritz, I wasn't even there. I'll swear on a stack of Bibles." Well, anyway, after three or four such lies, because he has to force me to go through a certain maneuver with him, he can finally bring himself to admit "O.K.! Here it is." He already knows before he starts that I am not going to hit him or punish him. But he has to go through these steps. Why? Not because of me–he has me figured out very early in the game–but because of what the other kids would think if they were around. *The invisible group is sitting right under my couch.*

This is now a group psychological session. I have to deal with an invisible group that is sometimes worse than handling a visible one. What it means in practice is that the youngster has to go through the motions of conveying to the invisible group that he will resist the "enemy" whatever adult shape this takes. He is oppositional not because he wants to oppose, or because he is in a state of resistance or in a state of transference, but simply because the group mores expects him to oppose as part of the code. In this case, the gratification from being oppositional is not derived from making you uncomfortable because he may even like you. He has nothing against you personally. It is all right for him to lose a battle with the confronting adult, but he has to fight first. He must not surrender easily. His prestige with the invisible group is at stake and he must preserve the group code.

5. Sometimes the phenomenon of "role-suction" occurs which is an interesting aspect of group psychology. In every teenage group there is

*Editors Note: Another brilliant example of Redl's colloquial style that gets his ideas so powerfully across to audiences.

a designated clown who is popular with other children but often a pain in the neck for the adult who has to manage him. Sometimes he is compelled to clown and almost addicted to clowning but there are others who become clowns under the force of circumstance. For example, this latter type may find the group too miserable, bored or tense with the teacher out of touch with them. This is too much for him. He is a group-psychologically conscious guy and cannot bear to see people squirm. (He will make an excellent group therapist someday.) Right now he has to relieve the tension so he might roll an apple down the aisle. He is sucked into this behavior and as a result becomes oppositional in spite of himself. He is not against anyone. He makes a fool of himself to help the group not to challenge the teacher.

If I am the teacher, I hope that the message comes across as to what this oppositional behavior means. He is helping me to realize that I am doing a bad teaching job and that my class is so apathetic and disinterested that they need a clown—and I need the sack! I should thank him, although of course not publicly.

6. There is a phenomenon I will call "play interruption frustration," that happens frequently with younger children. They are engrossed in play and you say "Dinner is ready." *For you,* dinner is ready but not for them. So they continue with their activity, not because they are born oppositional, not because they are angry, not because they are disobedient and not because they do not want their dinner. They simply want something else more. It is quite natural for all of us at times to be irritated by being interrupted. If the children are apathetic, we should thank God they are becoming interested again in something.

Another example is of children brought into an adult party to entertain the guests. They become excited and everyone dances around them like little prima donnas. All of a sudden, they are told to stop and go upstairs and do nothing. Of course they become oppositional because you, the adults started the situation.

7. The next phenomenon is a variation of this—the youngster tries to hang onto what he is doing to gain a respite before surrendering. It does not mean that he liked the activity so much, but he merely does not want to make a change. It is switching that is so difficult for this type of child and makes him automatically oppose it.

8. Another variation of this particular oppositional behavior involves children who are disinclined to interrupt their activity because what they

are required to do next is so boring, embarrassing or painful as to be unbearable. The parents demand that the shy child recite for the assembled guests and he would rather continue setting the table and keeping out of sight. He will resist to the last drop of his timid little heart! It is far from being a power play.

9. There is something akin to a dueling code that is demanded by the peer group, and which I have labeled "the choreography of the dare." With all tough, fighting gangs, there is always an element of dare. You dare somebody, and he has to respond or else he loses face. Let us imagine that you are in 19th century Germany sitting in a beer garden with your girlfriend, somebody comes up to you and says, "You are staring at me," and you say, "I'm not staring at you." He says, "You *are* staring at me." You say, "I am *not* staring at you." Finally, one of you has to use the irretrievable term "You are lying." Once he has said this, you have no option. You have to challenge him to a duel. You are not two people anymore but puppets in an associated drama, and the drama has to be played out to the end. One of you may end up dead, but there is nothing really personal about it. It is a choreography, a formal dance like a primitive ritual. The script is all powerful and the actors are faithful to the letter of it. The feuding gangs have taken over much of the cult with less of the *politesse*. The dare itself still cannot be left unchallenged, although the drag race has been substituted for the duel. Both have a lethal end in common, and both are ruled by the principle that it is better to be a dead Achilles than a live chicken.

The pathology of the dare is such that no one with a gang orientation can let a dare go unchallenged and be able to look at his face again in a mirror for the rest of his life. In the old days, such challenges were limited to fraternities, feuding gangs and delinquent gangs, but today it has become almost mythological. It is no longer a real group but a fictional imaginary one borrowed from the media and it takes over the lives of many of these kids. In this case again, the oppositional behavior is imposed from without and unavoidable.

In children's psychiatric hospitals, many of the incidents that end with kids getting dragged into the so-called quiet room are due to the skillful maneuvering of the kids and the unskillful response of the staff. The child care worker must act on his word. If he orders the child to go to the quiet room for disruptive, oppositional behavior, he must see to it that he goes. For both it becomes a dare. The child cannot allow himself to be segregated without a struggle or he would be dishonored and ashamed. The worker must stand up to the challenge. The duel has been arranged and neither can back out since they are the center of an audience of goggling children and the morale of the ward is in question. Neither party can afford to lose his self-respect or the respect of the onlookers. This oppositionalism is not directed against the adult. It is not a flaunting of authority. It is not a cutting down of an imaginary father. It is the working out of a ritual that could have been avoided with more skillful staff management.

10. I call the next maneuver a "displaced objection," a form of protest relating to former life situations, where the child is not realistically concerned with you but with some specter from his past life. It is like a *deja vu;* it has happened many times before and the child repeats his behavior compulsively although it is quite inappropriate to the present situation or present person. It has nothing to do with whether the person deserves such treatment now. The miserable life situations of long ago have to be worked over again and again. They have to make their objection now in a different place at a different time with different people, although it makes absolutely no sense whatsoever. Once again, the opposition is not aimed at you, the resistance is not against you and the bitterness has nothing to do with you. It is part of what the psychoanalyst calls the repetition-compulsion, and it is a way of mastering the past trauma by displacement. They do not as yet see you as a real person, only as a figment of the imagination and it may take four or five months before they begin to react to you as someone now rather than as someone then. One fine day after a reasonable period of living they will quite suddenly see you as "Bob," their worker, and know you for who you are. For a while you need to be patient and to accept their projections as they throw them on to you. This is what you are there for. Gradually, you will help them to disentangle you from their past and leave what's done where it belongs. They no longer have to be as oppositional and as objectionable as they resume their current life. One can therefore refer to it as a delayed and displaced oppositionalism coming out of a bad past.

11. Sometimes oppositionalism is a realistic issue concerned with testing the range of power and the setting of limits. If you are a newcomer in a group, how can you learn what really counts (and by this I do not mean the official rules and regulations). The youngster looks for evidence. He sizes up the situation and the people by putting them to the test. He tries out some unconventional and unacceptable procedures to see what happens. One could call it research, simple experimental research. One learns about sparking points, tolerance levels, grudge-bearing, reaction

times, avoidance behavior, escape routes, etc., etc. It is all done in the service of reality testing, and the tests are generally minor and innocuous. The child uses oppositional behavior first because that gives him a better picture of the situation and the "climate." It provides a more sensitive psychological barometer than other behavioral devices. Research needs to be done over a wide range and they have to try out many life situations before they learn how to live in this particular milieu. This type of oppositionalism is both harmless and necessary.

12. Another type of oppositional child generates complex considerations for the worker. He is happy in his delinquency until the worker comes along and raises new issues of right and wrong. They establish a relationship which they enjoy but they are afraid to change. What he conveys to the worker is: "You know that I am a somewhat tough, rough and not too well organized kid and you want to get me well put-together, but I am not so sure I want it, because right now, for instance, I have a lot of fun, and if from time to time I get punished for it, what the heck! Who cares? But I am no longer so sure about this. You like me and I like you, but do I have to give up my delinquency just because you make me feel guilty? Who wants to walk around with guilt feelings like a neurotic? Not me. I'm a delinquent! I better not commit myself before I know what I am buying."

What happens next is some oppositional behavior with the idea of cooling the worker off. "If you don't like me anymore, then I am safe again, and no longer need to be rescued. You don't like me anymore, and maybe you give up on me. I thought you were my friend but you are as untrustworthy as all the others." Such characterologically-disorganized cases try their hardest to put you in a bind where you can neither win nor lose. At the very point at which you think that you are successful with them, they turn on you, treat you as something to experiment with, treat you with indifference and do not seem to need you. *But they are far from invulnerable.* When they seem most aloof, they can become most scared and needy. They begin to negotiate: "If I really change, what is it going to do to me? What will the other kids think of me? They'll think I've gone soft, sissy. I'll lose all my pals. They'll say I'm crazy. They'll avoid me. I'll be alone."

It is a very difficult position. Improvement is one of the most difficult and disturbing experiences that can happen to a kid, because it is the hardest for the therapist to handle. Let us assume, as a kid, that I'm beguiled enough by the therapeutic process to let myself improve in areas relevant to the therapist. My whole development has made me sufficiently cynical about human reliability to test the worth of the new situation by being purposefully oppositional and provoking the therapist into doing the wrong things. "So, it wasn't worth it. It's the same thing all over again. I might just as well forget about it." It is the critical hurdle that every therapist, preacher, teacher, or reformer of any other category encounters at the time when he really comes close to getting places. It is the patient's "last stand." But here again oppositionalism is not simply to be equated with opposing. He does not oppose what you want him to do; he does not oppose the relationship; he opposes the hint of promise (so often broken in the past) that it seems to contain. So, because they are afraid, they try to "cop out" and thus evade the threatening need to change. Change, that mysterious unknown, is what they want to avoid at all costs.

13. Another interesting ploy is "the invitation to a game," and it arises in institutional children more from boredom than from oppositionality. They want to enliven the evening with some dramatic interaction, or "needed excitement and stimulation" which, according to Hebb, is age-appropriate. So they goad the child care worker for no other purpose than to have a game in which they can call the shots. They may end up in the "quiet room," but who cares? The child knows the worker does not want him to go there especially if he is in therapy with him. This allows him to be even more taunting. "You are my therapist, for better or worse. You certainly won't want to push the button and summon the ward personnel. I know this would embarrass you! I know, for intance, that you love me, but you're very scared that I'll hit your 'altar pieces.' " (Every therapist has certain "altar pieces"—his typewriter, his filing cabinet, his dictating machine, and some of the sentimental trinkets on his desk. The patient can smash other things and delight you therapeutically, but not these!) It comes out that this is aggression against father. The child knows that anybody else would knock his head off if he behaved destructively but his silly therapist lets him do it for some bizarre reason. But if he touches the "altar pieces" or tries to hang out of the window, it is quite a different story. The emergency button is pushed. What the child figures out is: "If the worst thing that can happen is for my shrink to push that button and have some lowly paid person from the child care staff pick me up and take me back to the ward because I am in no shape for therapy, then that's nothing." So he plays this teasing little game over and over again and it makes for liveliness!

Now this has little or nothing to do with transference or countertransference; it is strictly here and now and the children have no clue what this has to do with therapy. It is hard for them to figure out what we want in therapy anyway, and we are not often skillful enough to make them understand what the process is all about. What they do discover is that every therapist has his Achilles heel and that one simply has to learn how to play on it. I would not call this strictly oppositionalism. What they are doing is making use of oppositional behavior to bring about certain exciting interactions and events in which adults lose control of themselves and frequently make fools of themselves. It is intriguing to discover that lordly adults can also have tantrums! It is often only meant as an opening gambit but, as in chess, this can misfire and lead to more serious consequences—much more than bargained for.

14. In any institution, there are always youngsters who have a serious emotional illness, like schizophrenia. They too can be oppositional at times because of their illness but we should not, for the sake of clarity, label them oppositional children. Children who suddenly throw a temper tantrum *for no reason whatsoever* are not just oppositional. The oppositionalism is there to try and cover this up. It may make him appear to be more normal than he is.

15. In many instances, oppositionalism can be the most healthy reaction that youngsters can make to the most idiotic demands from adults. Take for example a bunch of kids who are tired, miserable and disorganized and you say to them: "Now, group, what would you like to do today? This is a democratic society, and I think you ought to decide. Now what's a good idea?" Nobody has the least idea, except to do nothing. So you say, "What's the matter now? I don't want to decide for you. It's up to you." You really put them in a miserable position. It is a sort of primitive democracy but it has nothing to do with the real meaning of democracy. And, of course, the first thing anyone suggests is immediately opposed by everyone else. If you have the sense to let them recover, regain their spirits and energy and then, when they are ready and responsive, to drop in a few preliminary suggestions for consideration—that is quite a different matter and is treated differently and not oppositionally by the children. At such times, foolish, insensitive adults need to be opposed to teach them better. If the kids sometimes want to do what they want to do and not what the adults want them to do, one might describe the adults but not the children as oppositional.

Conclusion

It is true that any child under certain conditions can become oppositional and that sometimes this is healthy and sometimes very unhealthy.
Children need to be oppositional for a wide variety of reasons, and these
sometimes lie in their case histories, sometimes in the situations confronting them, and sometimes in the adults they have to deal with. The gratifications they get out of opposition also varies a lot. It is not enough to
know why they developed an oppositional tendency; one must also know
something about the present provocation to opposition. The same youngster may be oppositional three times a day, and each time for an entirely
different incident and reason. This does not necessarily make him an
oppositional child. On one occasion, he may be oppositional because the
diet I am prescribing is wrong for him, and he naturally resists it. On another occasion, he has to be oppositional to prove to the other kids that
he is sticking loyally to the group code. There is rarely a simple answer to
the situation, but plenty of possible answers, and one has to explore them
along with the children. If you know your group and the predicament into
which the members have landed themselves and you do not jump too
rapidly from the observation of oppositional behavior to the diagnosis
of an oppositional child, you cannot go too far wrong and the kids will
forgive you for at least having your heart in the right place. We have to
remember that adolescents are very reactive, touchy creatures. In Vienna,
Anna Freud was misquoted as saying "You cannot psychoanalyze an
adolescent," which is not what she meant. What she meant was that
adolescence is a phase of normal developmental turbulence (at least in the
society existent in Vienna at that time) and that before anyone decided
that an adolescent required therapy, the question of whether this might be
a situation ought to be seriously considered and assessed. The child might
need some help and counseling but not psychoanalysis. He really needs to
be put together not taken apart. One has to remember these days that a
16 year-old is not crazy because he is adolescent or adolescent because he
is crazy; such synonyms become irreversibly fixed in the popular mind.

The same is true of younger children; one youngster may be age appropriately antagonistic or oppositional while another may have his oppositionalism rooted in pathology. To differentiate the two we need the help
of people who live with him—his parents, his teachers, and his counselors—
otherwise we may well miss the crucial distinction. It is not safe to rely on
tests—we need "living" tests, the tests of interaction with living people
in living situations. Life provides the best test of pathology.

CHAPTER 4

Panel Discussion on the Oppositional Syndrome

E. JAMES ANTHONY, M.D., CHAIRMAN

ALBERT J. SOLNIT, M.D.   FRITZ REDL, PH.D.
JAMES P. COMER, M.D.

Question: **In phase-appropriate, developmental oppositionality would intensity of the behavior be a clue to whether or not to be diagnostically concerned? Intensity meaning both frequency and volume. Would you discuss the relationship between infant energy levels and the intensity of later oppositional behavior?**

REDL: First of all I would say that the question is already based on an assumption that makes life much too easy. Not all opositional behavior that happens now is necessarily rooted in what happened when we were little. Some of it is a brand new arrangement. For instance, I have gotten over battling with mommy about "Do I finish the porridge even though it's cold by now and do I eat one more spoon for uncle Fred and for aunt Mary and for grandfather, until I hate my whole family?" But now I am 12 years old and they put me in a classroom with tougher kids and all of a sudden it is important that I'm not the baby anymore, that I've stopped mother from coming to school and licking my face in front of everybody else. Right now it is more important to me that the other kids know that I'm over all that and they don't think I am a sissy. So if the teacher acts unreasonably, or is a bit too fussy or if his demands don't respect my age or he wants me to be too obedient then I may want to balk. I don't really mind the teacher so much, and I'm not just out to get him. If I'm an average kid in a difficult situation, and if I'm difficult back, it isn't necessarily because I'm an oppositional character now or that they didn't handle me right when I was a baby or toddler. So there are always new situations coming up where opposition may be a relatively new phenomenon. Now let's look at a youngster who is unusually, unreasonably, compulsively oppositional out of keeping with all reality. Any child might say, "I don't want to go to bed so I'll give you a run around." But this child is different; he breaks the windows or spits in his grandfather's face! This is crazy stuff, and if he is so irrationally and slavishly dependent on having to be oppositional then I would assume that this didn't just happen yesterday, and that probably sometime, somewhere previously there were conditions that led this youngster to stick to an increased form of oppositionalism because his normal developmental opposition wasn't well handled. What we see now is inherited from past mistakes. But this is more than a theoretical issue; I still have the present problematical behavior to deal with. The present problem is a new problem and I have to try to get this kid off this specific form of being oppositional or this specific issue in which to be oppositional. I would sum up by saying that the more extreme and pervasive the pathology appears the more I assume that it probably didn't begin yesterday: that it probably has a long history. But even that doesn't have to be so because you can corner somebody in a situation now which is totally unbearable and no matter how reasonably you treated him before, right now he has to be oppositional. Let me use a crude illustration. A nice kid, who is anything but oppositional, holds onto the table when his parents say, "Look, it's time to go to school." He is not going to go to school and the parents get more and more upset. What kind of a kid is this who never behaved that way before? It turns out that he can't go to school because his grandmother knit long underwear for him and to go to school today when there is gym with long underwear is intolerable. He is not a compulsive youngster and it isn't because he wouldn't eat his porridge when he was three years old. On the other hand, if that kid has to act that way in lots of situations where there is no such reason then I would assume something happened before which increased his need beyond what is reasonable. Here again I couldn't say "yes" or "no." I would have to look into the details of the situation and at the degree of irrationality of compulsiveness from within. I would check the reality factors and then I would make such a hunch, and then I would act on it.

SOLNIT: I think that when it comes to phase-specific oppositional behavior, you cannot count too much on frequency and intensity of the symptom because there are times, especially in adolescence, when these criteria of normality and pathology can mislead you. I think we have to look for other criteria, and to gauge what kind of progression there has been in development along other lines. This is particularly true of adolescence. I would very much agree with Dr. Redl that at this stage criteria based on intensity and frequency alone could lead us diagnostically astray. The adolescent who is trying to define himself as an independent person will often have the need to be intensely and frequently oppositional and this may be part of his healthy development.

Questions: **Is there really such a diagnostic entity as an oppositional child? If so, why does such a child elect to become oppositional in his negativism rather than obsessive-compulsive? What is the relationship of passivity to oppositionality? Where did you get a spectrum of diagnosis ranging from the normal to catatonia?**

REDL: First of all I think we ought to be linguistically correct and say that when we use the term "an oppositional child," it's a headline, an eye-catcher. Let's not pretend we say much more than that about it. I once wrote a book and called it *Children Who Hate*, which is an idiotic title! What can one possibly mean by "children who hate?" Lots of kids hate who have nothing to do with that book and what these kids did wasn't just hating. But you have got to find something where you put together what you are *not* taught. You start by observing a phenomenon. Then you ask yourself what these kids are like who show this phenomenon. There is a whole youngster hanging on to any such label and whether you call him a bedwetter or a thumbsucker he is still a boy or a girl of a certain age, in a certain family, at a certain time, in a certain place, in a certain society. If it happens sometimes that he puts his finger in his mouth because he is not supposed to smoke cigars yet, does he become a thumbsucker? On the other hand, there is a youngster where that thumb is so important that even though everyone teases him and makes him feel miserable and even though he wishes he didn't do it, he has to do it. In this case I would say that, while it is far from hopeless and while he is still only a thumbsucker, in my clinical book I would note this ascendency over everything else and make sure that I take a much closer look at it, even though I keep in mind that he is a particular boy of a particular age, etc. So whenever we talk here about the oppositional child, we really don't imply that there is a single set of customers that run around (all five of them!) who can now be labeled precisely thus. Even when we label them, we have to ask ourselves, "When are they *not* oppositional?" We clinicians always look for the symptom, and once we have the symptom we are so happy with ourselves that we hang onto it with our teeth. It is much better that we wonder when they do not have the symptom. For instance, I have a camp for thieves but nobody steals all the time. They are much too lazy for that! There are some youngsters there I could trust with my car keys anytime but not with my wallet. But there are other kids I would trust with my wallet anytime (they would bring it back to the penny) but not with my car keys. And there are some I can't trust with anything unless I wear it. Then they take it off before I know because they really are magicians with their hands and by vocation pick-pockets and don't really care about the stuff they pinch. It's an art. Next time I come and ask for a pencil, they give me ten and half of them belong to me anyway. They don't care for possessions as such but what's more important to them is they they are card-carrying members of a gang. Well, what else do they do when are not oppositional? There are certain situations where I would expect opposition and don't get it. It is very easy to forget those situations where the expected characteristic does not occur; for the clinician both are equally important. I'd like to know when he wets his bed and when he doesn't, just as I want to know under what conditions and in what situations he is heavily oppositional and when he is passive. No kid is constantly oppositional, and almost every kid is at times oppositional. But every child is so much more than just his oppositional behavior. We need to look at the distribution of the behavior we are investigating and the reason why we need to break it into categories. First of all we ask the question, "How much of this behavior is normal or not?" The answer does not depend on theory but on what it looks like. Is that kid acting irrationally in response to the actual reality situation? If he cannot use anything else but this one behavior then there must be something wrong somewhere for which he needs some help. Or is the youngster oppositional because something is new to him, because he is going through a normative oppositional phase or simply because he has been in a passive situation for too long a time and is bored with himself. How can one snap out of too much passivity without first becoming a little oppositional or seemingly oppositional? If one suddenly stops being passive everyone knows that one is here and to be reckoned with. I would consider that behavior to be quite normal. Nevertheless, what he does to be oppositional may still be crazy. he may be simply oppositional, or he may have to act so bizarre that it isn't funny and it isn't necessary. So he is normal in terms of being oppositional but his form of opposition has a sick element in it that is quite different; they are not the same thing and I would have to look at it again.

SOLNIT: Let me emphasize one thing. Oppositional behavior and attitudes can only be understood in the context of an interaction with somebody or something in the environment. The same kind of behavior or attitude may be oppositional in one situation and not oppositional in another and if you think about that it may help you extract the richness of what Dr. Redl has said in regard to diagnosis.

Question: Can child rearing practices of Blacks, in spite of the poor malfunctioning power structure in which they are enmeshed, be changed? To what extent does Black language get confused with oppositionality? Why is it harder for the Black teenager to adopt an oppositional stance? Presuming a Black child at a young age had an opportunity to exercise his oppositionality and to develop his own skills, what special difficulties related to racial discrimination might yet occur in adulthood? In other words, do situational reactions still pose the possibility of oppositional behavior?

COMER: I want to stress the fact that there are many Black families that feel very much a part of American society and the parents are able to prevent the development in their children of feelings of rejection, and do not have the need to displace their anger and hostility onto their children. So although this is a problem affecting a disproportionate number of Black families for historical reasons, it is not across the board. I can see how speaking incomprehensibly can shut authority figures out and also be used as a way to be difficult. But Black language, if there is such a thing, is generally not used in an oppositional way. I disagree with the other part of the question. Rather than it being difficult for Black teenagers to develop an oppositional stance the reverse is true because adolescence is the period when the individual comes in greater contact with a society that is controlling, frustrating and difficult to deal with. It seems to me that it is very easy to become oppositional as a way of handling and managing a society that opposes one in almost every sphere of life. I think that many of the difficulties with Black soldiers and Black high school children around the country stem from the feeling engendered in them that those in power treat them in an authoritarian manner as compared with other groups.

Question: If the psychological development of a Black child is good and he does not pass through an early dysfunctional level of negativism, is there still a higher risk for him, as compared with the White child, to become socially or clinically oppositional when he soon learns that he has less leverage and opportunity to make society work on his behalf? In other words, is it inevitable that situations of racial discrimination will provoke oppositionality in even a normal Black adolescent? What immunity does his normal development afford him?

COMER: It seems to me that minority group children and minority people are always in a kind of a bind. In a majority group the individual is always able to identify with the authority system and with the people who control and have power in the system, so that at least they have the illusion of control and power in themselves. With minority group people there are too many instances in which you see the authority system deliberately closing you out of an opportunity, and making it only too clear that it is not acting in your behalf. There is a balkiness, a kind of oppositional stance that develops in response to this. Someone told me that I needed to work in a factory and have thirty employees under my command of which fourteen are Black and they are the first ones not to show up, and they always get excused for not coming to work. Blacks represented problem workers. I pointed out that this fitted the description of the poor White laborer during slavery in the south when they were deciding that they didn't want to use the White worker because he wasn't a good worker, and that they had to have slaves. The real issue is concerned with power, control and opportunity. If you cannot feel that you are a part of that and you do not feel that you are benefiting in a very real and important way then there is not much reason to cooperate. There *is* reason to make it difficult for whoever is in charge. Once this is established as a way of relating, as it was for the Black slaves in disproportionate numbers, then it becomes the life style and gets transmitted very directly to the next generation, unless the pattern is broken or unless you can establish goals and opportunities which are your own so you do not have to relate directly to the controlling power structure. This is in fact what the Black church enables many Blacks to do—to relate to another power system independent or separate from the overall social system of the country.

REDL: I have recently made two observations that may be interesting. One is struck by the fact that the Black child now in a school is sometimes confronted by a White teacher who frequently thinks that if she is nice and kind to the little Black child and even falls over backwards in treating him exceptionally that he will not think of her as prejudiced. But this is exactly what makes him think that she is prejudiced. I have observed a number of youngsters who have become oppositional not because they don't like the teacher but because they want to find out: "Does she respect me or not? If she respects me and I do something the White kid did, she is going to call me to task for it. She is not going to be afraid whether I am Black or White or whether I think she is prejudiced or not? she will take me seriously. The question is: Does she mean business and take me seriously or is she just mascoting me which is just as offensive as scapegoating. If she treats me as something very cute just because she wants to show that she really likes Black people, and that some of her best friends are Black, to hell with her! I'm a person. I don't want to be a mascot to indicate that someone has no prejudices? It is more insulting than if she actually shows prejudice." Prejudice may show itself as overreactions against prejudice and be perceived by recipients as such. The other observation has to do with the sensitivity of children to one another. Thus, for instance, a Black kid who had been very comfortable with his White group for years suddenly began to say to a White group leader whom he liked: "Please don't come to pick me up from school," and when asked "Why?" replied: "The other kids think it's funny. They tease me and say, 'What's the matter with you, Whitey, is that maybe your father or something?' " In such cases, a youngster may be very hesitant in public to show the same affectionate or obedient behavior. He has to act up, not because he doesn't like the White adult or because he wants to be objectionable, but because he has to watch that the other kids don't think he is brown-nosing the guy in authority. This has increased in the last 10 or 15 years.

COMER: I have had the same experience as Dr. Redl. A housemaster at Yale told me about Black students who would come in to talk with him but who would explain, "If we see you on the street, we might not speak to you," because it was important for them to have an oppositional stance. I can also underscore what he said about leaning over backwards in relating to Black people. This relates to the difference between engagement and running away; engagement means the need for the child to feel that you are taking him seriously and prepared to establish some kind of mutually respectful relationship.

Questions: **Pediatricians who previously had many toilet training referrals are now seeing problems from a later age (five to ten years). Has the battlefield been shifted, and is it the same battle with older troops using more modern weapons? Does oppositionality always have to be an external power struggle or can it be internal? Is oppositionality in the child ever an expression of the parent's feelings such as depression?**

SOLNIT: Pediatricians have also given me the impression that the struggle over toilet training and, more impressively than that, the struggle over the eating problems have sharply decreased. We like to think, although I don't know of any rigorous study that would document this, that oppositionality in regard to eating has decreased because parents have become more comfortable with a more flexible feeding schedule; not a chaotic schedule but one that represents a greater amount of mutual respect between child and parents as well as one that does not implicitly threaten the child with illness unless he complies with the schedule imposed by the parents with the backing of the doctor. I like to think that this change is associated with fewer feeding problems coming under the heading of oppositional. On the other hand, we cannot rest on our laurels because there is another kind of feeding problem that is coming up now. The incidence of a failure to thrive seems to me to be rising. This problem is thought to be associated with maternal deprivation, a lack of stimulation resulting from parental depression, a disorganized economic and social mode of living, or any combination of these. This deprivational syndrome, transmitted from one generation to the next, leaves the child disinterested in food. In place of active opposition we have apathy and this condition is even worse than negativistic food refusals. In these reactions, both active and passive, we are at an interface between individual and societal difficulties. In regard to toilet training, I suspect that the decrease is less and can be attributed again to permissiveness—not meaning, as sometimes understood, an absence of order and discipline but rather implying a flexible attention to the child's individual temperament and rhythms. In my opinion, oppositionalism is a vital part of healthy development and a characteristic of life; Therefore it is not a matter of avoiding it or getting rid of it, but of helping the child to express it in a way that allows him to move developmentally ahead. Gradually it can be transformed into socialized behavior and therefore past the point when opposition is an end point in itself. Now in regard to whether oppositional attitudes and behavior have internal as well as external components of motive and experience, the answer is "yes." When an individual has an internal conflict, one part of his being certainly opposes another; thus in a single situation, one part may wish to get ready to go to school and another part to dawdle. It is experienced both as internal and conflictual and the child may wish that the parent would come like a *deus ex machina* and take one or other side and relieve them of the responsibility of decision and the discomfort of indecision. They are therefore looking for an external representative of one side of that conflict and it is very burdensome, especially for the school-aged child, to feel that their own standards of autonomy and independence are opposed by something inside them that says, "Let's stay in bed a bit longer; why hurry to get ready; what's the matter with being late; who's running this show," and so on. This can be regarded as the external expression of an internal conflict; whether it is productive to call it oppositional or not is a moot point. It seems to me that we get into the problem of using a headline, in Dr. Redl's words that then overflows it boundaries, becomes amorphous, and loses the original crispness of its meaning. It is better for our clinical understanding to keep it within channels and not muck up the countryside with semantic ambiguity. The final question is whether oppositional behavior can or does represent the displaced expression of the parents' intent, attitude, wish or impulse? I would say yes. One frequently meets examples of a child expressing a parent's oppositional behavior, or accepting and complying with a parent's wish to be resistive or contrary. Often in a marital difficulty, the child becomes the unwitting tool or sometimes willing accomplice of one of the parents opposing the other by means of the child's resistant behavior.

Question: **How can teachers or principals handle an oppositional child without losing face? How does oppositional behavior develop in the therapeutic situation and how does one deal with silent opposition?**

REDL: These are not questions. These are invitations to a new dance! The first one bothers me most because the data which I need in order to say what would I do are entirely different from the data which is found in the case history that deals with etiology, diagnosis, and so on. The data I need to know must help me to decide what to do *right now*. I will give an example that occurs in a classroom of two highly disturbed youngsters with learning problems. The teacher is very friendly. Both kids sit with their heads bowed. She goes over to one of them and taps him on the shoulder and says, "What's the matter with you? Anything bothering you?" He groans, "Nothing." So she says to him, "O.K. Now it's all right. You can still sit for a while. Maybe you're upset. I'll come back later and then I'll ask you again." With just this communication the youngster will take about five minutes to come around. After a while, his head goes up and the teacher knows that it is time to come back and not say anything but simply to put the pencil in his hand and he will start working. She knows this kid; she sees him everyday and she can tell. In a case that looks identically the same, the same teacher goes over and says "Now come on kid, what's with you?" and he goes off like a rocket and has a forty-minute temper tantrum so that two people have to sit on him to hold him. This is what I would like to know *now:* which of my approaches will be perceived by the child as soothing and relaxing and which of them as panic starters? But these data are not in the case record. These belong to the living situation. The other point I want to make is that opposition often involves what I call the "dare" phenomenon. Let me illustrate this for you. One of the youngsters in a classroom is acting up and making too much of a racket. I am a teacher with too many kids; I can't bother too much; we know each other; it's a friendly outfit, and so I say to the child, "Look, I've told you forty-five times to be quiet; we can't work here; sit out there for a while and cool off and then come back. What's the matter with you today?" If that kid is well recognized in the group and tough, I have no problem. He just thinks, "Well, the old fool is tired today; maybe he has a hangover; well, no skin off my nose." If the kid, however, is insecure and if he thinks the other kids don't respect him enough then the moment I say, "Go out," he says, "Alright, make me." Now we are both in the "dare" bind and I then have to think fast of what I need to do to reduce its impact on the kid. First, I want to make very sure that the way I handle the "dare" is as free as possible from questions of prestige or losing face. This means I am not going victoriously into the situation. On the contrary, I may say, "Look, if you are so upset, it's O.K. to sit here and we will talk afterwards." I want to make sure that the rest of the "sons of a gun" know what has happened and if some of them giggle I jump down their noses and say "There's nothing wrong in being upset. I said he could cool off. That's all there is to it and don't you make any comments. Nobody has the right to say anything about that." But if they think he's a big hero when he comes back in again I remember next time and talk with them afterwards. I say, "Look, this is silly. I have nothing against that kid and I didn't want to punish him. It's just that he got high and if somebody gets high I want him to cool off and that's all there is to it." I want to also make sure that the kid gets the message either when he comes in the next day or sometime later when he is in better shape but not now when he can't listen. I'll say to him, "Look, what's the matter with you? I tried to get you out of here and I told you why. Do you have to get so upset about that crazy stuff?" So he knows what I am doing. My message is not, "I want you out of there," but "I want you in here, except if you act like that I can't let you be with us, but I want you back as soon as is halfway reasonable." That, by the way, is the biggest problem with lots of oppositional behavior which ends up with all the kids sitting in the principal's office. The message should not be, "Get out of here, we can't have you here," but the message should be, "We want you here as fast as possible, but this behavior we can't let you do and that's all we are interested in." The group worker who stays with the kid who was bounced carries the same message. "I know they want you in there. If you're that mad I'll sit with you and when you cool off, we'll go back again in there and join the other guys. It's too bad that you couldn't make it today." If everyone gets the message then the idea, "it's a big 'dare' if I get bounced," loses its punch. This may take a few months. It may take a few incidents before the message is clear to all—what bouncing means, which behavior is embarrassing, why should one lose face in a "dare," and how to behave in a way that has nothing to do with a "dare." The kid learns that this kind of behavior is not so great, not so glorious and so the issue disappears. This is how we handle oppositional problems in real life. One does not have to start a fight; one does not have to give in. One has to understand what it's all about and then tell it as one sees it. One doesn't have to worry about "losing face." If this is what worries one then one is no good with kids, especially oppositional kids.

Question: **Do you require special training to deal with Black oppositionality and do church affiliations help the problem?**

COMER: The problem with many teachers is that they are looking for some immediate and magical solutions to the problem of control and management. Many teachers also have the feeling that this type of behavior is a willful and unnecessary kind of response on the part of the child, that it has nothing to do with other issues and problems that the child is struggling with and, that it is unrelated to other things going on in the life of the youngster. The feeling is, "If he would just shut up, mind his business and do what he is supposed to and quit giving me a hard time, everything would be alright." Now if teachers can be trained to look at what is going on in the child, not as something good or bad but as a dynamic interaction with people, it would be very helpful to the situation. It is thinking diagnostically that is important and working out solutions that go beyond the minute-to-minute control.

In a program in which I am involved, we've worked out some approaches in this direction. We believe that difficult children are raising questions through their behavior. When the need is great enough, we have "expectation" meetings. These include the principal, teachers, social workers, and parents. We discuss what it is the youngster is saying, looking for and asking for. When necessary, we help them to find ways to meet their needs and handle their discomfort. They may go out of the classroom until they can get themselves together and come back in again. It is surprising to observe how well they manage when they are charged with the responsibility of controlling their own behavior. When you attempt to crush them into line you often get into a prolonged, angry struggle with oppositional behavior and alienation.

I don't think you need special training. There is, however, a responsibility on the part of Whites to look at their own prejudices and how they affect relationships with Blacks. It is important for people, White people in particular, working with Black kids, to look at their own feelings, attitudes and responses. This should deter them from looking at the child's behavior in a vacuum and conclude that he is reacting in a negative or difficult way without considering whether they themselves are actually helping to create this problem. There must be both a willingness to engage and a need to do so. Where this is absent, there should be a self-examination of conscious and unconscious attitudes toward Blacks that prevent us from responding to them or their children in friendly and civilized ways, or that generate stereotypes such as that Black children and adolescents are more dangerous, violent, destructive, dishonest and uncontrolled.

We have White teachers in our school program who are very effective for the very reason that Dr. Redl mentioned: their willingness to engage and to confront Black children, to set limits and above all to constantly examine their own attitudes and behavior. I repeat: there is no special training except in this vigilant self-examination.

CHAPTER 5

The Oppositional Child and the Confronting Adult: A Mind to Mind Encounter

FRITZ REDL, PH.D.

I want to start with a story about a youngster in camp. It was during the war. The camp site which we used didn't belong to us; it belonged to the state conservation department so no alcohol was permitted on the premises. Of course, in a camp you always need something for medicinal purposes so we kept a bottle of cognac. The only place to put it as there wasn't anything lockable, was in the filing cabinet under the letter "C." One day I came into my office and there was one of the kids there just trying to get a swig of that cognac. I said, "Hey, what are you doing, are you crazy? That isn't coke you know," and the kid said, "Can I help it if I'm a reading disturbance?"

Now, what did this stir up in me and, furthermore, what does such defiance and impudence and oppositionality stir up in all of us? You might ask me first of all, "Who is us?" It is easy to talk about us as people we know—the parents, the therapists, the teachers, or whoever is directly concerned with the child—but if we take the kid seriously and get involved with him, what I am going to say applies to all adults, both professional and nonprofessional who are confronted with oppositional behavior.

When I say, "What does it stir up in us?" I am not strictly talking about what we usually call our counter-transference. I find the term overused.

Anything or everything one feels as a professional with respect to a child is frequently called counter-transference which was not implied by the term originally. Not every feeling that hits us is counter-transference. In the clinical field we talk about counter-transference if the behavior or the pathology of the patient stirs up things in us which really have nothing to do with the situation now and which come from our own childhood, our own pathology, so that something of the child in us responds to what the patient produces. This is the more literal meaning of the term counter-transference. Now that also hits us but not only by itself. If I am nice to a child and he never says a word, I get mad after a while because I am helpless. That is not necessarily counter-transference. It is frustrating. I am frustrated by his oppositional behavior. As clinicians in the therapeutic situation we have elegant sophisticated problems of counter-transference which you can only afford if you are a clinician! A parent does not have counter-transference. But I am also in the same position as any parent, any teacher, any child-care worker, who reacts to oppositional children. I would like to make it clear that these affects I am talking about, that hit us from inside or stir us up from outside, are perfectly normal. In fact, it would be abnormal if we lacked these feelings and it could only mean that we don't care.

The question, therefore, is not, "What is stirred up in us?" but, "What do we do with what is stirred up in us?" First of all, let us admit openly that reactions to difficult, defiant kids are quite natural and not part of a neurosis. The more difficult the child the more feelings we have about him. We do not have to excuse them and we may even talk about them because they are not only natural but useful. They can often tell us what to do about the difficult behavior of the child. Of course they may also squeeze themselves between us and what the kid really needs and then they are a problem. It is not only my neurosis that sometimes messes up what I do to Bobby or Mary when he or she is oppositional; sometimes it is simply the normal reaction to the fact that I am getting worried by the situation. But is this normal reaction what the kid needs or is thinking that part of my hang-up? I have to take care of it. I have to ask, "What does the youngster really need at this moment?" So it is not only neurosis or the unresolved problems from earlier years that affect adults when they deal with children; it is also their normal and natural feelings although this is just what clinicians tend to underemphasize. Those of us who are loaded with a "professional self" have learned not to consider what it is natural to feel and so put it "out of mind." What the youngster needs now is to understand what and how we feel at the moment. This is our problem as professionals.

Let me list some of the most frequent affects which are likely to hit me if I am confronted with youngsters who happen to be, or produce behavior which we will agree to call, oppositional.

Sometimes the most visible oppositional behaviors are overemphasized. A few years ago, Anna Freud commented on a frequent misunderstanding in a similar situation. Social workers were trained to assume that if parents with a very disturbed youngster began to react negatively or unthinkingly to that youngster it was because they did not want him in the first place and rejected him. Anna Freud said it was necessary to distinguish between two different types of rejection—two different phenomena. The first is rejection from the outset; we know this happens. Then, there is rejection that develops later with experience. After you live for a period with a very difficult child, you can experience negative feelings. It does not imply that the child was originally unwanted. It does not even mean that you do not like him. It may mean that, but it does not have to do so. Secondary rejection can happen even though the youngster was not originally rejected. If you have a severely disturbed youngster who cannot respond normally to your mothering instincts, then this in itself creates a second wave of frustration. And it may be that this is what determines the inadequacy of the later loving or caring behavior of the adult. We should therefore bear in mind the different forms of rejections and some of the variations on this. For example, the child may have been unwanted at birth and then accepted; later the initial rejection may reappear and disrupt the relationship. There is a breakdown in the mechanism of denial dealing with the primary rejection which is reactivated and added to the secondary rejection. What I am emphasizing is what you know from experience: that it is not easy to live with a youngster who shows behavior that is unpleasant—no matter how well understood. It may be that some of it is even healthy reaction to bad circumstances but one feels like saying, "Will you please practice your 'healthy reaction' on somebody else and not always pick on me for a target!" I accept that there is a reality bound up with it but I may not always be able to remember it at the heat of the moment.

The Affects of the Oppositional Encounter

Let me remind you of some of the affects that hit us when we are confronted by the oppositional child. The list is by no means complete since the encounter can be very complex and generative.

First, there is *helplessness*—often a mixture of panic, helplessness and rage. When I am helpless in the situation either I get scared (and of course the kid smells that), or I get angry and not necessarily at the youngster. I may be angry at my own helplessness. Anyhow, the youngster has a scared or angry adult in front of him, and one cannot be surprised if he is affected, even though he may not know precisely what is the matter with you. His own reaction will be to become angry in turn, or anxious. (By the way, the only way I can rid myself of my own anxiety is to become angry. Rage is the way I cope internally with my own uncertainty, apprehension or fear.) Helplessness, therefore, occurs even in the normal course of living with youngsters from time to time, and when it happens, in addition to the rage and anxiety, the adult is likely to feel a certain amount of disappointment both in himself and in the relationship. He has let himself down, and let the kid down. How do we deal with this in ourselves? First of all we deny it. We become professional. We feel "neutral," God help us! And this is ridiculous! The consumer, however, has a sharper nose than that. We can smell somebody else's unconscious nine miles away while our own psychological body odor is not so noticeable. Obviously some peculiar affect of which we may be unaware gets across to others. This also happens in therapy. Even the most counter-transference-conscious clinicians can sometimes suffer from it. For example, I recall a case in which the child responded to the therapist in a negative oppositional way by keeping silent. Finally the patient brought in a can of insecticide spray and sprayed his therapist's face with it. The therapist was naturally very upset and insisted on the youngster being "gated" for four hours in his room. I think he should have been happy that at last the child was able to transform a passive into an active opposition. This is what therapy is about. What is the therapeutic situation for except to enable the patient to replicate his problem as closely as possible so we can take a close look at it. We do not want him to take his symptoms elsewhere. On the other hand, I can understand exactly what happened: the therapist was a child-care worker with not too much experience with these kind of children and obviously felt that such behavior only occurred with people who lacked understanding and experience, which is of course not true at all. With such children, under such circumstances, it could happen to Freud! But suddenly, when it happens to this therapist, he feels acutely disappointed and helpless. This reaction is natural. What the therapist then did was not natural and I would not advise it since it is punitive. The thing to do is to find some means of telling the kid, directly or indirectly, "Look, brother, there are certain things you can do and other things you don't."

Helplessness can also hit us in the area of communication. Let us say that you are a therapist trying to convince a youngster you are understanding him but he refuses to buy any of it; or a teacher, with a bedraggled kid in front of you, and you are attempting to show him that you really care and want to help him, and he behaves as if you were his arch enemy like everybody else. The inability to communicate what you really mean to convey can sometimes stir up a lot of feelings—mostly helplessness followed by anger. When you see that kid again anywhere, anytime, you are reminded of your helplessness and the anger comes back. I repeat that the feeling of helplessness is natural (especially if the kid is faster in biting, hitting and spitting than you are in holding him) but in the message that goes out to the youngster, the helplessness may be perceived only as anger. He sees you through his fantasies and may not recognize that you are different from others—that you do not shout back, do not kick back, and that you understand. And even when you are being "so nice," the kid lumps you in with the rest of the hostile world. You are entitled to your feelings because you put up with a lot of buffeting and garbage!

Parents do not have to be neurotic, do not have to be crazy, and do not have to be stupidly tied to old-fashioned methods when they let off physical and verbal steam at their children. Like the therapist, they react with anger out of helplessness because something needs to be done *right now*. (For myself I find that the more primitively and simplistically I respond—and this I think is peculiar to all of us—the better I feel about it. If I try gentle persuasion, it may be good for the kid but it does not take care of my affects.) Consequently, you frequently find people becoming cruder in their behavior to children or more simplistic in their selection of rewards and penalties because they have a theory and not because they are too helpless and unable to face the helplessness. They try whatever makes them feel less helpless at the moment. Whether it has anything to do with the client they are trying to influence is of course a secondary problem, but generally speaking, the more extreme the opposition the less helplessness it induces. The smaller and less noticeable and more undefinable the resistance is, the more it irks us. If the youngster is so crazy that he throws the furniture at me, I duck, but it does not make me feel helpless. I could not have helped it anyway; no skin off my prestige, knowledge or skill. But if the youngster, simply by the way he looks or talks or acts, suddenly starts another chain of contagion or by his silence sets me up for something, this really gets me. It is the little things that have the biggest effects. I cannot seem to influence them and they get me more and more helpless. The youngsters of course know this and have developed skillful little techniques to break us down. For instance, in the technique of slow motion, you ask the kid to bring you your pipe from over there. He starts off and on the way over he fiddles here and he fiddles there, and by the time he gets there, and looks out the window, a good deal of time has passed and finally you say, "What's the matter? I asked you to bring me the pipe." He answers, "I'm going, aren't I?" It is often pure torture and extremely rage-provoking. But when someone asks "What has the kid done?" you are at a loss to tell him.

A second affective phenomenon I would call *complexity shock*, to which we are becoming more prone as our theories and practices become increasingly simplistic. Behavior modification would be a case in point; M&M candy will eventually cure childhood of all its disturbances! As a result, clinical complexity becomes liable to produce shock. Some years ago, a study of child guidance procedures revealed the observation that parents tend to become more "primitive" during their attendance at the clinic and I would imagine that this is due to *complexity shock*. For a long time before the referral, the parents deny that their child has a problem. If he refuses to eat the parents do everything which their parents and grandparents would have done before them using every old-fashioned and well-tried trick in the family repertoire. Finally, when none of it works, the teacher advises them to take him to the local clinic. And there it all turns out to be much more complex than the parents ever thought. First of all, they are under the impression (or delusion, as the clinic thinks) that there is something the matter with the child and that the therapists will set it all right. That's their job, so let them do something about it.

The next thing they know is that *they* are on the hook! They are informed in no uncertain terms that it is up to them to change and not take their feelings out on their poor little children. When they come home at five o'clock and find half of the kids gone and the other half have not washed the dishes, no anger must be shown. "There is no such thing as a problem child, only a problem parent (A.S. Neil)." So what is the matter with them? And this means dragging themselves and the child twice a week to the clinic with all the people in the neighborhood saying "What's the matter? They have a child who needs a child guidance clinic. What kind of parents must they be?"

At this point, they may reach a critical understanding and decision, telling themselves, "This is ridiculous! How did we make a mountain out of a molehill? What went wrong from there. It must be simpler than they say it is."

Well it is complex, and the parents have to realize it and face it. But the first response to "complexity shock" does create helplessness and oversimplification of attitudes and behavior. As a result, the professional in the child guidance clinic may have to spend some time arguing against primitive and obsolete notions of reward and punishment that went out with the deluge! The parents may accept the fact that the youngster has a disturbance but nothing that a smack of a gift of candy cannot settle once and for all. They may accept that the child needs to be seen at the clinic but not that they need to go. If they are expected to attend, they would prefer to deal with the problem at home. But all of a sudden it gets bad again and once again they are overwhelmed by "complexity shock," and escape into primitivized behavior management and maneuvering. (One should mention that society as a whole can also suffer from "complexity shock" with the awareness of what is really necessary to do for children—not just provide them with extra playing fields! Society, like parents, is more inclined to recognize material deficiency than emotional disturbance; the latter is regarded as a behavioral deviation and dealt with effectively by behavior modification without bringing in society, parents, etc.)

This simplistic approach is not the same as the issue itself. The issue is "complexity shock." When faced with it, we react. We become or look for obvious causes or scapegoats. The professional reacts similarly if more sophisticatedly. He may say, "I think the parent ought to handle this" or "It's more complicated than I thought and we must admit the child," or "I should not have taken him in. It is a wrong referral! He needs a more structured environment, a larger therapeutic program." "Complexity shock" hits us, both parents and professionals, and forces us to do things that are not the most appropriate, but not because we do not like the child.

Another affect that hurts even the best motivated people arises when we rescue a child from an horrendous environment and he turns and bites (metaphorically) the helping hand. It can bring up very angry, vindictive and even sadistic responses that indicate a certain residue of the primitive under the professional skin. The child is treated as rejected but he is really being punished for the narcissistic injury he has inflicted on his rescuer.

A third affect that oppositional behavior generates is a fear of the future. This comes about when the child changes from one developmental phase to another and has already been described by Dr. Anthony.[1] As he mentioned, the two main ages when it is developmentally important to display oppositional behavior are between about three and five years and then again in early adolescence. There is also, I think, an intermediate phase of negativism at preadolescence between the fifth and seventh grade, and which appears to be on the increase at least in this country. The migration from childhood proper and the need to act like somebody three years older provokes some parents to react to this pseudo-precocity. He has no right to behave like an antagonistic adolescent when he is still to be labelled a compliant child. He is metamorphosing into a junior delinquent while still a grade school child. As the parents settle down with one step of development, prodromal signs of the next appear to haunt them when they are not even prepared for it. These affects, therefore, in parents and professionals stem from confrontation with age-inappropriate behavior, either regression or precocity.

The clinical behavior can be equally perplexing since our patients do not read out of textbooks, they mix the most varied syndromes together that really baffle us. We are worried by the fear of what they are likely to become in the future and we worry as to what we must do now to forestall that. We react therefore not out of anger at what is happening now but out of fear at what will take place next. So in the first instance we react not to the present but to what happened in the past and in the second instance we react not to the present but to what might happen in the future. In fact, we seem to avoid dealing with what is going on in the present, in the here-and-now.

This is an argument that no horticulturist would be so ignorant as to even hold, namely, that you must pamper your plants now and preserve them in a greehouse or else they will be unable to stand up to the rigors of outdoor life later. No horticulturist does that to a plant but every parent wants to do just that to his children. They cultivate a special kind of behavior as a safeguard against the hard times to come and find to their chagrin that the child begins to exploit it for all it's worth, and this begins to scare them. It is the Frankenstein story as developed in the nursery. He is growing up faster than he should under the special regime and soon he becomes too big and strong for them to deal with comfortably. If we are not helpful enough to parents, it is usually because we counsel them about developmental problems that are almost past; we should talk rather about the next phase while they are still in the previous one, so the parents can form a developmental perspective of what lies ahead and what will be normative. This will help to relieve them by giving them a time perspective. It is panic that makes monsters out of parents. As a result they fail to interpret behavior in the present but worry about its consequences in the future. For instance, we know that a certain amount of oppositionalism is normal, and that saying "no" first is important for the child to be sure that he is doing it and not somebody else. When we know this we can relax a little about it. We may do something if it goes a bit out of hand, but we don't have to become scared about it.

Our next affect creeps up on us from our own case histories and it happens to all of us if we are clinically trained. If you are not clinically trained, it would seem to be the most normal thing to have happen, namely, that children remind us of things from our past. There are two possibilities open to us. We can try to reproduce the same situation that worked wonderfully and helpfully in those early days except that we inevitably find that it no longer seems to fit. Or, we can try to do the exact opposite to save the child from our own less happy experiences. When I had to undergo retraining after working with neurotic, anxiety-ridden cases, to working with children who were delinquent, this was one of the lessons I had to learn. In my own life I was obviously a neurotic and not a delinquent child which explains why I have so much fun now living and working with delinquents. I was never allowed to play with "bad" kids. Now I can play with as many bad kids as I like and nobody can say anything about it. As a result of my particular upbringing, I assumed, for instance, that if a youngster had to admit to stealing something, that he would be embarrassed. I would therefore produce all kinds of behavior designed—imagining myself to be in his shoes—to make him feel comfortable. What it does do is to make him feel I am crazy. What he thinks is, "I swiped the stuff to get a good reputation so the other kids could trust me and let me into their gang and so I want everybody to know what I've done."

I had to first realize that I had entered a different world with different inhabitants, and that entirely different attitudes prevailed in the delinquent as compared with the neurotic thief. What may have been appropriate in my life if I had been caught doing this and someone wanted to make me feel comfortable is not appropriate here. This kid is comfortable. He does not want me to make him comfortable in this way. What I think makes him comfortable in fact makes him uncomfortable. We promise him privacy, and what he wants is publicity. He wants the gang to know. He wants his delinquency to be advertised.

In our zeal for empathy we must be careful not to confuse our past with the child's present and foist our past solutions onto his present problems. Empathy is fine. Without it we cannot do our job but we must avoid counter-identification with both the patient and his predicament. His situation is not our situation and never was. But we can try to understand and even to experience his feelings; however this also sometimes comes out the wrong way because we forget the radical differences between then and now. Our empathy may be adequate but our understanding deficient. We must stop seeing him in terms of our own life and more in terms of the current reality for this youngster in this social environment under these conditions. Unless we do this, we will suffer from the psychological fallacy of anachronism—the mindless assumption that what went for us goes for the child today.

Affects associated with what I will call the Abraham complex, which is also a natural response, and is as old as the Bible story if not older.*

> There was a guy called Abraham and he was a nice, friendly and good guy and God knew it. But you know most nice people get worried after a while. "Am I nice enough or good enough?" So the guy had some depressive phases. He thought, "Maybe God doesn't know how good I am. I've got to do something dramatic to show him." So what does he do? He goes to his Cub Scout age boy and says, "Look, kid, let's go on a trip, like father and son. Take your scout knife along." So they walk up the mountain and when they finally get there, the father says, "All right, now give me that scout knife and lie down on this nice little slab." He then pulls the knife and goes after the kid. But God is watching and by this time he has had it. He can't keep quiet. "Now look, brother, are you crazy or something? What is the matter with you? What are you doing here? If you want to show me you are a nice guy, then show me, but leave the kid out of it. Kids are not made just to prove your own righteousness. What is the matter with you? Why are you so depressive? Why not call a shrink?" (Pardon me, God, but this is 2,000 years ahead of time and shrinks are not yet born.) But it was crazy stuff even 2,000 years before Christ, and it is still crazy. Abraham said "All right" and he just took the kid on a little hike and went back home and they started collecting flowers and stamps and other things and everything was fine again.

So things have not changed much although they may be less dramatically conveyed. The message still comes through. The Abraham complex continues to lean on us heavily to this day. It is not explicit in the literature because it lies so close to the bone. But it seems important for us from time to time to show our righteousness, in terms of our moral values or our clinical training. We have to do it because we have to show somebody this is the way to run an interview. We have to be permissive because people watching might mistake me for a school teacher instead of a therapist whose job is to be permissive even if the youngster is begging him to set some limits. If I am not permissive somebody might think I am not clinically sophisticated and that would be a terrible loss of self-esteem! In short, at times we use the children in our care as props to demonstrate our professionalism, our competence, our integrity and our

---

*Editor's Note: This free rendering of the story of Abraham and Isaac gives some impression of Redl's style and his skillful intermingling of the sacred, the profane, the clinical and the colloquial in the service of insight.

loyalty to principles that may have nothing to do with that kid right now or his particular problem.

The situation is further exaggerated in supervision, when the hot breath of the supervisor goes down your neck as you wallow helplessly with a patient or a group of patients. Very often it is the wrong breath because if the supervisor knows his business, he will never say, "You should do this or that," according to the rules. He would be talking about another situation. He wants to be loyal to the letter of past lessons and apply it to the present even though the situation now is quite a different one. In fact, it is fortunate that we only get supervised occasionally or else treatment would become truly confused. In actual fact there are a wide range of things to be tried out and a lot of mistakes to be made and learned from. We do not know enough to be nonpragmatical, and we would never learn under constant supervision. Supervision is fine in its place, but not for every ubiquitous moment of therapeutic life.

So, in relating to children, feelings that they provoke in us are quite appropriate and normal provided we do not go to the extremes of hiding all our affects and pretending they do not exist or shooting the child. We should not get too scared of our feelings or else we will end up frightening the children as well. We must deal with our feelings as real, as normal, as natural and as expectable. When we fail to show our feelings, the child may be surprised. "Doesn't he care? Isn't he concerned about me?" The expression of feelings is therefore part of the appropriate management of the provocative oppositional child.

Here-and-Now Management

In giving advice to professionals "fighting in the trenches" one must first try to appreciate what they are going through and not simply assume certain developments on theoretical grounds. One should *never* give pious advice on what to do from the pulpit, speaking *ex cathedra*. It must always be translated into a dialogue. The worker must first describe the specifics of the event. This you must know in detail before you can make any sense of the situation or put yourself in his shoes. The general public is often angry at us in our field because our theoretical expositions sound quite helpful until they come with a specific problem and ask for operational advice. Then we hesitate and say tentatively, "Let's wait and see. He is only expressing himself symptomatically at the present moment. We'll have to see what develops further." "But he is smearing his feces all over the wall and we have to live with it. The other kids just hate him and beat him up."

It is obvious, if not imperative, that we have to say something. On the other hand, we are wise not to pretend that the situation can be fixed easily by some facile practical recommendation. We must let the parents know that it is not a simple matter like turning off a faucet. First of all, let me remind you that a symptom, like a sausage, has two ends. At one end is the primary symptom, such as oppositional behavior which you cannot eradicate by legislating against it; in fact, it is better not to fight it since it may even represent a symptom of a healthy development. But at the other end it is something else. This is the secondary gain from the primary symptom.

Let me illustrate this with a familiar-sounding vignette:

> As educational consultant I refer an oppositional child to a good teacher with an average-sized class of 30 that she manages very efficiently. I know her to be tolerant and understanding. I tell her that he gets episodically difficult especially where his "rights" are in question and that this tendency has a long history. This was his symptom. Obviously what the teacher has to know is: "Can I afford to buy this kid or will it disturb the other children who might interpret my leniency with him in terms of weakness, permissiveness, and discrimination and resent both me and him. Why should I let him be a spoilt brat and not them? Can I explain him to them?" I tell her that this is my business and not to worry about it. When the kid starts to play his piece, I tolerate it and ignore it while his self needs to assert itself. But once he moves beyond the bounds of needed autonomy and the secondary benefits begin to accrue, I let him and the group know that this is as much as we call all put up with. Before that, the teacher is helping him, the children are helping him and he is helping himself. After that point, nobody can help, nobody can be helped and everything is chaotic. When opposition becomes a secondary gain it is time to blow the whistle. Like all of us he is trying to get a little extra mileage out of his primary symptoms, and we cannot let him get away with it. It is also important for the other kids to understand the difference. Such management, carried out quietly but firmly, will also help to mollify the primary symptom.

In general, therefore, a teacher or parent of a youngster who produces a lot of really hard-to-take behavior must be helped to differentiate an unavoidable symptom that often needs to be tolerated for a while and secondary gains from the symptom that can be managed and modified with some reality testing. Clinicians rarely inform parents or teachers, once the diagnosis is given, what they are supposed to tolerate and what to interfere with. Children often become oppositional as a secondary symptom when they are admitted to hospital units and their whole routine of life is suddenly turned upside down. The child understandably responds by refusing to comply with any of the new rules. It is important for nurses and doctors to be aware of this and handle it with a maximum of tact and sympathy.

Another golden rule of management is never to talk in clinical esoteric terms with lay people, such as parents or teachers. We *do not* talk about the "oppositional child" as some new virus infection; we *do not* allow the parent or teacher to get away with saying, "What do I do about this oppositional child?" Instead, we get down to brass tacks. "What does the child do? What does he say? What bothers you about his behavior? What does he look like? How does it start? Where does it end?" Try to translate into an actual anecdotal incident– "an event-system." There is no other way to get at the clinical facts. It is easier with naive parents who generally stick to description. However sophisticated parents tend to speculate and hypothesize which generates a lot of muddle. What is worse is that they quote from the latest textbooks of psychology and may trap the clinician into an embarrassed confession of ignorance (No, he did not read the article by Bumke in the *Archives* of 1928, page 14, paragraph).

Even with one's collegues, one has to bear with their professional narcissism and indirectly worm the fact out of them, unadorned with theory. We want to know the details of opposition–not what Levy[2] or Spitz[4] or Anthony[1] has to say about it. Stick to the here and now, the actual process, the demarcated event and then you will begin to understand. The here and now approach puts the patient himself back into the picture.

One also has to consider the traditional oppositional systems of the parents that may be heavily opposed to "new-fangled" psychological laissez-faire. The therapist and youngster may find themselves on the same side. The parents will probe the ethical system of the doctor: "Do you believe in punishment?" or "Do you believe in overpermissiveness?" or "Are you one of those people like Spock[5] who wants to let the kids do everything they want?" Avoid such traps. Admit that the questions are academically interesting and pertinent but that right now you yourself are more concerned with what the child actually did or said, and how did they see it as a problem. You tell the parents that you will be happy to discuss the philosophy of child rearing with them when the present crisis with Tommy has subsided.

Sophisticated teachers and parents can set other traps of an either-or variety. Is the child sick or does his behavior just need modifying? Is it internal or external? Is it neurosis or just naughtiness? Is it clinical or simply psychological? If it is the latter can it be simply modified by behavior therapy? I call this an either-or syndrome–usually runs a course of from one to two decades before it is resolved. In such a period, especially, a professional worker must help his clients to come to grips with a host of such false dilemmas with regard to handling a child's behavior. You cannot hope to alter their thinking. It is based on deeply ingrained beliefs. The father tells you proudly, "I wouldn't be the man I am now if I hadn't been well and truly spanked as a child." Well let him hang onto that belief, but try to indicate as well what he should do with Tommy *right now* not only because the times have changed, or the world has changed or that children have changed but because there is a real value in dealing with many problems as if they are predominantly and even exclusively situational or "existential."

Then we come to the therapist's ungained beliefs which also need to be heard but which are often put forward as panaceas without reference to their strengths and weaknesses. It is a truism that therapists become invested in their systems and may come to regard them as cure-alls. A wrong system may be injurious to a child but even a right system may be inappropriate for a particular patient at a particular time. There is no medication "good for everybody" and the rigidity of such an attitude may be harmful. Good treatment is essentially flexible and adjustable, especially in child therapy.

Techniques for Oppositional Behavior

One should begin by pointing out the obvious: that it is not easy to live with a youngster who is oppositional, even for a mere fifty minutes. Secondly, one should be clear in one's mind that diagnosis is a different business from treatment—in one we try to discover how things come about, and in the other we try to do something about it now, firstly, and then something that will stop it from happening again. Reeducating the child's oppositional character is an entirely different business from dealing with an oppositional crisis when the kid suddenly challenges us defiantly. What can we do to relax him, to make him feel more amenable not more antagonistic? The most important thing is to help people to understand the difference between overpermissiveness and limit setting. Limit setting is not imposing penalties or prohibitions. Limit setting must be part of a conversation, a dialogue. When the child is oppositional, your first business is to talk to him and to get the facts straight from his side and from yours.

The most frequent mistakes are made in connection with timing. People either use the wrong time to say something (when the youngster is not in shape as yet to take it), say it much too late, or say it for much too long. The second mistake is that penalties cannot be added together as in a court of law. It is nonsense to state that it will be half an hour in solitary for saying "shit" and three quarters of an hour for "fuck" and that if you put in the two together and bring in your mother, it will be two hours. This is bureaucratic craziness! Timing has to do with the amount of time a youngster needs to reap the benefit from a penalty. He should not have to sit endlessly and pointlessly feeling sorry for himself, get miserable and lonely, develop claustrophobia, or become increasingly enraged. It is surprising that people pay little attention to psychological things whereas they are very punctilious about physical medication.

After the question of timing comes the nature of the message to be communicated. The parents want to stop a behavior but the way in which they say it may tell the child something quite different. It may encourage him to continue or to try something different. I can tell the teacher, "You don't have to take that from the kid. If he gets that high it's not good for him or anybody else. He ought to be somewhere else. Somebody ought to take care of him." But then the teacher bounces him in such a way as to say that nobody likes him and this embarasses him. This is what I mean by giving an unhelpful message. The kid needs two messages: one from the bouncer informing him why he is being sent out temporarily and another from the worker who stays with him and prepares him for his return once he feels and behaves more reasonably. The composite message is that we both want you back but this is difficult to convey in words. Our language is not adequate for conveying the psychological flavor of such a message; it does much better with material and mechanistic reward-punishment pronouncements, such as, "three candies," or "half-an-hour isolation."

In conclusion, I cannot do better than to counsel against impatience too early with the efforts made by either parents, teachers or whoever is spending 24 hours of the day with the child. We assume far too quickly that they are too hostile, lacking in understanding, or too full of their own problems. This may be true, but we should remember that the task of surviving this behavioral output can be extremely exacting and exhausting. Our situation is comfortable by comparison. We have the children for a limited time; they are brought to us; we see them in one room; and sooner or later somebody else has to take over. We do not have to face quite the same kind of helplessness. This is the point that must be made. We professional therapists need the help of others. To treat a youngster with severe forms of oppositional behavior, an hour in our office is not enough. We require strong allies in his normal environment, parents, teachers, counselors, who can help us at times to pick up the situation. We need a total preventative environment if we are to stop him from becoming a chronically oppositional character. We may look for additional help in "life space interviews." In these procedures the therapist enters the "life space" (Lewin) of the patient and deals with the crisis as it occurs and whenever it occurs.[3] Such crises may never appear in the regular treatment. We need more of both approaches—the regular and the critical. The patients in our own clinics today are different from those we saw in the 1920s in having both internal and external pathology. This means that no matter how competent we are we can do with the extra help; that is no reflection on our skill. We are dealing with a different type of difficulty. Children now appear to have more ego disturbances and other problems in the same neurotic package. They may need the possibility of living somewhere other than at home. So that at least some supportive therapy can be obtained in addition. This is hard to get today since it is costly although not as costly as armaments or space travel but more humanly meaningful. With lack of funds, there is a lack of adequate therapy. We must inform parents that the ideal treatments are not financially available and that we can do less than what is fully needed. Since we can only do less the kid may catch us with out counteroppositional pants down from time to time. But if we do the right thing only five times out of ten, we are still doing well.

In general, the child senses our attitude and is not simply judging us on our performance. They can even forgive us for many of our mistakes provided our hearts are in the right places. The same is true for the parents; they may be unable to do necessary things not because they do not care but because they themselves are not implemented enough. What it takes to implement the facilities needed to help a child with deeply ingrained oppositional tendencies may be highly complex. If the youngster is running around putting houses on fire or raping people then we call on many resources that public authorities are only too ready to provide, but if he is only oppositional, help is less available—yet the complexity of the need is as great. We know what to do from within, and clinically we know how complex it is. There is a wide gap between knowledge and implementation. In general, short-term or long-term therapeutic management needs time, money, space, personnel, patience, gradualism, continuous dialogue. It is thought in some high-up circles that all this can be replaced by suitable medication or operant conditioning. There is a pressing need for quick and easy techniques and only time and trial will tell us how amenable the human mind is to the immediate onslaught or gadget and how permanent or transient the effects are. The world is in so much of a hurry these days (going nowhere in particular except to perdition, perhaps) that all human operations, including treatment, must become part of the mad rush.

References

1. Anthony, E.J. The Genesis of Oppositional Behavior. This volume.
2. Levy. D. (1955) Oppositional Syndromes and Oppositional Behavior. In Hoch, P. and J. Zubin, Eds. *Psychopathology of Childhood*. New York:Grune and Stratton
3. Lewin, K. Field Theory and Experiment in Social Psychology: Concepts and Methods. *Am. J. Social Psychology*, 44:873-884, 1939.
4. Spitz, R. *No and Yes*. New York:I.U.P., 1965
5. Spock, B. *Baby and Child Care*. New York:Pocket Books, 1947.

CHAPTER 6

Symptomatic Oppositionality as Seen in the Clinic

DORIS C. GILPIN, M.D.
JULIEN WORLAND, PH.D.

Introduction

Since September, 1976, our clinic has had a weekly seminar on the oppositional child. At first we merely followed process notes on the treatment of one such child. We then became interested in an overview of many such cases. We were able to pull the charts of all children with such a label or a passive-aggressive label who had a diagnostic conference at the clinic since July 1, 1968. There were 36 cases which constituted almost 12% of the children. Thirty-three were boys and three were girls. These clustered at age six, age eleven and age fourteen. Half of the children were in the first two clusters. These two clusters are what we are reporting on; we are reporting only on the boys.

When we had the charts we tried to read them with open eyes and to notice anything possibly significant. We then discussed the children and worked out questionnaires to be answered from the charts.

Cluster Number 1

A group of eight boys first seen at ages five through seven. Half were Black which was in proportion to the number of Blacks at our clinic. We chose a group of 8 controls by pulling the next chart, matched for age, sex, and presence of psychological test material.

History. The referrals on these boys came from many sources. There were all socioeconomic groups represented. (See Figure 1.)

An unusual finding was that four had grandmothers in the home who were the mothering figures. The four other cases had no father in the home. In other words, not all the mothers had to work and therefore didn't have to call on a grandmother to be the mothering figure. In the control group there were again 4 out of 8 cases with mothering figures other than M but only 2 out of 8 fathers were out of the home.

Almost all had as presenting symptoms, temper and physical aggression toward people. There were descriptions of fighting, scratching, slapping parents and fighting at school. There were two exceptions to these presenting symptoms who were also different in other ways. One presented with enuresis and had depression as his only other symptom. The other presented for negativism and poor school performance.

Additional presenting symptoms were encopresis and resistance to attending school. All of the controls presented with temper and physical aggression and 3 had in addition poor school performance in the control group onset, varied from always to 1 year, with 3 being "always" whereas 5 control children were not described this way.

The age of onset was variable from always to four years. Five had onset at eight months to two years which corresponds with an impression or oral aggression and anal stubbornness. There were no precipitating factors in common; mostly there were none at all. Another symptom was wanting mother's attention. There were only two children who did not seem to want this, whereas 5 control children were not described this way. These cluster children were described as standing around pulling at mother. Other symptoms included fears which were absent in only one case (p.005), nervous habits, short attention spans, and school discipline problems. Depression was mentioned in three cases and was not known in the remaining five. The depressed children would say such things as "you don't love me." In the control group depressive statements were mentioned only once, fears once, and short attention span twice.

Of the eight in the cluster, half were definitely unwanted. They usually precipitated an unwanted marriage and were conceived out of wedlock. Only one was definitely known to be wanted. This one also was the only one with a passive mother and had the presenting complaint of enuresis rather than aggression. There were no unwanted children in 8 controls.

There was no consistent pattern to the first year of life in the cluster

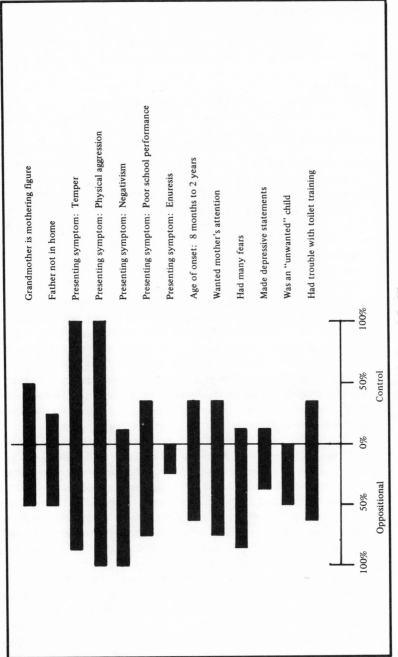

Figure 1. Boys 5-7: History

61

but five had trouble with toilet training in the second year of life. One mother described her feelings about toilet training as "you are not going to do that to me" when the child would eliminate in his pants. The children were described as refusing to sit on the toilet seat or sitting on it, doing nothing, and then, as soon as they got off the toilet seat, they would soil or wet. Only one had an easy toilet training. In contrast, there were toilet training problems in only 3 controls.

Mother. (See Figure 2.) As far as we know, six of the mothers or main mothering figures were from chaotic backgrounds or deprived background. Fairly typical was one mother who lived with her grandparents and whose schizophrenic father would visit every few months, stay for a month at a time and was very disruptive. Another mother had to keep house while her mother worked. In controls there were 2 deprived or chaotic backgrounds.

At least five of the mothering figures were controlling, aggressive and masculine, and two others may have been (p.001). One was passive. There was ambivalence about controlling in these women where it was known. Many liked the boys to be mischievous and tough and encouraged their sons to act out. One mother, for instance, was always in a hurry to take snapshots of the boy whenever he was in trouble or showing mischievous behavior. It may be that all of the women were this way. This was true in none of the controls. While there was 3 controlling mothers in the control group, they were not described as aggressive or masculine. There was no consistency as to whether girls or boys were liked better, nor was there consistency as to whether fathers were called on to discipline.

All of the mothers seemed to have been arguers (p.001). One mother said, "He gets on my nerves, screams and cries, throws fits until I lose my temper and I begin screaming too." This was not mentioned in any of the controls. Six mothers were known to be depressed and all may have been. One was so depressed that she cried in an interview when talking about her father's death. Two mothers in the control group was depressed.

There was no consistency as to whether these mothering figures were closer to their father or their mother. One factor noticed, the significance of which is unclear, was that two of the mothers had been exposed to sex with their father or stepfather. This was not noted in the controls.

Most of the mothers were hard workers; this was not true of controls. Only one was considered physically attractive in both groups.

Note: p values were calculated on all items and are indicated whenever < .01 which can be considered significant to differentiate the two groups. However, since this is a descriptive study, items with higher p values are also presented.

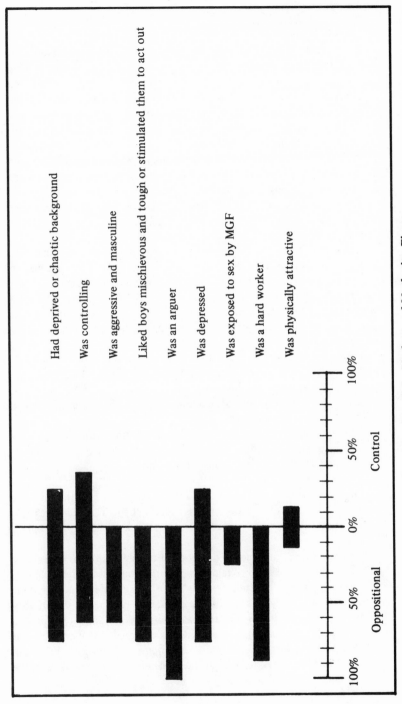

Figure 2. Boys 5-7: Mothers and Mothering Figures

Had deprived or chaotic background

Was controlling

Was aggressive and masculine

Liked boys mischievous and tough or stimulated them to act out

Was an arguer

Was depressed

Was exposed to sex by MGF

Was a hard worker

Was physically attractive

100%   50%   0%   50%   100%

Control

Oppositional

Father. (See Figure 3.) There was little or no information about three fathers. In controls there was little information on 2 of the fathers. Over half in the cluster were from deprived or chaotic backgrounds. There were 3 deprived backgrounds in controls. A typical story was that the parents were divorced when the father was two years old and he had to live with his mother and grandmother; he was not close to anyone. These fathers also worked long hours, only 1 control father did. One father worked at three jobs for twelve hours a day, seven days a week. These same fathers from the deprived chaotic backgrounds who worked long hours were also loners; there was only 1 loner in the controls.

Over half these men were or had been heavy drinkers in contrast to only 2 who were in the controls. Interestingly enough, these were not the fathers from the deprived or chaotic backgrounds.

There were three passive-aggressive fathers and one passive father. The rest were undiagnosed. In the control group 3 were definitely not passive-aggressive nor passive, one was passive and 4 were not diagnosed.

Only one father in the cluster identified with his son. This was the one with a passive wife and enuretic depressed son. Two of the fathers identified their son with a disapproved of sibling of the father's. One control father identified with his son.

Four in the cluster were felt to be loners and two were felt to be depressed; one was both. Among the controls, there was 1 loner and 1 depressed. Of the three in the cluster who showed little warmth for the patient, two were from the deprived or chaotic background. Absence of warmth was seen in 2 controls.

Four out of five cluster father's main interaction with their son was discipline (p.007). Exception was the boy who was easy to toilet train. In sharp contrast, this was true of none of the controls.

Parents together. (See Figure 4.) There was lack of affection in every marriage but that of the dependent enuretic boy. The marriages also lacked in mutual trust and respect. There was lack of affection in only 2 controls.

Four sets of parents were felt to control the child for their own needs, not for those of the child. Again, an exception was the enuretic child as well as two others. In three families there was clear evidence that the parents felt autonomy was bad for the child; they felt that he should obey them. In one family it was also felt that autonomy was bad for the parent. In three additional families it seemed to be accepted that it was just not possible to be autonomous. Clearly, autonomy was no issue in 5 controls and not known as an issue in the remainder. In four families in the

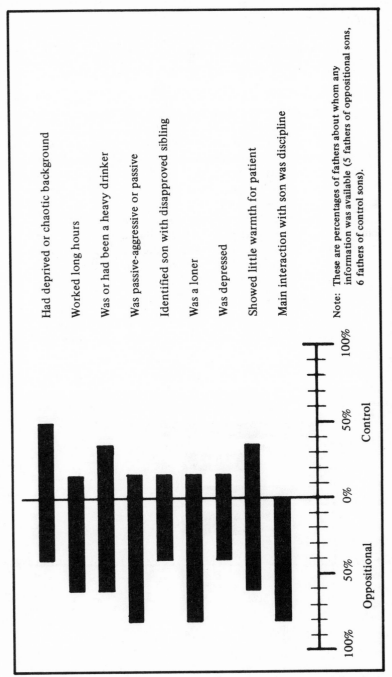

Figure 3. Boys 5-7: Fathers

Had deprived or chaotic background

Worked long hours

Was or had been a heavy drinker

Was passive-aggressive or passive

Identified son with disapproved sibling

Was a loner

Was depressed

Showed little warmth for patient

Main interaction with son was discipline

Note: These are percentages of fathers about whom any information was available (5 fathers of oppositional sons, 6 fathers of control sons).

100%   50%   0%   50%   100%

Oppositional   Control

65

cluster it was noted that the parents did not respond to small cues. This was not noted in any controls.

Psychologicals and psychiatric interview. (See Figure 5.) These children were seen similarly by psychiatrists and psychologists regardless of the sex of the examiner. One child had no psychological testing.

Most psychologists noted slightly lower visual motor scores but did not attribute these to organicity. Instead, they attributed these lower scores to the oppositionality of the child. Two children had adequate scores in this area. There were 3 slightly lowered visual motor scores in the control group.

Half of the cluster were definitely noted to have trouble with autonomy. One of these was the enuretic child of the passive mother. The other child who was enuretic was noted to have quite a dependency problem and had onset of some symptoms in regard to separations. Presumably he did have an autonomy problem of sorts. The control group yielded only 1 child with autonomy.

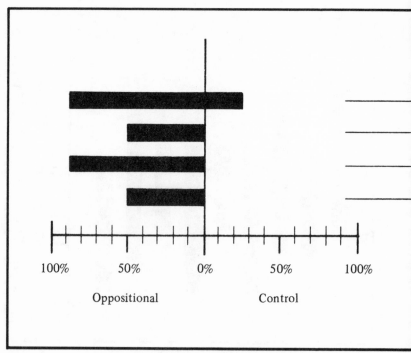

Figure 4. Boys 5-7: Parents Together

All the cluster were noted to be controlling (p.001). This was manifested in such ways as refusal to talk, telling the examiner what to draw, and starting without waiting for directions. No controlling behavior was noted in the control group.

The psychiatrist felt that the child was not withholding in only one case. This was the case of the bedwetter with a passive mother who had previously been seen as having no trouble with autonomy. This seeming contradiction may mean that his controlling worked to maintain autonomy so there was no trouble.

Aggression was expressed openly in the cluster group. For instance, when asked what he should do if a smaller child started a fight with him, one boy answered, "I'd beat him." Another child told of slapping his mother. There were quotes such as "I'll knock you off, I'll kill you." This open aggression was seen in at least four cases; it was expressed covertly in the rest and both ways in one. The control cases showed 3 children with open as well as hidden aggression.

Depression was noted in three cases. For instance, one boy talked about

Lack of affection, mutual trust or respect in marriage

Parents controlled child for their own needs

Autonomy was an issue in the family

Parents did not respond to small cues from child

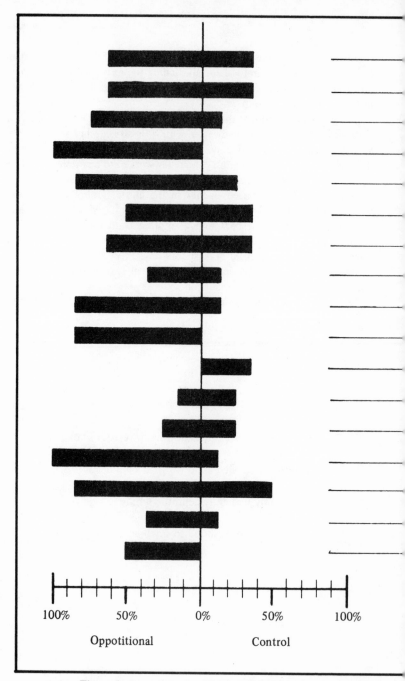

Figure 5. Boys 5-7: Psychologicals and psychiatric Interview

———————— Slightly lowered VM scores

———————— Outwardly turned anger

———————— Trouble with autonomy

———————— Controlling

———————— Withholding

———————— Open aggression

———————— Covert aggression

———————— Depressed

———————— Anal defenses

———————— Primitive and external superego

———————— No evidence of superego

———————— Well-internalized superego

———————— Trouble with reality testing

———————— Father and mother not well differentiated

———————— No evidence of satisfying relationships

———————— Masculinity seen as attacking

———————— Mother seen as superpotent; father less potent

having all of his toys given away. There was depression in only 1 control.

All but one of the boys were felt to have anal defenses (p.005). This was the boy with the passive mother who was also perceived as having some phallic oedipal features which none of the other boys had. Anal defenses were present in only 1 control case.

The superego was seen as largely primitive and external where it could be delineated at all. The one phallic oedipal boy with the passive mother had more of an internalized superego. In contrast, 3 of the controls were felt to have no superego and 2 to have a well internalized superego.

There was minor trouble with reality testing in two of the cases. One very interesting observation was that in no case were father and mother seen as well differentiated (p.0007). For instance, both were seen by their sons as spiders with big teeth and no heads. Or in another case, both mother and father puppets would say the same thing such as "no" and "go to your room." This lack of differentiation was seen in only 1 control.

In only one case did there seem to be evidence of satisfying human relationships. A typical story was that of a chicken left outside in his crib during a storm who might get wet and even die. Four of the controls found relations satisfying.

Masculinity was seen as attacking in three, not at all in one; attacking males were seen in only 1 control. There was no pattern as to whether femininity was seen as caring or uncaring.

Where it was noted, the mother or mothering figure was always seen as superpotent and the father as less potent. Also where it was known, the father was seen as less involved. These items were not noted in any of the controls.

Summary. The evidence seems to be that these are boys with mothers or mothering figures who are ambivalent about controlling and who argue with the boys and seem to stimulate the boys to act out. The mothers seem to discipline for their own needs and are depressed. They tend to project blame onto husbands. The fathers are not as consistently alike.

The boys were noted to be controlling with a largely primitive and external control system. They did not differentiate father and mother well but mothers tended to be superpotent and fathers less potent. All of the boys showed the above characteristics where it is known.

The ones with presenting symptoms of temper and physical aggression were also more alike in other dimensions than those with other presenting symptoms.

One subtype seems to be the child who presented for enuresis and had depression. He was the only wanted child and the only one with a passive mother and the only one whose parent's marriage was felt to be adequate. These parents did not seem to control for their own needs. They did, however, feel that autonomy was bad for the child. He seemed to need controlling to maintain autonomy. He was perceived as phallic oedipal with more of an internalized superego.

Another subtype may be the more or less symbiotic child with minor problems in reality testing who had been brought in for negativism and school problems rather than physical aggression. His mother was perceived by him as an eagle—very ferocious about protecting her children but also dangerous.

Therapy. The fathers were mainly seen by female social work students. Missed appointments ranged from 40 to 90%. In the control group missed appointments ranged from 75 to 90%. Only in one case still in therapy is it felt possible there may be successful therapy for the father. There is no information on another father apparently still in therapy. Of the completed therapies, none were felt to be successful with the father. No father stayed with the therapy except the two still in therapy. There were of course, four families where there were no fathers to involve. Lack of success does not seem to be related to whether the father was seen with the mother or separately. The one father still in therapy with possible success is being seen by a staff social worker. The focus of therapy in this case has been to develop trust and lessen marital conflict.

Mothers also by and large were seen by female social work students with missed appointments in the range of 27 to 40%. There were 75 to 90% who missed appointments in the controls. One mother, however, missed 75% of her appointments as did the father in that case and this was the reason for closing the case. Even though the major mothering figure was the grandmother in four cases, she was not seen.

The three cases still in treatment have had mothers who were major mothering figures. Thus, every treatment failure involved a family with a grandmother who was important but left out of therapy. Two families with a grandmother who was left out of therapy were considered successful.

In a case still in treatment where we have information, parents and patient are missing 40% of appointments. The focus in this case has been various. With the first social worker it was to develop a relationship and trust; with the second social sorker it was to work through terminations with previous social workers and to establish trust and support for the child's therapy.

One of the successfully terminated cases was that of the more dependent boy. Another mildly successful case involved helping the mother, not the mothering figure, in seeking satisfying relationships with adults and in developing better control of her own impulses. The evaluation of success was that she developed self-esteem. These two cases were seen 21 and 16 times respectively with good attendance.

One case still in therapy involves a mother who was sent elsewhere for psychiatric treatment because she seemed to be getting psychotic. This was the mother of the symbiotic boy.

Another case was considered successful for the boy but not for the parents. The boy was the only one seen more than once a week. He was seen for 113 visits over 66 weeks. The focus of therapy was on relationship and he gained in control of impulsivity, basic trust, and school behavior. The father pulled out of therapy early. The mother, not the mothering figure, became very dependent and was unwilling to terminate.

The dependent boy who improved with successful termination had been helped mainly with self-esteem. The other improved boy was also helped with self-esteem and development of internal controls. It is interesting to speculate why self-esteem was focused on in the treatment when it was not picked up as being a particular problem by the psychologist or psychiatrist.

The three cases still in treatment are showing slow improvement. Self-esteem is again mentioned in two of them as well as the development of relationships. In all three cases, they are being helped to experience autonomy; two of the therapists mentioned helping the boys to understand oppositionality.

Thus, of eight cases, one was sent elsewhere to a special school, one was unsuccessful and terminated when parents failed to come, and two were terminated with the improvement of the boy and mother after relatively short term therapy. Both of these had absent fathers and in neither case was the mothering figure seen. One was terminated with improvement of the boy, not the parents, after a long term intensive treatment in which the mothering figure was not seen. Three boys are still in treatment for a longer time than the terminated cases and none of these sessions involve the mothering figure.

In the control group 1 was referred elsewhere, 3 did not come for therapy, 1 did not have a therapy recommendation, 2 improved in individual therapy and 1 did not improve in group therapy.

Cluster 2

This is a group of ten boys first seen at the ages 10 to 12. There were two ten-year-olds, six eleven-year-olds, and two were twelve years of age.

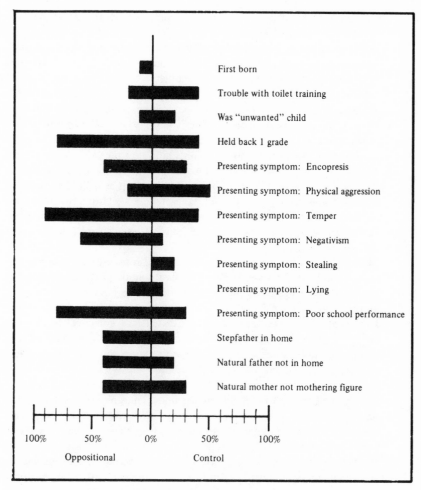

First born

Trouble with toilet training

Was "unwanted" child

Held back 1 grade

Presenting symptom: Encopresis

Presenting symptom: Physical aggression

Presenting symptom: Temper

Presenting symptom: Negativism

Presenting symptom: Stealing

Presenting symptom: Lying

Presenting symptom: Poor school performance

Stepfather in home

Natural father not in home

Natural mother not mothering figure

100% 50% 0% 50% 100%

Oppositional   Control

Figure 6. Boys 10-12: History

History. (See Figure 6.) We noted only one Black family represented. This is much lower than the black representation in our clinic, which is 40%. Again the referral sources were varied; three came from schools.

In contrast to the five- to seven-year-olds, only one in this cluster had a mothering figure who was not the real mother during the preschool years; only one had no father in the home. These facts signal what later seems to become clearer—that these boys are different and they represent a different problem than the younger group. The control group had all mothers as mothering figures.

The most common presenting complaint of eight out of the ten cluster patients was poor school performance. Comments from the teachers were such things as "he does not try hard enough," "written work is confused and messy," "does not follow instructions." Many of the children hated school. In six of the children with poor school performance it was felt this was due to "I won't" rather than "I can't." Half of the controls were brought in for poor school performance.

Lying was one of the chief complaints in four of the cases. The description of the lying was somewhat unusual. For instance, one mother said that the boy imagined he had done something such as going fishing with his father; another said that the boy exaggerated to get attention. One boy told his mother that a policeman used foul language and was rough with him when the policeman brought him home. Three control children were brought for lying.

Two children had been stealing cans of food from the pantry or money for food and the other was stealing pencils at school. There was stealing in 5 controls and negativism was seen in nine of the boys in contrast to 4 controls. One mother described how the child got a pale deadpan look of determination on his face and "you can tell he's not going to move." Another mother explained how she could never say, "you must" or he would withdraw and do nothing. "We don't expect too much but we get nothing."

Temper was described in six, but in 1 control only. One boy became angry and threw a bottle of milk on the floor. Thus, physical aggression to people is no longer a prominent feature; however, three cases were destructive of things. Physical aggression was a problem in 2 controls. Two were encopretic and the encopretic cases started at school age. There was 1 continuous encopretic in controls; one was suspicious. There was a long list of other complaints such as wanting mother's attention, nervous habits, discipline problems at school, destructiveness, somatic complaints, bullying, enuresis, and accident proneness.

In line with a poor school performance, eight had been held back a grade; five of these (the majority) in second grade. One of the two who had never been held back turned out to be the only one helped by our therapy. In controls, 3 children had been held back a grade—the 2nd, 3rd, and 4th respectively.

Four of the ten boys were definitely unwanted children and in only two was there good evidence that they were wanted. There were 2 unwanted boys in control.

The boys were equally divided between those who had a difficult first year of life and those who did not.

Toilet training was easy in three cases and difficult in four; two of the controls had been difficult to train. In every case this was just the opposite of the first year experience. That is, a difficult first year is correlated with easy toilet training and vice versa. One mother spoke of how she dreaded bowel training as her pediatrician had told her that the boy had a mind of his own.

Four of the boys were the oldest in the family; one was an only child, two were middle children and one was the youngest. There were 3 first-borns in controls and no youngest child.

Mother. (See Figure 7.) The mothering figure had a deprived or chaotic background in half of the cases. In 4 controls she was described as controlling, aggressive and masculine in eight of the cluster, but controlling in only 3 controls. The fathers would call the mothers bull-headed or say, "she wants to wear half my pants." Two mothers were passive. Four mothers seemed ambivalent about controlling but two were not. Only one definitely liked girls better than boys and only three definitely liked boys to be mischievous and tough. Two of these definitely stimulated their sons to act out. No controls wanted tough mischievous boys and none stimulated sons to act out. One mother described her father as always making sure he was late and others had to wait for him but as soon as he started his joking, "you can't get angry at him anymore." She wanted her son to be like this grandfather.

Three of the mothers called on the father to discipline, which was not true of controls, and three argued before or instead of punishing. Controls did not argue but 4 parents physically punished their sons. Three seemed seductive with the patient and one of these was one of the passive mothers. For instance, the boy and mother had the same horoscope which the mother pointed out as very meaningful. This horoscope was conflictual with father's and the mother explained that this was why the father rejected "us." The mothers would allow the sons to sleep with her when the father was not there.

Two mothers had had psychiatric help and five were depressed; this included the two who had had help. There were 4 depressed control mothers; three had had psychiatric help.

It was noted that two mothers were closer to their maternal grandfather than maternal grandmother and one was the opposite. Six had definitely always been hard workers. Controls showed that 2 had been hard workers.

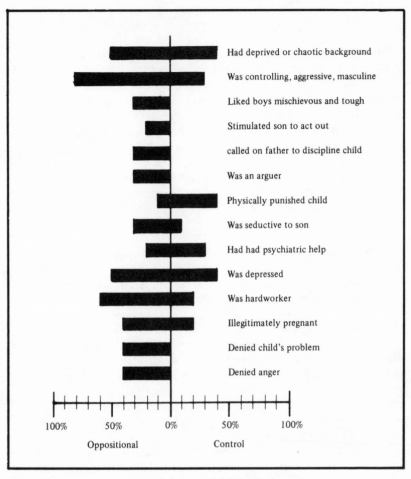

Figure 7. Boys 10-12: Mothers

Four were illegitimately pregnant and one additional may have been, but only 2 control pregnancies were illegitimate.

There seemed to be a range in intelligence and a range of physical attractiveness.

Four mothers tended to deny the problem. One mother said that her son just didn't have anyone to play with; another said he was "momma's boy." They also tended to deny anger. The denial was not noted in any control. One mother was felt to be symbiotic and this was the case where treatment was later successful.

Father. (See Figure 8.) Not much is known about two early fathering figures as one left the home when the boy was one-and-a-half and the other had a stepfather about whom the history was taken.

Again, as was the case with the mothers, five fathers came from a deprived or chaotic background; one control father came from such a background. One father said that his mother never had a kind word for him. He had signed his report cards himself as his parents hadn't bothered to look at them. In only one case were both parents free of a deprived or chaotic background. This was the case where the father was noted to be quite carefree and the mother was passive.

Father was a hard worker in six cases and in half of these he worked long hours. There were only 2 hard working men putting in long hours in the controls. In contrast to the six-year-olds, only one father was a

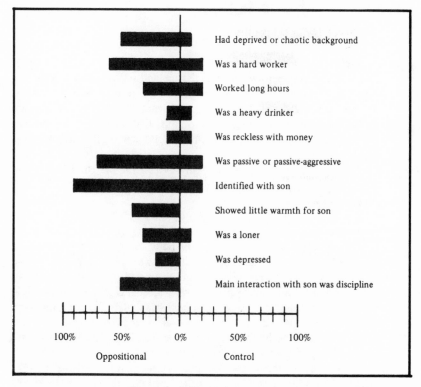

Figure 8. Boys 10-12: Fathers

drinker and one was perhaps reckless with money, the same as the controls.

There were seven passive or passive-aggressive fathers, in contrast to 2 in controls (p.007) One father claimed he got along well with the patient because he gave in to him. This is a higher proportion than the six-year-olds. The one father who was not definitely diagnosed as passive or passive-aggressive was a carefree father who owned a motorcycle. Most of the fathers identified with their sons; in fact only one did not. Two controls did. For instance, the father would say, "Oh he just tells white lies which is normal . I do it." This is in contrast with the younger group where only one father identified with his son.

These fathers tended to minimize the problems of the boys. Four were lacking in warmth for the boy, but no control fathers were. There were three loners and two depressed fathers with one overlap. In controls there was 1 loner and no depressed fathers.

The main interaction with the boy was disciplinary in five which was not true of any of the controls (p.007).

Parents together. (See Figure 9.) Only three marriages were felt to be adequate and the rest lacked mutual trust and respect. Controls showed only 3 adequate marriages, too. In five of the relationships the parents exercised control for their own needs and not the child's, this was also true of 3 controls. As an example of this, the parents would continue to use corporal punishment even when they knew it effected no change in the boy.

Three of the parents saw autonomy as bad for the child but two of these saw it as good for the parent. In the controls autonomy was an issue in only 1 case.

Psychologicals and psychiatric interview. (See Figure 10.) Again there is no striking difference between the psychological and psychiatric evaluation. Perhaps the most unexpected finding was a lowered visual motor score in seven of the nine cases where it was tested. This was quite serious in two. One additional child had relative acalculia. One examiner said that the lowered visual motor score could have been related to oppositionality rather than a true deficit. The remainder of the lowered visual motor scores seemed to be because of a genuine handicap. There were only 2 lowered visual motor scores in the control group.

To jump ahead for a moment, it should be pointed out that psychotherapy helped, nor remediation. The successfully treated case was one of the ones with a lowered visual motor score. He received no direct help about his visual motor performance.

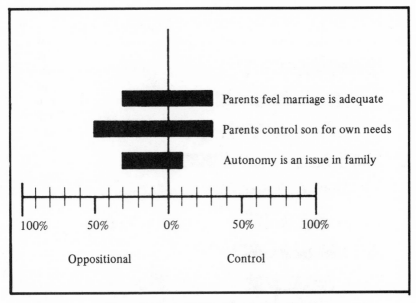

Figure 9. Boys 10-12: Parents Together

These boys were not noted to be impulsive; they showed outward turned anger in five cases and projected anger in four. Controls showed outward anger in 4 of the boys and projected anger in 5. Aggression was the big concern in nine cases, and in 8 of the controls. This was expressed in many ways. One boy would like to be a ferocious lion even though he turned off to TV violence. One boy kept a BB gun under his pillow so he could shoot a tiger if it attacked him. Sometimes before going to sleep he would shoot at a picture of a tiger to protect himself. Aggression was expressed covertly in five; four controls expressed aggression this way. This was displayed in many ways. The boy would point out the nonessential details of a task or criticize the composition of the test materials or ask to go to the toilet or mumble or complain of tiredness or give very brief answers. In the rest, aggression was expressed openly; there was open expression of aggression in only 2 controls. Eight seemed to be depressed in contrast to 3 of the controls. There would be talk of the boy's grave or suicide. Four were deprived as was true of the controls. Eight were seen as withholding, but not true of controls where only 2 were. Trouble with autonomy was seen in only two and only 1 control. Five cases were controlling in contrast to 2 controls. Anal defenses were seen in five. One boy for instance, liked to read the encyclopedia. Three controls

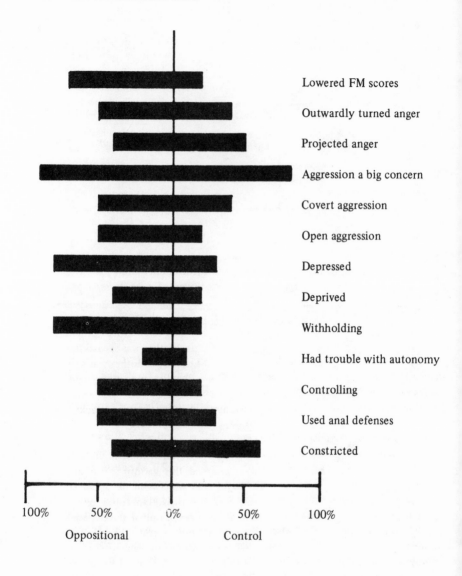

Figure 10. Boys 10-12: Psychologicals and Psychiatric Interview

were anally fixed. Four of the boys were constricted as were 6 of the controls. One showed withdrawal. Others showed withdrawal by wanting to be astronauts to get away from people or an ostrich who keeps his head in the hole.

The controls, where commented on, were largely external and also primitive this was true in five of the cases. (See Figure 11.) The one child with a severe superego who had parents with neither a deprived nor chaotic background, had a separation problem from his mother and major trouble with reality testing. His mother was noted as more intrusive than anything else. There was absence of superego in 2 controls, clearly intern-alized superego in 3, and a still somewhat external controls in 3.

Minor trouble with reality testing was seen in one of the boys with a passive mother and also in a boy who had a lot of dependency needs. Only 4 controls had this problem.

In only two cases were the human relationships felt to be satisfying, whereas this was the opposite in 6 of the controls. These boys saw people as statue-like things in their descriptions or they wouldn't draw people at all saying, "I can't." The story characters they invented were shot, robbed or attacked by sharks.

These reports did not say nearly as much about relations to parents as the reports on the younger children. Father was seen as less potent in four, but not so in two of the cases. One control father was seen as less potent. The males were decapitated or turned into boys. Mother was seen as super-potent in two but it was not known how she was seen by the rest. Two controls also saw their mother this way. Occasionally she was seen as devouring, "an anteater." Again, though masculinity was seen as attacking in three and femininity as uncaring in three, it was not known in the rest. These facts are the same in the controls.

A striking finding was that four of the boys were felt to be femininely oriented and were seen as homosexually oriented; this was not true of any controls. This included the one successful case which will be discussed later. In addition three more had poor sexual identification; four controls had poor sexual identification. Thus, a total of seven out of the ten boys had problems in this sphere. A majority of the boys (seven), were felt to have reached the phallic stage. This was manifested as drawing motor cars although there was emphasis on exhaust fumes which showed some anal characteristics still. The phallic stage was not seen as a phase dominant theme for there was always considerable remaining evidence of anal difficulties such as rockets blasting off or of oral difficulties such as tape-worms or mouths (p.002). In two cases there was nothing noted past the

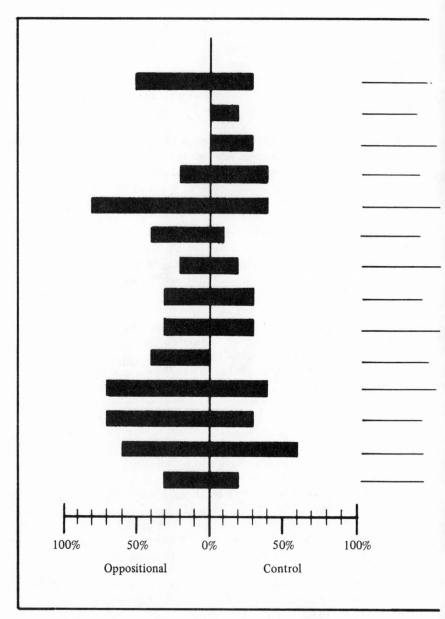

Figure 11. Boys 10-12: Psychologicals and Psychiatric Interview

————————— Primitive and external superego

————————— No evidence of superego

————————— Well-internalized superego

————————— Trouble with reality testing

————————— No evidence of satisfying human relationships

————————— Father seen as less potent

————————— Mother seen as superpotent

————————— Saw masculinity as attacking

————————— Saw femininity as uncaring

————————— Femininely and homosexually oriented

————————— Poor sexual identification

————————— Reached phallic stage

————————— Felt self inadequate

————————— Had difficulties breaking ties with mother

anal stage. Oral fixations were present in 4 controls, 3 were anal, and 3 were oedipal.

Six boys felt themselves inadequate, as did 6 controls. They would say they didn't look very good or that a character they identified with looked like he wouldn't be very strong. They were self-critical and four felt they had little control over what happened in their lives.

Three had difficulty breaking ties to their mother as compared with 2 controls; this included the successfully treated boy. He also felt adequate.

Summary. There was a group of boys with poor school performance and visual motor deficits who also presented with negativism. They had failed second or third grade. They were unwanted children with a controlling mother who was also depressed. Fathers were passive or passive-aggressive or carefree and identified with their son and minimized his problems. Aggression was a big concern. The boys were withholding and depressed with a largely external superego. They felt inadequate. Human relationships were seen as unsatisfying. They tended to have problems with sexual identification. Although most showed some evidences of phallic interest they tended to be in anal phase dominance.

Five cases had all of the previously mentioned characteristics as far as is known.

Again there seemed to be subtypes; was the symbiotic boy who was a wanted child and did not have school difficulty. He seemed to have more of a separation problem. This is reminiscent of the symbiotic boy in the six-year-old group. Another possible subtype was the school refusal boy who also had trouble separating from his mother, lacked sexual identity and had identity confusion.

Thus the boys with separation problems differed in other ways from the majority.

Therapy. Six families refused suggested therapy. These six included the five most typical cases plus the school refusal boy. Four controls refused therapy and 2 controls were referred elsewhere. One control did not have a therapy recommendation while 3 controls received successful therapy.

The two boys with passive mothers were taken into unsuccessful therapy. In one case the parents were placed in a parent's group and the boy in a boy s group. They dropped out after 26 weeks, 13 sessions—a 50% absence rate. The parent's groups focus is not known. The boy's group focus was to help with self-esteem and support male identification. In the other cases of a boy with a passive mother who was taken into unsuccessful therapy, the father missed 93% of appointments with a female staff social worker. The mother missed 37% of her appointments but did become able to set limits better and see the patient more clearly. The boy in a group only missed 12% of the sessions for 42 weeks. The group focus was again to develop self-esteem and help in the struggle for masculinity. The boy made some gains. This case was terminated because the family moved.

The boy with good visual motor equipment and no school failure was seen in treatment but the case was terminated by the mother. The parents had been seen together by a social worker for 20 weeks and then separately for 20 weeks. The father did better when seen alone, listening better to his son and getting involved. He himself gained in self-confidence. The social worker tried to get the mother to support the father without success. The mother pulled the family out of therapy apparently being unable to tolerate her loss of control over the family.

The case deemed successful had no father available. This was the symbiotic case. The mother was seen 82 times over a period of 108 weeks. for the first 24 weeks she was seen every other week. She missed 24% of her appointments. She was helped to see her son more clearly but only intellectually until she and her son were seen together for the last 48 weeks. At that time she was able to extend more freedom to him. When he was seen alone the female social work therapist had as her aim to develop a relationship and help him understand his oppositionality. She felt he did well. There was no mention of any aim at changing his sexual orientation and it is doubtful that therapy was successful in this area. In the control group attendance was 75-81%.

Conclusion

Thus, we seem to do much better at getting children into treatment who are in the younger age group. We seem to be 100% unsuccessful at getting the typical 11-year-old into treatment.

It would help to highlight the ways these two clusters of boys were alike and how different.

A big difference is in the presenting complaint. The younger boys were brought in for their physical aggression toward people; the older boys were brought in for poor school performance.

Both groups tended to be unwanted children with controlling mothers who were depressed. The fathers tended to be passive-aggressive; they did not identify with the younger boys but did relate to the older ones.

Both groups of boys had primitive and external control systems. The younger group was more controlling, the older group was more concerned with aggression, withholding and depression. The older boys had problems in sexual identification, the younger group did not differentiate mother and father well.

The older boys showed more phallic development but both groups were mainly anal in phase dominance.

Both groups had visual motor problems but in the younger group these were felt to be a result of opposition; this was not so in the older group.

CHAPTER 7

Psychotherapy of the Oppositional Child

DORIS C. GILPIN, M.D.

The psychotherapy of the oppositional child is grounded on two generally accepted therapeutic canons for the treatment of children: firstly, that one needs to understand the factors that have made the child what he is and are keeping him that way; and secondly, that if the impediments to healthy development are removed from the path of the child that his further progress along healthy lines can often be left to his own inner resources without the need for any massive reconstruction from the outside.

From the point of view of the therapist, the oppositional child represents a patient who is, by definition, not going to be easy to handle, not going to be cooperative, not going to accept clarifications and interpretations gladly and gratefully, and not going to surrender to the therapeutic process without a considerable amount of fight. The intrapsychic conflicts of the patient become the interpersonal conflicts of therapy and may be equally unrelenting and bitter.

History inevitably repeats itself in the therapeutic situation. The child who has been bossed around by a mother almost totally unsympathetic to his growing need for autonomous control anticipates the same treatment at the hands of his therapist and is ready to understand every rule and regulation pertaining to the treatment environment and procedure as an attempt to control him. The therapist must expect an automatic resistance that is sometimes overtly defiant but often covertly passive to the point of inertness. The "will not do" oscillates with the "does not do" but both amount to the same thing in the end—opposition to the therapist and to the therapeutic procedures and processes.

The Goals and Stages of Treatment

What should be the goals of therapy? Obviously there is an overall need to free the child from his defensive style of automatic opposition. The achievement of this goal, however, includes several other aims. The patient will need to develop enough confidence about himself as someone to be counted and, therefore, not have to rely on his negativism to have his viewpoint considered. He will need to understand his lack of cooperation as therapeutically counter-productive. He will need to recognize his manipulative strategies as a system of controlling devices unconsciously set into action when he himself is threatened with controls. He will need to appreciate that the therapist is there only to help him to replace outer with inner controls, unconscious with conscious controls, and false independence by real autonomy. He will need to understand this in the context of reliving, at least in a symbolic way, the training experience of early life but this time without trauma. He will need to discover that his autonomy does not have to disturb the autonomy of others and that others, in general, and therapists, in particular, can function as allies in his autonomous development. He will need to become consciously aware of who he is and who he wants to be so as not to be caught by unconscious identifications as his only choice.

The period of treatment can be divided into three stages. The first of these is mainly devoted to developing a good enough therapeutic alliance to withstand the oppositional pressures. The child needs to discover that his autonomy is not at risk. He is therefore given a carte blanche to explore what interests him, to talk or not to talk as he chooses, to disagree with and to contradict the therapist whenever he thinks necessary. The therapist, on his side, should concern himself with clarifying the developing situation and with conveying his deep and abiding respect for his patient's need for autonomy. He does this not by eschewing all activity on his own part but by acknowledging the child's potential from the very beginning. Thus, a child who asks, "What's that for?" can be told, "I bet you can figure that out." This does not imply a refusal to satisfy the child but an understanding of the fact that his unmet needs are at a higher level plus a feeling of respect for his abilities. Questions of "should" such as, "Should I do thus and so?" need to be dealt with in the same way. The child must be made aware of his own autonomous rights with regard to "should." It does not have to come from the authority figure in the room, namely the therapist. Even with respect to certain things that are in reality not permitted, the patient can find out that he can become the authority in this as well; by accepting certain limitations, he can use the situation better to his own advantage. The therapist can systematically convey the feeling that he is very much on the side of the child in the furtherance of his individuation and independence. For example, he can reflect this with the statement: "You really do like to choose for yourself, don't you?" Even the most oppositional child may momentarily abandon his negativistic posture to agree with such a sympathetic understanding and noncritical comment.

When sufficient trust and confidence has been built up, the therapist can call attention more directly to the oppositionality in the same understanding and noncritical way. "Have you noticed that if I seem to want something one way, you always want it the opposite way?" There will be, as in most therapy, some contrasting by the child of the parent and therapist and this is, of course, brought to his notice: "You seem always to take the opposite tact to me as you do with your mother and you expect me to react like her." Again it is useful to think of this in the context of autonomy and control. "You can care about your mother and you can care about me. You do not have to choose between what she says or what I say. You have to choose for yourself when you have understood the situation better. I am here just to help with the understanding.'.

The Course of Treatment: The Initial Stage

The patient, a Black boy with a fairly typical constellation of oppositional symptoms, was first seen at the age of six and continued in treatment for a period of two years. He had been expelled from three separate schools within a month for being uncontrollable. I decided to place him in a special class for emotionally disturbed children and arranged with the teacher to manage him more flexibly with regard to choice and time of assignments.

He communicated with me from the beginning by means of drawings. At the very first session, after completing his picture he asked if I wanted it. I said that it was his picture, that I would like to have it, but he must decide what to do with it. He said that I could have it but then he decided to take it with him. However, after some indecision, he gave me a second picture that he had made. I again repeated that it was his but that I would be pleased to have it. This illustrates his ambivalence about being given open control.

However, even when this was done, his automatic oppositionality could be provoked. For example, he wondered which color I wanted him to use and I said, "Well, whichever one *you* want to use. It's *your* picture." He asked if I wanted him to use green and again I said, "If you want to." He decided to use red and I said, "Fine," at which point he put the red down and decided to use blue.

He also communicated through play with toy soldiers. For example, he seemed very pleased at finding a captain for the soldiers, and I commented that he seemed to get some pleasure out of having a captain. He didn't say anything but he gave out with a little exchange with the captain ordering some men to go someplace and one of the men saying back in a very hearty tone, "Oh, you go." I said it seemed as if some of the soldiers had feelings about the captain. This would seem to illustrate some of his concern about bosses. There was also interaction among the soldiers about getting in line.

At a later session, he was drawing a picture for his mother but would not let me see it. I said that it must be an important picture because it was taking him so long to draw. He then drew another picture, a helicopter, that was for me and kept it separate from the other. I wondered whether he needed to keep things for his mother and things for me separate, and perhaps he tried to keep feelings for us separate also. It looked as though he did not want me to know what he did for his mother. After some hesitation, he showed me the mother's drawing which was a flower with the words, "I love you" under it. I said it was very nice and made me understand the sort of feelings he was having for his mother and also the feelings he had for me. He then went on to draw a dinosaur that was very dangerous as if in reaction to the tender feelings for his mother that I had remarked upon.

There were also interactions to and from the waiting room. At first he was very positive about showing me a shortcut which turned out to be longer but he insisted that it was shorter. As he became less oppositional, the decision to take his "short cut" became less preemptory and more open to negotiation and eventually he was able to admit that the "short-cut" was, in fact, the longer way round. I would follow him whichever route he took until he reached his final conclusion.

Next came the guessing games where once again he had me at a disadvantage with him having complete control over the situation. He had the answers and enjoyed this power as I floundered around. I pointed out that when he had me fooled, it made him feel big and strong; not letting me know things was like not letting me have things. Perhaps he wanted to show me what a super-boy he was. This led him to pretend that he was driving a real car. I said that this was still another way to be big and powerful. I could understand why he wanted to drive himself and not be driven by others. He said that he thought I might not like it if he drove his own car but he still would do it. No one could stop him. This was defiance in fantasy.

Later (in about the fifth month), he was making it more explicit that the powerful wish was connected with masculinity and his identity as a male but there were clearly problems associated with this. He began drawing racing cars that could never win races. I would comment about all the trouble he was having getting into the race and yet not being able to win it. He drew two types of racing cars, black and white, and it was the black cars that could not win. He also, for the first time, drew in people watching the race which suggested that an observing ego was developing in relation to the conflict. I remarked on the black and white cars and wondered whether he had thoughts and feelings connected with them. He said suddenly, "Oh, I made a mistake." He hadn't left room for the lines between the cars so there was bound to be smashups. I asked what he thought about smashups between black and white if they raced against each other or anything. I said it must be hard to be black if you were never allowed to win or have anything good happen to you. It would make you feel they were against you and so you would have to be against them. At this point, the black cars decided to challenge the whites and he then boldly challenged me to guess what was going to happen. I said that his challenging me reminded me of the black cars challenging the whites. Would the black cars get the better of the white cars? Would he be able to win?

He went on to play tic-tac-toe in which he would play both positions and always had me win. I pointed out that even when he was in full control of the game, he let the other person win so perhaps he imagined himself winning even when he seemed to be losing.

He was reported as settling down at school and this appeared to be closely associated with his bringing more open opposition into therapy. At this point the therapeutic alliance was strong enough to withstand it.

The Middle Stage of Treatment

In the middle stage the causes for the automatic oppositionality began to be sorted out although there was some interference with the process by extraneous events that affected the whole family such as the birth of a new sibling, the hospitalization of the father for ulcers, and his running around with another woman. The main sorting out had to be done in the therapeutic relationship. As he was able to perceive more clearly, his fantasies about "significant others," particularly how they handled mess and rage and self-control, in turn controlled him and this realization freed him to imagine and experience outcomes other than oppositionality. As he progressed, further options opened up on his expanding emotional horizon. The motivation for this came from inner urges to go on to manhood and growth. He could now face feelings about his enraged, bossy mother, his impotent father, and the whole Black predicament and try to work through these in the transference. He had now been in therapy for eight months and had come approximately 40 percent of the time (which is a good average for the oppositional case).

He began to use puppets to show some of the interaction within the family. For instance, there was a play involving the father (who is ill) and a boy and girl being afraid that they too would become sick like him. It was hard for him to deal with his father's illness and he would disrupt the play or train of thought to turn to something more pleasant. He turned to clay but as he talked about his father he began making long pointed structures. I told him that all boys had worries on occasion about their fathers and so I expected that this was also true of him. I also said that boys often think about tall pointed things because they have a tall pointed thing on their bodies, namely, the penis. I asked if he knew what I meant and he said he did. (At this time he was responding to almost all my comments and questions instead of ignoring most of them as he did earlier on.) He then drew a parade. I said I bet that it made him feel tall and important to be in a parade and he agreed. He next drew a racing car and I wondered whether this was also another long pointed thing that could make one feel tall, powerful, and important if one drove it and once again he agreed. I said that boys liked to feel tall and important and one thing that made them feel that way was the penis and the fact that it could be long and tall and proud and important. He had some concerns about giving me the long pointed things that he had made, and I was able to discuss with him his feelings about me doing something with his penis.

There was some indication from his play that he felt I was not helping enough with the real things that were going on at home. Finally, there came a session where he stayed out in the hall and peeked at me from time to time to let me know that he was close enough for me to talk with him. I told him that I thought he was angry with me for not being able to help with the things going on at home and that I could understand his feelings about this. This brought him back into the sessions but they were fairly silent. He seemed vaguely unhappy. This was in the period when his father was out of the home and mother was angry at him because of his affairs with other women. I told the patient that one could have long, tall, pointed things without necessarily being chased out of the house or getting into trouble but I could imagine that he might be worried by such thoughts. His father was now becoming quite ill and some of his drawings suggested that the possession of pointed things made one vulnerable to illness.

Then came a session in which he said nothing and I told him a story about a little boy who was scared about his mother and father and wondering what he could do about their quarreling. He abruptly got up and left the room. When he returned, he drew a vampire and said he sometimes felt that I was a vampire trying to suck words from him.

Then there followed five sessions when he did not come into the office but hung around the door to listen to me and at times throw stuff at me. I talked of how very angry he felt with me and what I would do to him if I became angry in turn. It would be hard to assure him that I would not hurt him. I had known for a long time that he had these hating, damaging feelings inside of him and that he would like to make a mess on me because he felt like a mess with all the awful feelings inside of him. He wanted to throw it all at me. I also knew that there were good feelings inside of him too. I said that he was used to being around people who would try to hurt back if you got them mad. At the end of each session he would indicate how I could put things away and he would wave good-bye. Finally at one session he bagan to say loudly enough so that I could hear, "Fuck you" and "Shit." I said quietly that "shit" sounded like a big mess to carry alone by yourself. From then on he came back into the room and continued with his drawing. While we did this we talked and I told him how good it felt our working together. We recalled the times when he was out in the hall both mad and scared at the same time. I said that I knew that he was trying to be himself and not be just someone who's so mad and scared that he has to be against everyone.

The Final Stage of Treatment

In the final phase of termination, the problem has to do with facing life armed with his new knowledge and attitudes but without his therapist. Once again, his autonomy should be respected when it comes to choosing the time and length of termination. A patient like this needs to try out various separations and returnings partly because of what he has had to cope with in his family where opposition often begets rejection. He may attempt for the first time various nonoppositional ways of dealing with others and may at times get discouraged and lapse back into opposition. The time is therefore taken with recapitulations and further clarifications of the oppositional issues.

In one of his final sessions he was engaged in the construction of a very large building and I told him that he could be proud of himself not only because of being able to build something so tall and strong but also because of being able to learn about his feelings and behavior. It took a lot of guts trying to understand what made you mad.

At another session he reminisced about some pleasant events in his life and I, in turn, reminisced about the early days of therapy and how angry and scared and unhappy he was when he first came to see me. I said that perhaps he would soon be ready to talk about when he would not be coming to see me anymore. At that exact point he said, "through" and handed me the paper on which he was working. He had drawn a tree and a house. He then decided to clean out his box. I talked about the times when he had really made a big mess and had thrown it all on to me. And here he was now cleaning out his box without anybody saying anything about it. He had decided himself that it was a good thing to do and he was doing it. I thought it was great.

When we played games, he was now able to win and to lose without it being a problem. He thought that I would be a good person to take care of his turtle if he ever needed anyone to look after it. He also wished at times that he could go home with me. Talking about termination got him a little upset and he needed to go out for a short while to recover his poise. He listened very carefully when I talked about one part of him that really wanted to make a mess like the child who wanted to make a mess with his shit instead of putting it into the toilet. This part of him really wanted to be two years old and do this but there was the other more grown-up part that was too old for this and could notice all this. I said children really are in charge of their shit and can make decisions themselves. They are in control. They can do this when they decide they want to be grown-up or when they decide they want to please their mother or for any reason. He was still listening very intently to all this, standing in the doorway. As we cleaned up I talked about how making a big mess could sometimes be fun even when we were grown-up. The next time he turned again to the construction of pointed structures as if underscoring a developmental advance. Termination was not easy for him. On one occasion he had the toy soldiers out and "talked it over" with them about "when the war would be over." He spoke of one day becoming a junior policeman who helped people. At school he was reported by the teacher as being exclusively verbal in expressing his feelings and no longer an angry, automatically oppositional child.

CHAPTER 8

Summing Up on the Oppositional Child

E. JAMES ANTHONY, M.D.

In this comprehensive review of the oppositional syndrome, we have dealt with a wide variety of its aspects, covering such facets as the normative view, the situational response, the characterological defect, the undertone of psychosis, the association with delinquency and the cultural artifact. It is a protean state that varies with the individuals concerned and the circumstances that force them into opposition. In his work, Levy had stressed the fact that oppositionalism was a "method of choice" to cope with threatening situations. According to Comer, the Black adolescent male, for historical reasons, had been compelled to make this their choice so that there was a "kernel of truth" in many of the stereotypes, active as well as passive, that were used habitually to stigmatize the Black minority. The matter further aggravated by the inability of the Black parents to identify with the White power struggle and have therefore refused to relinquish power over their children. They crush opposition in their offspring just as their own opposition was once crushed by the White masters. Antagonism and resentment would rife even more among the younger Blacks if the Black church, like the Black parents, had not thrown in its weight on the side of law and order and obedience.

The educational impact of opposition had even greater importance than the cultural deflation since many of the autonomous ego functions associated with learning belong with the general suppressiveness. Opposition became an unwillingness and eventually an inability to learn. Among the other casualties of opposition were motivation and communication. There appeared to be a real resistance to speaking the White language that had held them so long in subjugation.

Comer was of the opinion that a free and open society, coupled with "reasonable behavior" on the part of the parents, was the only answer to chronic Black resistiveness. By "reasonable" parents, he meant those that acted for the good of the child's development rather than in response to society's pressures and required an understanding of children and childhood which was often lacking in the Black parent.

At the same time, Comer wanted White people to become more conscious of what Black treatment did to them. They should understand that if Black adolescents turn out to be antisocial, it is mainly because in a predominantly White society they have not been subjected systematically to the socialization process.

Black parents are not unlike Martin Luther when he said: "I should rather have a dead son than a disobedient one." This same Luther, however, remarked in another passage that "children should not be too severely flogged; for my father once flogged me so severely that I fled and became averse to him . . . my parents treated me so harshly that I grew quite dispirited. My mother once flogged me till the blood flowed all because of a nut, and the hard and severe life they made me lead caused me later to enter a monastery and become a monk." As Mitscherlich remarked:

> To Luther's parents the "evil" that they did was morally justified and good. The childish ego was faced with the tremendously difficult task of obeying two unalterably opposed introjects, one of which called for obedience, because his parents intentions were "for the best," while the other, the remorselessly punishing, humiliating, intimidating, irreconcilable element, was destructive to his self-esteem. Disobedience is sometimes the only way to save face and preserve some measure of self-respect.[3]

Comer calls himself a pessimistic optimist since he feels he has seen enough social change occurring in this country to stimulate some hope for the future. Yet, pessimistically, he is aware how deep and tenacious roots of prejudice are.

He offers us an interesting formula for appraising the Black child in the clinic: one has to ask oneself what one would say about this child if it were White and not Black and what the blackness in itself meant to the diagnostician. By labeling qualities Black, we begin to create mythologies and stereotypes; in calling anger Black, we do not really need to treat it any different than we would deal with White anger; we would negotiate with it until something satisfying was worked out. By deeming something a Black problem, there is a tendency to suggest it is insoluble.

Redl's remarkable outpouring of experience makes one wish for an "instant playback," so memorable are the comments that he has to make. Where else, but in Redl, would one find such remarks as "the invisible group under the couch; parents don't have countertransference like us—they just get mad. We can smell else's unconscious miles away but not what's happening in our own. It's no skin off my prestige nose; every child immigrates from one developmental phase to another and goes through all the pains of immigration; some kids have a penchant for torturing the friendly adult; they never let me play with delinquents as a child and now I play with bad kids all the time. The kids may often catch you with your counter-oppositional pants down. Advice has to be a dialogue; it can never be given from a pulpit" etc., etc. Redl writes as he feels, and he feels as he writes and his audience feels along with him. His greatest talent is for categorizing human behavior in completely nonjargonized terms as if he made them up spontaneously as he went along.

In his summary of the oppositional state, he tried to tell us something of what goes on in the oppositional child, pacifying both his oppositional and pseudo-oppositional behavior; then he turned to us, professionals, parents and teachers, and attempted to understand what stirred us up in our confrontations with oppositional behavior. Finally he addressed himself to the vital question of what we can do about oppositional behavior when directly in contact with it. He was not concerned with analyzing its roots but in resolving its present disturbing manifestations.

What was the reason for its appearance—it certainly gratified the child to provoke exasperation in the frustrating adult; it certainly saved face when what Erikson[2] referred to as "the humiliation of being a child" came into question; it certainly informed the world that one had a mind of one's own and was a person to be reckoned with.

The oppositionalism, on the Redl stage, revealed itself in a series of dramatic movements—the group offstage, the sucking into roles, the deliberate "slow motion" that infuriated all adults, the sharp confrontation of the dare, the experimental testing of limits, the "invitation to the game," the use and misuse of the "opening gambit" and the strategic outmaneuvering of the adult: all these combined with transference-countertransference leftovers from the past created a vivid choreography that comes to life in Redl's terminology.

Redl makes the important and, for him, almost central statement that not all counterreactions are countertransferences and, furthermore, that not all counterreactions are clinical; they may be quite natural and necessary responses that demand or deserve opposition.

These counter-feelings to opposition may take many forms involving rejection, helplessness, "complexity shock," apprehension about the future and resonances from the past. What Redl warns us about, and we need to heed this warning, is that we should not act or react in certain ways toward children merely in order to demonstrate our professionalism (amusingly, he refers to this as the Abraham complex in which the supervisor is allocated the role of God who speaks out of the clouds to remind the therapist that he is, first and foremost, a human being and should behave as such).

When Redl talks about treatment, one is reminded of Aichhorn[1] discussing treatment: the treatment that they advise can, for the most part, be done only by themselves. With others, it generally falls flat. It is based on a charismatic contact which is hard to duplicate under ordinary circumstances by ordinary people.

In paraphrasing this therapeutic advice, much of its flavor flies out the window. He tells us, for example, in his tempestuous way, listen to the facts in detail, talk to the protagonists directly, and bear in mind that even the simplest behavior has complex roots. We should then reclassify oppositional situations into those that are unmodifiable and need to be lived with and those that are modifiable and can be acted upon. At this point, all generalities must be translated into specific events and incidents. When things can be acted upon, a "life-space interview" should be constructed in which the specifics of the here and now are related directly to the immediate urgencies of the child and his situation. It is also important to remember not to create either-or confrontations that may lead the child to act up in order to save face. A final matter of importance is not to feel so grandiose as to avoid obtaining additional help when the situation gets beyond our own capabilities.

With regard to limit setting, Redl has some wise things to say: one should legislate limits from the beginning and not on an *ad hoc* basis. Once the limits have been established, a good therapist can deal flexibly with deviations and departures. Before limits can be set, however, they must be fully discussed and found acceptable by the group and after full group discussion, changes can be made where required. A parliament of children, even oppositional ones, can often function better in this respect than the adults who constitute the United Nations Assembly.

References

1. Aichhorn, A. *Wayward Youth.* New York:Viking Pr., 1965.
2. Erikson, E. *Childhood and Society.* New York:Norton, 1964.
3. Mitscherlich, A. *Society Without the Father.* New York:Schocken Boots, 1970.

PART II: *The Inhibited Child*

CHAPTER 9

The Genesis of Inhibition

E. JAMES ANTHONY, M.D.

In 1926, Freud published a paper on "inhibitions" that dealt with a restriction on ego functioning that developed either as a defensive measure or because of an actual diminution of energy. It did not necessarily have a pathological implication but was assumed by the ego for the purpose of avoiding instinctual or moral conflict. It could be simple or complex, partial or massive and the functions affected were those concerned with eating, motility, work and sex. Inhibition, therefore, is characterized by an absence of reaction and can almost be regarded in negative terms as a mode of nonbehavior. For this reason, it is more frequently overlooked by the parent, the teacher or the clinician since the child, for the most part, does nothing to annoy or provoke his environment. Yet, sooner or later, even the least empathic parent will become troubled by the lack of involvement in the everyday situations of life and all their efforts at stimulating or interesting obtains very little response. The clinician is faced with a similar situation when he comes to investigate the case and soon discovers that the behavior he is observing is not based on stubbornness or oppositionality; the child is not refusing to cooperate. He appears not to understand the meaning of cooperation or, alternatively, he has no drive to cooperate.

This unforthcoming type of behavior is both etiologically and phenomenologically complex. It is difficult to unravel the many antecedents that present themselves from very early on in life; it is difficult diagnostically to separate the inhibitory response from reactions of withdrawal, passive aggression, obsessive-compulsive negativism, ego constrictedness, anhedonism and a constitutional lack of energy and drive. What is clinically apparent is that there are certain individuals who characteristically show little enthusiasm for life and tend to respond to internal or external impingements by disengagement. In this way, they radically reduce the amount of contact with the outside world so that the area of interface is small, sporadic and tenuous. If it is a defense and not a constitutional lack, the conflict appears to be deeply buried. The patient is only conscious of his inability to respond in any way commensurate with the emotional and social expectations of the other person. He simply feels he has nothing to say, nothing to give and certainly nothing to reveal, and after battling with this interminably, the clinician is often prepared to give up and agree with the patient that there is an internal vacuum. The personality has been summed up as self-annihilating; most of the positive elements in life appear to be missing—spontaneous exchanges, pleasure in mastery, curiosity and exploration and the joyousness that is so much the hallmark of the emotionally healthy child. The impulse is constantly under surveillance and the natural exuberance of childhood is replaced by the severe constriction.

The Predisposition to Inhibition

The question facing the theorist in this area has to do with the nature of the barriers on the afferent or efferent pathways of the stimulus-discharge system. Ever since Freud first postulated the existence of a hypothetical structure that he called the "stimulus barrier," investigators have attempted to give more substance to it. Benjamin carefully researched the vicissitudes to barrier formation on the afferent side.[3] He described a maturational crisis at the end of the first month of life when there seemed to be a marked increase in overall sensitivity to external stimulation. Without the intervention of a caretaker, the infant tends to become overwhelmed by stimuli and evinces a considerable amount of distress. According to him, the crisis represented a rapid maturation of sensory apparatuses at this time and pointed to the existence of a "critical period." Sometime in the third month, a more active stimulus barrier was constructed and was probably related to neurophysiological developments that took over the inhibitory function. The development of a well-regulated inhibitory mechanism was imperative for normal living. Anthony speculated on the clinical effects of an hypertrophied barrier resulting from innate causes or the absence of adequate mothering.[1] Whether a disturbance in this primary inhibitory regulatory mechanism can predispose to later inhibitions is still a matter for conjecture.

This brings up the problem of the relationship of innate to experiential factors in the genesis of such phenomena as inhibition. There is much experimental evidence to suggest that experience alone can produce marked variations in behavior in genetically homogeneous animals and, as Benjamin pointed out, the work of such psychoanalysts as Hartmann, Kris, Rapaporte and Erikson "has made an interest in the innate respectable again."[2] It is hardly possible to discuss inhibition without considering both sets of factors although, at the present time, the evidence from the experiential side is weightier and more convincing. The recognition of experience in creating character is no new discovery: it was recognized in Roman times by Lucretius, the poet-philosopher, who wrote as follows:

> Though education may apply a similar polish to various individuals, it still leaves fundamental traces of their temperaments. It must not be supposed that innate vices can be completely irradicated: one man will still incline more readily to outbursts of rage; another will give way a little sooner to fear; *a third will accept some contingencies too impassively.* And in a host of other ways men must differ one from another in temperament and so also in the resultant behavior. . . . I cannot even find names for the multiplicity of shapes that give rise to this variety of types. But I am clear that there is one relevant fact I can affirm: *the lingering traces of inborn temperament that cannot be eliminated by philosophy are so slight* that there is nothing to prevent men from leading a life worthy of the gods.

As matters stand today, innate factors in the development of the third man, who accepts contingencies too impassively, should be considered and must be investigated but experiential factors from early life are undoubtedly major sources of etiology.

According to Bowlby, a child of 15 to 30 months who has previously had a reasonably secure relationship with his mother and has not been parted from her will commonly show a predictable sequence of behavior in separation from her.[4] There are three phases, described as protest, despair, and detachment. It is the third phase of detachment that is of special interest to the subject of inhibition. The child, on reunion with his mother, appears on the surface to have recovered from the separation, but his behavior is oddly different. He may hardly seem to recognize her *and may remain remote, apathetic, listless and disinterested.* If the separation is repeated, he will in time behave as if neither the mothering or contact with humans has much significance for him. He ceases to show much feeling, becomes disengaged from people and curiously detached which Spitz referred to as an "anaclitic defense." As time goes on, the child's psychological life becomes woefully constricted and the degree of inhibition seems designed to guard against the dreadful reexperience of abandonment. The most striking thing about the "detached" child is his behavior under conditions of stress, fatigue or pain. The normal child on such occasions will almost certainly go to his mother, but the "detached" child tends to fall back on his own resources as if he had lost faith in his environment and could no longer base his security on what Benedek refers to as "the relationship of confidence," Erikson as "the relationship of basic trust," and Klein as the situation created by the "introjected good object."

If inhibition is self-imposed under conditions of threat, the next question that arises has to deal with the nature of the threat. At one time, anxiety was thought to constitute the predominant threatening affect that the organism needed to guard against but today depression is obtaining equal attention in this regard. Both affects have their origins in the regulatory mechanisms for arousal and inhibition; both affects have to deal with loss, either threatened, fantasied, or actual; both affects have preoedipal and oedipal roots; both affects generate symptoms representing a compromise between wish and defense against the wish; both affects are pitted against the ego that tries to master, diminish or contain them; and both affects, subjected to such defensive operations, can give place to severe inhibitions. It would seem necessary, therefore, in the clinical investigation of any given case of inhibition to find out which of these basic affects can be held responsible for the outcome. In tracing the history retrospectively, the clinical landmarks passed on the way would include the characterological development, the defensive symptom formation, the primal affect of anxiety or depression, the somatic components behind each of these, and the original psychobiological experiences in the earliest symbiotic relationship. The affects of anxiety and depression as signal systems lose much of their value as a result of the blanketing influence of inhibition.

The Life History of the Inhibited Child

As mentioned earlier, both genetic and constitutional factors play a significant role in the predisposition to inhibition. Various developmental psychologists, such as Fries, Wolff, Thomas and others have each described a type of infant who, from the neonatal period onward, is underactive and unreactive. Where other infants reach out eagerly to the environment, these withdraw. Heider described a group of infants who appeared to be at high risk for inhibition and characterized by poor physique, inadequate energy, and a poorly functioning autonomic system.[7] The baby was different from other babies by its lack of interest in exploration, its inactivity, its narrow range of reaction, its low energy drive, and in the absence of trust and confidence. Any discomfort seemed to drive the child even further into itself.

Fries and Wolff carried out a longitudinal study of a particular child in whom they were able to link later inhibitory defense operations with early constitutional factors.[5]

> Anna was born to an orally-dependent, depressive and sadomasochistic mother whose attitude toward her baby was intensely ambivalent. From the beginning, Anna was underactive, anxiety-prone, slow to react and quite unconcerned with exploration and experimentation. When she was four years old, her mother became even more depressed and uncontrollably enraged and at this time Anna herself began to look subdued and somber. There was a frozen, almost catatonic quality about her behavior. In her fifth and sixth year, she was given to repeated bouts of vomiting and in her seventh year, she was afraid of being bitten by crabs, kissed (because of the germs), and tried to pull out her eyelashes. She seemed preoccupied and unable to grasp external events easily. She was still grossly underactive. At fourteen, she appeared extremely self-conscious and withdrawn. "Blind" readings of her Rorschach indicated the presence of severe inhibition and passivity. And there was evidence of earlier readings that these character formations were on the increase. She seemed to be giving up the struggle against internal and external factors and was becoming increasingly quieter and disengaged. Her posture especially pointed to the severe degree of inhibition.

Fries and Wolff have suggested that there is a "constitutional complex" that determines much of an individual's later development and even his interactions with the environment. The evolution of the inhibited child was especially predictable.

The Fully Developed Clinical State of Inhibition

The fully developed inhibitory state presents a devastating picture even in childhood. All the spontaneity, flexibility, good humor, freedom and color appear to have been snuffed out. Trying to meet the child's authentic self, one merely encounters a dull representation of it. He is unable to respond to any overtures. Like the caged bird, he is unable to emerge even when the door is open and remains a characterological prisoner within himself. Life within the cage of inhibition is tedious and boring beyond description. Nothing happens within it and nothing takes place between it and the outside world. Every now and then, there is evidence of an internal volcanic eruption that is rarely permitted to see the light of day. At best, spasms of rage are felt and at night there are dreams of tornados and storms. Shame and guilt are the prevailing affects.

The inhibition invades and pervades the therapeutic situation and renders it equally, dull and lifeless. The therapist tends to become discouraged as if there was a law of reciprocal inhibition and the treatment can be interminable. A lot of therapeutic time is passed "in the doldrums."

One of the most vivid descriptions of the inhibitory syndrome in childhood has been provided by Griffiths who writes:

> The child begins to fail cognitively, emotionally and socially. She begins to experience disappointment in herself, fear, humiliation, rage, hatred against objects, negative self-feeling and despair. She projects a good deal of this onto the outside world believing that it is deliberately thwarting her. As her experiences accumulate, the chronic condition is imposed, made up of a general state of unhappiness, slowness to undertake anything, an inhibition of thinking, feeling and speaking, and *a shrinkage of personality.*[6]

The inhibited child is often silent and inwardly turned. There is an element of depression and it is often stated that *inhibition is the depression of childhood.* The conscience is severe and tyrannical and the inhibited child is often a "morally battered child" who lives fearfully and conscientiously by rule of thumb. His inner moral programming is fixed and largely inaccessible to reason. His life is often overshadowed by the need to avoid sin and he goes about over-anxious, guilt-ridden and scrupulous. It is difficult for him to enjoy anything easily and naturally for its own sake without first having to assess its moral worth. He is more at home with parents and adults than with peers and evoked aggression in other children may provoke anxiety in him. He is tied to his parents through guilt as a result of a suffocating upbringing.

Conclusion

What has been emphasized in this chapter is the importance of considering the complex factors responsible for the genesis of inhibition. In every clinical study, one must bear in mind the reciprocal interactions between genetic endowment, intrauterine experience, the birth process, the "constitutional" temperaments, the vicissitudes of the symbiotic unit and the outcome of separation-individuation. To understand these interactions better, the clinician must turn investigator and conduct prospective studies into such clinical phenomena. Only then, can etiological statements be made with any confidence. There is a long way to go, but we should not be disheartened or overly optimistic. A letter from Freud to Pfister in 1926 suggests the right balance appropriate to our state of knowledge today:

> A new pamphlet of mine, *Inhibitions, Symptoms, and Anxiety*, is now being published. It shakes up much that was established and puts things which seemed fixed into a state of flux again. Analysts who above all want peace and certainty will be discontented at having to revise their ideas. But it would be rash to believe that I have now succeeded in finally solving the problem with which the association of anxiety with neurosis confronts us.

It would certainly be rash for us to believe that we have finally solved the problem of inhibition. We are only on the way, but the situation is not discouraging.

References

1. Anthony, E.J. (1958) Recent work on the psychopathology of perception in childhood. *Psychol. Bull.* (British Psychological Society), Feb. 1958.
2. Benjamin, J.D. (1959) Prediction and psychopathologic theory. *Dynamic Psychopathology in Childhood.* (Eds. Jessner, L. and Pavenstedt, E.) New York:Grune & Stratton.
3. Benjamin, J.D. (1963) Further communication on some developmental aspects of anxiety. *Counterpoint: Libidinal Object and Subject.* (Ed. Gaskill, H.S.) New York:I.U.P.
4. Bowlby, J. (1961) Separation anxiety: A critical review of the literature. *J. Child Psychol. and Psych.*, 1:251.
5. Fries, M. and Woolf, P. (1971) The influence of constitutional complex on developmental phases. *Separation-Individuation: Essays in Honor of Margaret S. Mahler.* (Ed. McDevitt, J. and Settlage, C.) New York:I.U.P.
6. Griffiths, R. (1935) *A Study of Imagination in Early Childhood and its Functions in Mental Development.* London:Kegan Paul.
7. Heider, G.M. (1966) Vulnerability in infants and young children. *Genet. Psychol. Monogr.*, 73:1-216.
8. Tarachow, B.S. (1947). The syndrome of inhibition. *Psychiatric Quarterly.* 21:233-252, April.
9. Wenar, C. (1957). The therapeutic value of setting limits with inhibited children. *J. Nerv. Ment. Dis.*, 125:390-395, July-Sept.

CHAPTER 10

The Nonengaging Child

PETER B. NEUBAUER, M.D.

A Matter of Definition

Initially, the topic of this chapter was "the restricted child." I had intended to differentiate the restricted child from the inhibited child, but after thinking about the clinical data, it seemed to me that the term "restricted" is also not quite appropriate. Therefore, it is necessary to define the terms. "Inhibition" should be used for those conditions in which conflict leads to interference in psychic functioning. Certainly Freud's monograph on *Inhibitions, Symptoms and Anxiety* gives a detailed discussion of the role of inhibition.[2] In this paper, he outlines the relationship of inhibition and symptom formation to anxiety as the major motivating force. He speaks of inhibition as a defense and thus keeps it both as a part of normal function as well as an indication of pathological conflicts. What may be inhibited is the aim of an activity or drive which may either undergo complete repression or be relinquished after its inception. Thus, inhibition should be understood in connection with a variety of behavioral phenomena and drive discharge patterns.

The conflicts that lead to inhibition may be based on a neurotic constellation involving superego, ego and id components or stem from the interplay of ego and drive or between various ego functions. This definition assumes that the child's potential was toward a freer form of functioning but then undergoes various degrees of interference.

The term "restriction," on the other hand, refers to those conditions which lead to a withdrawal of ego function. This can be seen as a defense against exposure to situations that cannot be mastered or conduce to anxiety. This modality of defense avoids symptom formation and internal conflict by limiting the ego in its development, its functioning, its differentiation and its adaptive capacity. We must assume that this occurs as a result of internal and external interactions.

In *The Ego and the Mechanisms of Defense* Anna Freud differentiates between restriction and inhibition as follows:

> A person suffering from a neurotic inhibition is defending himself against the translation into action of some prohibited instinctual impulse, i.e. against the liberation of 'pain' through some internal danger . . . . In ego restriction, on the other hand, disagreeable external impressions in the present are warded off, because they might result in the revival of similar impressions from the past . . . . The difference between inhibition and ego restriction is that in the former the ego is defending itself against its own inner processes and in the latter against external stimuli.[1]

The Concept of the Nonengaging Child

The child, about to be described, falls into still another category. It concerns itself with the child's inability from infancy on to engage himself strongly in an interaction system with the environment, whose involvement stays limited, and who shows few signs of phase-specific expressions of conflict. I have not found a word for this form of psychic function except to use descriptive terms such as "unengaged," "uninvolved," or "inappetent." When we see such children during latency or later, we may wrongly assume that their behavior is based either on inhibition or restriction. Furthermore, as I shall demonstrate, these children can in addition to their "unengaging" disposition later develop inhibitions and restrictions that will further blur the clinical picture.

Over the last twelve years we have been able to study children from birth on. We did a careful evaluation three or four times a year in the first years and later twice a year. The data which we accumulated were based on psychological testing, observations, interviews with the mother, observations of the mother-child interactions and, finally, filming of the child. These children were adopted and we could observe them first in a foster home up until the first few months of their lives and later in their adopted homes.

It should be understood that the condition illustrated by the case presented is not a specific outcome but an incidental finding in a prospective study of adopted children.

Prospective Study of an Adopted Child

The foster mother was very pleased with Jerry because he made few demands, was easy to feed and handle, generally did not signal distress, fell asleep easily and did not awake during the night.

At a little over six months of age, Jerry was adopted by a family with a girl of two, also adopted. The adoptive mother presented herself as an active, energetic woman with everything under control but nevertheless gave the impression of being under strain, with a tense, anxious involvement with the children. This tension increased from year to year until Jerry's fourth year when the mother became involved in outside activities which were apparently responsible for the new air of vigor and purposefulness the observers noted in her at this time.

In caring for Jerry as an infant, the mother followed a rigid schedule for feeding and sleeping, expecting the child to adapt to it. She saw him as being very demanding and determined in what he wanted and did not seem to have an understanding of his developmental needs. She was restrictive and overly controlling. She tried to discourage him from feeding himself until at 17 months he refused to eat until given table foods (at the adoptive father's suggestion) and again a few weeks later until given a fork (at his sister's suggestion). Although she expressed the wish that the children be more independent, the mother was threatened by any interest Jerry showed in mastery and exploration. When he tried to do something for himself, she immediately forbade it, and although he usually obeyed her, she described him as being "stubborn as a mule."

By three years of age, Jerry's slightest attempts to assert himself were perceived by the mother as great stubbornness. She inhibited any expression of aggressiveness and assertiveness and fostered dependency; yet she was proud of what she saw as his "tough boy" qualities, and even while complaining about him to the observers, her gestures and tone of voice conveyed admiration and pride. She felt he was brilliant and possessed many intellectual virtues. She was thus contradictory and inconsistent in her handling of the child. It should be noted that Mrs. A presented herself as more severe in her child-rearing practices than she actually was. Her screaming, scolding and threatening of the children were more attempts to mold herself to her conception of the maternal stereotype rather than any real ill feelings toward the children.

The father traveled extensively on business, every other week during Jerry's first two years and almost continually thereafter until he was seven, when he began to spend more time at home. In the intervening years, even when he was at home, he worked in his den and only joined the family for meals.

Jerry was above average in fine motor skills and motor-visual coordination during the first months of his life, but motor activity diminished to the low average range and remained so throughout the first year. He began to walk at 13 months, but reverted to crawling two months later. By the end of the second year, he was slightly behind in gross motor coordination, but did extremely well in fine motor manipulation. Up to the age of seven, his overall motor activity remained in the low average to average range with his greatest strength in fine motor tasks. In films at the age of four, it was noted that he held his body in a constricted manner and moved in a rather jerky, marionette-like fashion. At age five, he reported that he did not like to run and could not jump. Beginning the following year he was reported to dawdle a great deal at school over his work, at home over food, and around getting up in the morning and going to bed at night. His mother reported that he took an hour-and-a-half to get dressed in the morning. *The observers described him at this time as a restrained, passive and unexuberant child.* By seven he had become a little more active, enjoying such physical activities as playing ball and bike riding.

Over the years, he was found to be sensitive to various sensory modalities: visual, auditory and tactile stimuli as an infant; touch and body experiences and taste at two; sounds at three. By the age of seven, he was sensitive, to the point of being fearful of auditory (thunder), visual (lightning or lights going out) and painful (needles, scrapes) stimuli.

The most salient aspects of his physiological functions centered around eating, sleeping, and bowel and urinary functions. As an infant, he was easy to feed, but the adoptive mother found him to be a picky eater and was concerned that he did not eat enough. He had definite food preferences, from time to time refusing to eat those he did not like.

In early childhood, he slept soundly, except when ill, but beginning at age four, he resisted going to sleep in order to stay up to watch television. He would also wake up during the night and roam around the house with his sister.

As an infant, he did not signal when wet or soiled. His mother put him on the potty at twelve months of age to "condition" him. He complained about this but remained seated until his mother decided to take him off.

He was bowel trained by 23 months and completely trained at three-and-a-half years. Being a task-oriented child in general, his urinary training was accomplished via his fascination with getting his penis through the opening of his pants. At the age of six, he refused to use strange bathrooms and at seven wet himself while playing at a friend's house because he "forgot" to ask to go to the bathroom. At home, he was reported to remain in the bathroom up to 45 minutes when having bowel movement.

From the early months on, it was apparent that he related more easily to "things" than people. This tendency was reinforced by the adoptive mother who would offer a toy for gratification rather than make herself available. He gradually did become increasingly interested in people and more responsive to social demands but remained predominantly "thing" oriented throughout the period under study. *His primary mode of interacting with people was to "react to" them rather than initiating social contact.*

At 15 months, he needed a special blanket in order to be able to go to sleep, and at 20 months, as soon as he saw or touched the blanket, his fingers would go into his mouth. He also had a little stuffed bear with which he slept until the age of three and a half. He gave it up for a time, then used it again until age six.

As already noted, his relationship with his mother was a difficult one. Her controlling management fostered dependency. by the time he was three years old, he would confront her in a calm, detached way when she threatened him, but in the next two years there was pronounced aggression directed toward her as they became firmly entrenched in a continual and acute power struggle. The pattern was relatively consistent with either a request from him and a harsh refusal from her or else a request from her and a passive disregard by him, eventually followed by compliance. The intensity of the involvement between mother and son, even though of a negative nature, appeared to be quite high. At the age of five, there was an upsurge of aggressive outbursts and destructiveness. The tension, passive resistance and anger in the relationship continued into the sixth and seventh years. However, he enjoyed being babied by her when he was ill at seven.

The relationship with the sister was easier. During the early years, he played with her and imitated her activities. At two, he clung to her when she returned from school, and at three he went to her for help and comfort. By the sixth and seventh year, he was quite competitive and aggressive with her, both verbally and physically.

The relationship with the father was consistently positive. At first, Jerry did not show any particular response to father's overnight absences, but as the traveling increased, he began to miss him. By the third year, he had developed a close attachment to his father, missed him when he was away, enjoyed "rough play" with him when he was at home, and was reported to prefer him when both parents were present. By his fourth year the mother considered herself to be the favorite person in his life, but Jerry reported that he was lonely and that his parents gave him headaches. At six, the father was still away from home most of the time, but during the following year, he began to spend more time at home and Jerry enjoyed helping him with his work. The new closeness between father and son seemed to relieve some of the tension in the mother-son relationship.

Regarding strangers, he was reported to differentiate familiar from unfamiliar faces by the four-month visit, and by nine months, he inspected strangers carefully, then would either smile at them or ignore them. He did not show any particular stranger reaction until 23 months when he hid from them and would inspect them from a distance.

He showed interest in other children before three, played with his sister, but liked to have one of his parents nearby while playing alone. He gradually lost some of his shyness and would play with other children, but was described as neither a leader nor a follower, but as a loner. His friendships dwindled from a few at his fourth birthday to one at his fifth, and it was at this time that he was more aggressive with his peers. After a fight with a friend, he usually did not continue the relationship. In the sixth year, his circle of peer relationships once again widened. He fought verbally and physically with them but would leave the scene if the aggression became too violent.

Within a narrow range, Jerry did have strong affect, but few channels of discharge were available to him. As an infant, he was in the low range of intensity of affect except in the areas of rage and anger where he showed considerable intensity. At 15 and 20 months, he held his breath and banged his head when frustrated. There was *a pronounced flattening of affect at about the time he was placed in the adoptive home*. His affect remained generally low, peaking at the age of four when the observers described him as charming, sociable and spontaneous. By the next year, he was again withdrawn, overly compliant and trying hard to control underlying anger. This underlying anger and tension were readily apparent in the seventh year from projective tests which also showed constriction, possible difficulty in reality testing and a strong tendency toward reaction formation with many defenses against affect.

In the early years, Jerry was not an aggressive child, making few demands on the environment. He was physically and verbally aggressive with his sister and peers by age five and was also reported to have brief, uncontrolled outbursts of aggression. Most of this was directed towards the mother and expressed by passive resistance rather than overtly. In the sixth and seventh years he did calm down a little in this respect.

In the area of cognitive development, he started out as average but by the fourth year he was in the superior range with highest scores in concrete, structured tasks. At five and six, he was above average and superior in nonverbal performance subtests. Anxiety intruded, interfering with his ability to concentrate. His language development hovered around average, slightly above at times, and at six, dropping to slightly below average. It is interesting to note that by the end of the second year he had stopped using the few words he had at the beginning.

During the period under study, he was consistently reported to be "adaptive" *because he showed little or not reaction to changes until the the age of four when he became rigid, inflexible and passively resistant.* When settled on a course, he was said to remain on it unless forceful measures were taken to deflect him.

As an infant, he could stay in one place for twenty to thirty minutes without fussing but became more distractible as he grew older. By six and seven, although capable of a long attention span, his anxiety level was such that it diminished his ability to concentrate.

His superego development proceeded much as might be expected. He internalized the mother's rather rigid standards to the degree that he insisted that things be neat and orderly before any new activity could begin. The Rorschach at six indicated an overly harsh superego with some tendencies toward sadistic fantasies and masochistic behavior.

He was consistently in the low range of libidinal drive, deriving most of his pleasure from mastery of tasks and interactions with things and materials rather than people. By six and seven he enjoyed ball games, playing with toy cars, watching TV and being active with his father.

Over the years, one could see hints of various conflicts, but specific phase conflicts were never clearly delineated. One had the impression that the mother did not permit him to resolve conflicts at any stage and he therefore had to carry them from one stage to another without resolution. At the age of six, his fantasy life was somewhat constricted and indicated low self-esteem, fear of punishment and rejection, and a marked preoccupation with aggressive themes. The testing also indicated a tendency to withdraw from aggressive situations and to deal with them mainly on a fantasy level. There were no indications of oedipal conflicts. By the next year, he had not asked any questions about sex nor had he given any indication of being interested. There was little sex differentiation and nothing "boyish" about him. On the TAT he focused on issues concerned with bodily harm, anger, retribution and ambivalence. He seemed very concerned with somatic responses and almost obsessive about bodily damage.

Discussion

This clinical vignette, which is based on a large amount of accumulated data over seven years of the child's life, provides an outline of a child whose major characteristic is one of noninvolvement. It is possible that such a quality could find its particular expression in a particular area of functioning while leaving others relatively unaffected. In the same way as inhibition can express itself in cognitive, sexual or other areas of the ego, so can "nonengagement" be restricted or limited to specific spheres. When we use categories such as inhibition or restriction to describe a child, we generally assume that this refers to a characteristic of the child's overall functioning.

As the case indicates, the "nonengagement" is a function of limitations in all major areas of the child's functioning and development. It can be observed in his drive expression in both aggressive and libidinal components, in the absence of assertive ego function, in object relations, in the motility discharge pattern and in his cognitive style. All these would then have further repercussions on the development itself. If development is seen as proceeding from phase organization to new phase organization with discrete conflicts and achievements of primacy at each phase, particularly phallic primacy, there appeared to be an absence of such developmental conflicts in Jerry's case. It would thus seem that his "nonengagement" with the outside world was reflected equally in a "nonengagement" in developmental conflicts. One cannot see distinct steps in his passage through phases.

It may be of some interest to speculate about the primary cause of this development. Is it based on an original (constitutional) limited availability of drive energy? Is there a growing preponderance of "nonengaging" ego defenses such as repression, avoidance and denials? Or is there some still undetected developmental entity that generates this individual variation? Jerry's developmental history would incline us to the view that the weak involvement manifest in his psychological functioning is dependent on his individual makeup rather than to any defensive maneuver against undue external or internal influences, but this conclusion at the present can only be regarded as tentative. One requires evidence from more such prospective studies.

In discussing the various deviations from normal development and the disorders that appear to stem from deficiencies, there is an obvious need for further careful delineation before specific disorder forms can be isolated. In this presentation an initial attempt has been made to differentiate "restriction" from "inhibition" and to point to still another characteristic that also seemed to originate from faulty development, namely, a child with insufficient capacity for appropriate engagement in the essential areas of psychic functioning. A similar and perhaps related clinical disorder would be the case of the child showing "a failure to thrive." Genetic studies together with an understanding of outcomes of therapeutic interventions may lead to further clarification of the way in which later symptoms and conflicts become coordinated to this general "absence of struggle." This should help us to disentangle the mixed clinical phenomena, to determine the underlying disorder and with it the choice of treatment.

References

1. Freud, A. *The Ego and the Mechanisms of Defence.* London:Hogarth Press, 1937.
2. Freud, S. Inhibitions, Symptoms and Anxiety. In: *The Standard Edition of the Complete Psychological Works of Sigmund Freud, Vol. XX,* 1926. London: Hogarth Press.

CHAPTER 11

The Inhibited Child: A Family Therapy Approach

ARTHUR MANDELBAUM, M.S.W.

A Metaphor

In D.H. Lawrence's short story masterpiece called "The Rocking Horse Winner," he describes a child who is inhibited, shy and reserved, and who destroys his life because of his unrequited love for his mother. Because of intense and desperate desire to gratify his mother's needs, the young boy exerts tremendous physical and emotional effort, transcending the limit of his powers. The story begins with profound insights into the mother.

> There was a woman who was beautiful, who started with all the advantages, yet she had no luck. She married for love, and the love turned to dust. She had bonny children, yet she felt they had been thrust upon her, and she could not love them. They looked at her coldly, as if they were finding fault with her. And hurriedly she felt she must cover up some fault in herself. Yet what it was that she must cover up she never knew. Nevertheless, when her children were present, she always felt the centre of her heart go hard. This troubled her, and in her manner she was all the more gentle and anxious for her children, as if she loved them very much. Only she, herself knew that at the centre of her heart

was a hard little place that could not feel love, no, not for anybody. Everybody else said of her: 'She is such a good mother. She adores her children.' Only she, herself, and her children themselves knew it was not so. They read it in each other's eyes.[7]

I quote this passage not only because it describes a woman frightened of loving and her husband who is unable to be a husband and a father, but also because of the extraordinary way it describes a sensitive, restricted and inhibited child within the matrix of a deeply torn and unhappy family. The child is vividly aware of his mother's unhappiness with her life, with her children, and most of all with her husband. The house in which they live whispers the mother's complaint, "There must be more money; there must be more money." In the darkness of his room, the boy climbs on his rocking horse, which he has outgrown, but refuses to give up. He clings desperately to it, rocking back and forth, until the name comes to him out of some hallucinatory vision of a horse likely to win the race at some local racetrack. The child persuades the family gardener to wager a small sum for him and slowly he accumulates a large sum of money. Extending the secrets of the family, he swears into confidence a maternal uncle, who arranges for a lawyer to give the mother the winnings, disguising them as coming from an inheritance left to her by an unknown relative in a far off country. To the child's astonishment, his mother keeps this "inheritance" a secret from all others in the family, and although she improves the family's living status, the house continues to whisper "Not enough money' There must be more."

Once again, the child rocks on his magic horse, although exhausted, for he must please his insatiable mother by grasping for the elusive name of the horse who will win the Derby. As his horrified mother watches, drawn to his bedroom by the thumping noise of the rocking horse, the child falls into a major seizure, and dies in his mother's arms. Sadly, and with guilt, his uncle says to the shocked and grieving mother, "My God, Hester, you re eighty thousand to the good, and a poor devil of a son to the bad. But poor, poor devil, he's best gone out of a life where he rides his rocking horse to find a winner."

Individual Dynamics

This unfortunate child might be understood as an individual entity, and from the content of his conscious dreams, it is possible to surmise his instinctual wishes and his early development. His rescue fantasies toward his mother show his masculine strivings, his desire to replace his father. His rocking back and forth on his toy horse, its masturbatory nature gives some glimpse of his erotic fantasies toward his mother. The torturous treatment of himself and his horse may point to the developmental phase of his fixations and sadomasochistic aspects of his infantile sexuality. Just as there are secrets in this family, the child has his secrets also. These are his forbidden wishes, hidden by repression, covered by compliance, an undemanding, uncomplaining nature, an ascetic denial of his own impulses, aggression and greedy strivings. These are the danger signs of a serious neurosis, in a quiet, depressed and, in short, an inhibited child.

A Family View

It is also possible to view this child within the system, structure and uniqueness of his family.

In 1948, in his introduction to the *Psychoanalytic Study of the Family*, Flugel wrote:

> . . . it is fairly obvious that, under existing social conditions the psychological atmosphere of the home life, with the complex emotions and sentiments aroused by and dependent on, the various family relationships must exercise a very considerable effect on human character and development. Recent advances in the study of human conduct indicate that this effect is even greater than has been generally supposed; it would seem that, in adopting his attitude towards the members of his family circle, a child is at the same time determining to a large extent some of the principal aspects of his relations to his fellow men in general; and that an individual's outlook and point of view in dealing with many of the most important questions of human existence can be expressed in terms of the position he has taken up with in regard to the problems and difficulties arising within the relatively narrow world of the family.[3]

In his eloquent way, Winnicott also touches on the profound importance of the family, in which the child must see his mirror image.

> When a family is intact and is a going concern over a period of time, each child derives benefit from being able to see himself or herself in the attitudes of the family as a whole. We can include in all this, the actual mirrors that exist in the house and the opportunity that the child gets for seeing the parents look at themselves . . . . This could be one way of stating the contribution that a family can make to the personality growth and enrichment of each one of its individual growth.[9]

Here Winnicott emphasizes how self-concept has its roots in the reflec-
tions a child gets back from his parents, his siblings, his grandparents and
other close relatives who make up his family. And parents also add to their
self-concept in the ways they see themselves mirrored in the eyes of their
children, and in their view of each other. This is why in many troubled
families one notable characteristic of their interaction is their difficulty in
looking at each other's faces and eyes lest they see their own image, their
own angers and their own pain.

Erikson described in *Childhood and Society* his treatment of a child
with a convulsive disorder, and defended his "acceleration of a spontaneous cure," by saying this was, "No mean contribution when one considers
the damage done by the mere habitualness and repetitiveness of such
severe neurological storms." But was he pointing to the direction family
treatment was to take when he stated, "But in claiming less than the cure
of epilepsy, we would in principle like to believe that with the therapeutic
investigations into a segment of one child's history, we help a whole family
to accept a crisis in their midst as a crisis in the family history. For a
psychosomatic crisis is an emotional crisis to the extent to which the sick
individual is responding specifically to the latent crisis in the significant
people around him."[2]

Family Dynamics and Treatment

Thus, Erikson turns our focus even more to the "significant people"
surrounding the child and their important impact upon him. In family
system terms, however, a new dimension of meaning is given to the symptoms of the inhibited child, their position in the structure of the family,
their particular architectural place in the circle of family life. Jay Haley
would point to the *necessity* of the inhibited child in the dynamic system
of family life described in "The Rocking Horse Winner" and he said
in 1962:

> Psychopathology in the individual is a product of the way he deals with
> his intimate relations, the way they deal with him, and the way other
> family members involve him in their relations with each other. Further,
> the appearance of symptomatic behavior in an individual is necessary
> or the continued function of a particular family system. Therefore
> changes in the individual can occur only if the family system changes
> and *resistance to change* in the individual centers in the influence of
> the family as a group.[6]

If this conception of symptoms and symptomatic behavior is valid (and there is abundant evidence to demonstrate its validity) then the inhibited child may be understood from new perspectives and new treatment approaches. The repression in the child, his rejection of drives and impulses from coming into consciousness, his refusal to entertain sexual thoughts, the rigid constrictions imposed on him by his environment, may be a requirement of the collective family, its myth, the expression of collective unconscious fears—one of the control mechanisms for maintaining family harmony. It is an unsatisfactory one at best. For the child, it leads to a constriction of personality so that he might be regarded as good, as lovable, as wanted. Externally, he must maintain the facade that he is loved, but internally his life is impoverished, his development at a standstill. Since the child has developed this kind of personality in response to family interaction, to the insistence of the family on its particular style and shape of functioning, what better way to intervene than to change family homeostasis for a new level of functioning which might permit growth not only for the identified symptomatic child, but for others as well who upon diagnostic perusal, may have symptoms of equal severity when compared with the child designated for treatment. It is in family interaction that we open a host of intimate data about a child's mysterious life experiences, the direct observation between the concrete environment and the development of the child's capacities. Although this is accomplished in psychoanalysis as well, it is not achieved by direct observation of the family in interaction and its members serving as observers and participants. We may then observe *some* of the following family dynamics, especially in the case of the inhibited child as he interacts with his parents, his siblings, possibly even with his grandparents if they join the group:

1. The disappointment and unhappiness in the marital relationship, with frustrated expectations causing anxiety and anger, detoured and expressed toward the inhibited child on one hand, with encouragement for him to be silent, subdued, the container of family secrets and its forbidden impulses. On the other hand, another child may be selected for opposing family needs, to express the aggressions in the family, its explosive quality, its wishes to act out its great anxiety. Both children then serve a binary function, giving the appearance of belonging to an integrated family which is held together with fragile bonds.

2. The seductivity of the parents is not contained within the marital relationship. Its infantile qualities are expressed through the children; the children in turn are vulnerable, demanding and tenacious because of their frustrated needs.

3. The parents are weak and inconsistent in setting boundaries, the children often assuming the role of adults; the parents often assuming the role of children. Roles are diffuse, inconsistently defined and enacted, highly fluid.

4. There is encouragement of superego defects, with corrupt acts, bribing to please and to be loved, contradictory messages given which cause splitting and confusion.

5. There are irrational role projections, causing the rejection of qualities seen in others, which belong to and are disliked in the originator of the projections.

6. Secret sexual inhibitions in the adults of the family cause intense anxiety when children express sexual curiosity, and strive for individuation and autonomy.

Resistance to change in the child does center on the influence of the family as a group, an influence which conveys to the designated patient that his pathology is an essential part of the family system, that his role in the family is fixed and immutable, that it must remain habitual and repetitive, and be maintained so that other family members can hold onto their own equilibrium, no matter how tenuous and ungratifying. As early as 1946, Anna Freud pondered the same problems in the analysis of children. She struggled to solve the dilemma of how to free the child so that he was receptive to analytic treatment. In her analysis of a gifted and sensitive girl she triumphed in freeing the patient from the influence of a destructive relationship with a nurse. Miss Freud then goes on to say, "but consider how impossible such a situation is when one has an opponent who is no stranger but the child's parents."[5]

It is no longer sufficient, however, to win the parents over as allies in the child's treatment. Neither is it sufficient to affect modifications in the parental attitudes which will enable them to understand the treatment, their own attitudes and conflicts in relationship to the particular patient, nor even their own intrapsychic dilemmas. While these goals are in themselves ambitious, and sometimes achieved in skilled and sustained casework or individual psychotherapy for the parents, neither the patient nor his family members have sufficient opportunity to deal with the primary, interacting, dysfunctioning family system which should be one of the major mediums for conflict resolution. Nothing less will do for a significant number of children than to quote Dr. Ron Rinsley "disciplined family analysis and therapy carried out by expert therapists, capable... of full engagement with the incredibly difficult patterns of pathogenic interaction long established within the skewed or schismatic family."[8]

Family therapy is a psychotherapeutic approach to the family as the unit of treatment. The major focus of this work is to intervene and alter a family system which hampers and indeed halts the mature development of a majority of family members. The goal of the process is better family functioning as a social unit and of benefit to each individual who participates. Family therapy is based on the assumption that many of the identified patient's difficulties have their origins in family conflict, and working within that matrix, many of his conflicts might be resolved. It is not unusual to find that in many of these families, where one member is designated as the patient, that other members—the mother, and/or the father, and/or the siblings, have a good many severe problems as well, all interacting at great cost to the family's effectiveness as a group and as individuals.

A good many of the children who come for treatment play a pivotal role in their parent's marital life and in their roles as father and mother, creating either new opportunities for heightened and mature intimacies or distances and withdrawals away from old conflicts too complex and painful to face. Children also resonate for parents repetitive patterns and characteristics over which the parents' own development stumbled when they were children and caused their parents anguish. One father stated with angry emphasis that his son was "like me to a T. I did poorly in school, so does he. I stuttered badly, so does he. I recall an aunt of mine telling me that one day I would bring out a string of words and that they would turn around and slap me in the mouth." The father then proceeded to angrily tell his son to speak up in the family sessions, but scolded him for whatever he had to say. There is no better way to observe the phenomenon of irrational role assignments or projective distortions than to observe a family unit as it functions in a treatment situation. Framo has suggested that psychopathology usually seen as an insoluble intrapsychic conflict now may be seen as "a special form of relationship event which occurs between intimately related people." He goes on to postulate that "symptoms are formed, selected, faked, exchanged, maintained and reduced as a function of the relationship context in which they are embraced."[4]

Parents relate to their children, based on their own parental introjects, assigning to their born and even unborn children powerful feelings which had their origin in the parents' own experiences as a child. Thus, a designated patient is often compelled into the role of the scapegoat, the child who will not speak, the crazy one in the family, the clown, the stupid one; whatever role, he yields his uniqueness and individuality in order to cover some deficit in the family system, some distortion, out of some ill-conceived notion that this would preserve and save one or both parents from destruction or from desertion and divorce.

Boszormenyi-Nagy makes a related point when he states:

> If we assume that then the homeostases of the pathogenic system is regulated by the loyalty bound regression and arrest of development we can expect the child's guilt to increase to the extent he lets his parents down, so to speak. Leaving them behind to struggle, already borders on disloyalty; if in addition, he would improve symptomatically, it could amount to psychological treason. Guilt over his familial loyalty is not simply a regressive fixation, anchored in an internalized situation; it is rather validated by interpersonal reality of the parents' own messages. To keep his guilt down, and also to protect his parents, the child has to appease the system by (1) preserving his symptom and (2) trying to help his parents through sharing with them everything he can enjoy in life. Thus, it would be unrealistic to expect the child to progress too far in the face of actual disloyalty and a mounting guilt feeling over it. [1]

In a family therapy process the identified patient has the opportunity to do the following in a direct interaction and transaction with his family members:

1. To experience, but in a controlled and observed environment, how the family assigns him a role which he accepts, with their collusion as well as his own;

2. to begin the arduous process, with the help of the therapist and others in the family, to disengage himself from the role to which he has become accustomed and to take on a new role which will offer him growth opportunities hitherto unavailable;

3. to experience and witness how he and others in the family take turns in scapegoating and its negative values for growth;

4. to experience and witness irrational role projections and their defensive meanings against assuming awareness and responsibility for ones own behavior;

5. to examine and experience the power divisions in the family, the division into subsystems and their defensive importance against anxiety, conflict and risking change in the direction of autonomy;

6. to become aware of role confusions, and their importance in maintaining the status quo in the family, not only for the designated patient, but also for the parents and his siblings;

7. to experience the strengths and frailities of his parents in their marital and parental roles and to not assume inappropriate responsibilities and pseudo-mature roles which have as their function the rescue of his parents;

8. to disengage himself from his parents without risking their anger, their resistance, their rejection of him as he changes and as he undesignates himself as *the patient* and yet maintains his responsibility for whatever changes he wants for himself;

9. to experience and become aware of where he has assumed responsibilities out of misconception about what is loyalty and disloyalty and to note and feel the relief in being psychologically free to be an individual.

It is quite impressive to observe how quickly the inhibited child may change in family treatment; for the first few sessions he is quiet, reserved, withdrawn. If the therapist is skilled in establishing a positive relationship with the family, dissolving resistances as they inevitably appear and must unfold, the inhibited child will reveal his other side—his anger, his impulsiveness, his competitiveness with his parents, perhaps principally with his father. He will, if given sufficient time and support by some subsystems in the family reveal his sexual curiosity, his disillusionment with his parents, his secret contempt and idealization of them. Hopefully, as the family argues, pleads, scapegoats, projects and negotiates, the dysharmonic elements in the child and his parents will modulate and become more synchronized with the total family's best developmental thrusts. In any case, as he changes, a whole family changes. This may, in the long run, be sufficient and best, for the intimate environment around him, his family, is the best guarantee of support for the arduous developmental changes the future will demand.

References

1. Boszormenyi-Nagy, I. (1972). Loyalty implications of the transference model in psychotherapy. *Arch. Gen. Psychiatry.* 27:374-83.
2. Erikson, Erik. (1950). *Childhood and Society.* New York:W. W. Norton Company, Inc., p. 33.
3. Flugel, J.C. (1948). *The Psychoanalytic Study of the Family.* London:Hogarth Press, p. 4.
4. Framo, J.L. (1965). Rationale and techniques of intensive family therapy. In Boszormenyi-Nagy, I. and J.L. Framo eds., *Intensive Family Therapy: Theoretical and Practical Aspects.* New York:Harper and Row, pp. 143-212.
5. Freud, Anna. (1946). *The Psychoanalytic Treatment of Children.* New York: International Universities Press, Inc., p. 13.
6. Haley, Jay. (1962). Whither family therapy. *Family Process.* 1:69-100.
7. Lawrence, D.H. (1961). *The Complete Short Stories,* Vol. III. New York:Viking Press, p. 790.
8. Rinsley, Don. (1973). From an unpublished paper presented to Grand Rounds, Menninger Foundation School of Psychiatry, March 28, 1973, p. 8.
9. Winnicott, D.W. (1967). Mirror-role of mother and family in child development. *The Predicament of the Family.* (Ed. Lomas, P.) London:Hogarth.

CHAPTER 12

Symptomatic Inhibition
as Seen in the Clinic

DORIS C. GILPIN, M.D.   PAMELA MALTZ, M.S.W.

JULIEN WORLAND, PH.D.

There have been seventeen children who have been given the diagnosis of overly inhibited personality disorder at the Washington University Child Guidance Clinic from July, 1968, to the present. The criteria for this diagnosis was taken from GAP (Group for the Advancement of Psychiatry) Manual classification under the heading of Personality Disorder:

> These children show superficial passivity, with extreme or "pathological" shyness, inhibition of motor action or initiative, and marked constriction of personality functions, including at times diminished speech or even elective mutism, among other features. They are distinguished from the children with so-called schizoid (isolated) personalities by the fact that they seem to wish for warm and meaningful relationships but are inhibited from achieving them. They may be less inhibited in the home than at school or in other social settings. Some conscious anxiety may be evident, but the frozen, inhibited quality is ordinarily paramount. Some negativism and other oppositional features are frequently

a part of the picture, although these do not seem to predominate, and such children exhibit considerable self-doubt and lack of achievement or autonomy.

Although their inhibitions, related primarily to unconscious fears of losing control of aggressive or sexual impulses, render these children somewhat dependent upon others for initial action, they are not ordinarily overdependent in many respects and may be able to function quite independently under special circumstances in which they have come to feel comfortable. Their inhibitions frequently spread over into areas of academic learning. There they may show difficulties in assimilating knowledge, as well as reproducing it, because of their fears of aggressive or competitive action and their constricted, unspontaneous personality trends.

Particular behavior, such as learning inhibitions, elective mutism, etc., should be specified from the Symptom List.

This diagnosis represents 3% of the total diagnoses made during this time at the clinic. Of these seventeen children, thirteen were boys and four were girls, which is approximately the ration of boys to girls in the clinic. Nine of the boys met the stated criteria for the diagnosis. Of the four remaining boys, one was dropped for lack of data, one was completely mis-diagnosed and two will be discussed later in the chapter. One of the four girls met the diagnostic criteria and the remaining three will be discussed later in the chapter.

Discussion of Cases

The following discussion is limited to the nine boys and one girl who met the diagnostic criteria. A control group of nine boys, chosen by pulling the next chart of a boy in the same age group with psychological testing, is also presented. Again, p scores $\leq .001$ will be indicated.

Referral Source and Presenting Problems (See Figure 1)

Four of the boys and the girl were referred by the school. Five control boys were school referrals. The girl presented with refusal to speak in school. Four of the boys presented with learning problems, three with effeminate behavior, one with sibling rivalry and one with sibling rivalry and encopresis. An example of a school problem from the chart reads:

(Patient) is described by his parents as "less of a problem at home than at school." Father states, "He's not very communicative and things

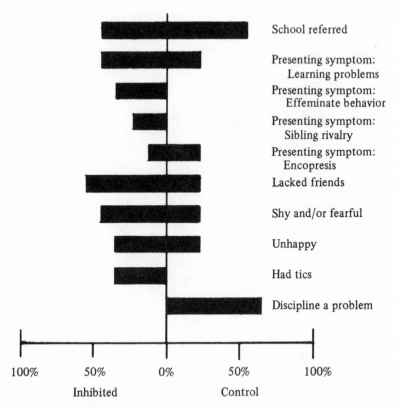

Figure 1. Boys: Referral Source and Presenting Problems

bothering him don't come out until much later." Parents feel he doesn't rise to the challenge of life, rather passively "wishes for things." Parents note that he will not even try something where the risk of failure exists at all.

The school reports that he has an IQ of 109 on the WISC, is not working up to his capacity, is restless, daydreams, has difficulty concentrating and fails to get along with other children.

In the control groups there were two with learning problems as presenting complaints, none with effeminate behavior, two with encopresis and none with sibling rivalry. This group of ten had additional similar problems. Five of the boys and the girl lacked friends, compared with two controls, three of the boys and the girl were unhappy compared with the two controls, and three of the boys had tics occuring in no controls. Only

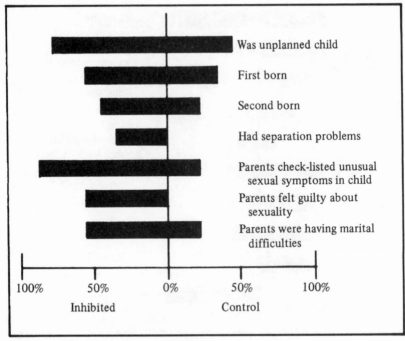

Figure 2. Boys: Psycho-Social History

one boy who did not talk, lacked any of the three symptoms of lack of friends, shyness and unhappiness. No control had all three symptoms (p.0002). Discipline was not among the problems mentioned by these families, but was in six controls.

Psycho-Social History

Seven of the boys were unplanned children as were four controls. Five of the boys and the girl were first-born, the remainder were second-born. In controls three were first-born and two second-born. Three of the boys and the girl had separation problems. There were no separation problems in controls. Unusual sexual symptoms were check-listed by eight of the nine boys' parents (p.007). Three were unnecessarily modest, three touched and handled their genitals at inappropriate times, two were overly interested in sexy pictures (of which one was a teenager), one was upset by references to sex in boy-girl relationships and one dressed like a girl. Five of these nine parents of the boys and the mother of the girl felt guilty about sexuality and had difficulty discussing or dealing with it in the family. There

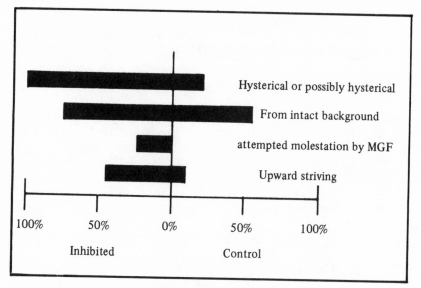

Figure 3. Boys: Mothers

were concerns about sexual symptoms in two controls but no parents were reported as feeling guilty about sexuality.

There were marital difficulties in the families of five of the boys and the girl. In only two controls were marital difficulties known. All nine of the boys' mothers were noted to be hysterical or possibly hysterical (p.0011). (See figure 3). The diagnosis of hysterical is that given in the edition of the *Oxford University Press Psychiatric Dictionary*.

Some examples from the chart read:

Mrs. T is described as an obese thirty-one-year-old woman who has multiple somatic complaints and sees a doctor for various illnesses at least once a month. She maintains telephone contact with a group of cardiologists who reassure her that she does not have cardiac problems. From intake, mother considered herself the patient, got bogged down in petty detail and became very dependent upon the worker making numerous phone calls between appointments. She is flirtatious with other men and is then shocked when they respond to her behavior.

Mrs. L is a forty-year-old woman who was scared to death about sex by her own mother. She dated a feminine, impotent man for seven years until she finally met her husband which she considers lucky; otherwise she probably would never have gotten married at the rate she was going. Mother was determined not to be like maternal grandmother, so when she married, she acted the part of a sweet wife who always pleased her husband at her own expense until she had a nervous breakdown. Mother states that she had numerous physical problems including heart trouble, female trouble, dislocated knees, etc. She is described as immature, insecure, constantly worrying about life and death. She spreads her energy so thin in many different areas that she has little time for her children.

This was true of only two control mothers.

Seven of the boys' mothers and the girl's mother came from an intact family background as did five control mothers. Two of the boys' maternal grandfathers had attempted to molest their mothers not noted in controls. Four of the boys' mothers were upward striving noted in one control. Five of the boys' fathers were from chaotic backgrounds as were four controls. (See figure 4). Four were said to be passive and five were said to be constricted whereas only one control father was described this way. The girl's father was described as isolated and constricted.

He was also seductive. An example taken from the chart reads:

> Father feels that he and his wife waited so long for children (3 years) that they "love" them too much and both parents recount the daily scenes where the girls are held in daddy's lap and they stroke his hair and he tells them how much he loves them.

The father of one of the boys had homosexual experiences and feared impotency. Six of the boys' fathers were anxious (p.0045) and four identified with their sons, but no controls were this way. The girl's mother overidentified with her. Six of the boys' fathers were good providers as were three controls and four had better than a high school education as did two controls.

Thus we are getting a good picture of the families of these children. The parents of both the boys and girl are similar in their dissatisfaction with marriage and their inability to deal with sex in a comfortable way. The mothers of the boys are possibly hysterical and therefore both seductive and frigid, that is promising but not providing, whereas it is the father of the girl who is seductive. The boys' mothers may have had sexual stimulation by their own fathers but have come from intact family backgrounds. The fathers of all tend to be good providers, but are constricted, and the fathers of the boys are anxious, passive and from chaotic backgrounds. For the boys, one can speculate that the men tend to let the women run the family, whereas for the girl, there is conflict over control and the father runs the family through guilt. These parents have sons who are effeminate and children who have learning problems, and are shy, lonely and may have tics. These are children from the early years of marriage who are not particularly wanted and who have developed problems in sexual areas.

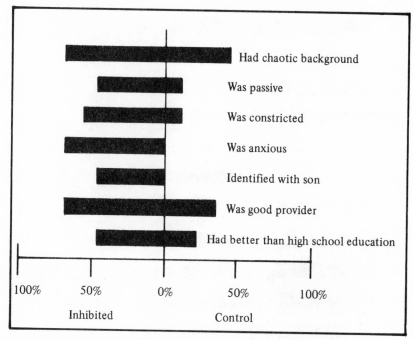

Figure 4. Boys: Fathers

Psychological and Psychiatric Evaluations (See Figures 5 and 6)

The data from the psychological evaluations and the psychiatric interviews have been combined. Seven of the boys and the girl were anxious about aggression and in all but one of the boys this aggression was said to be oral. There were 5 controls anxious about aggression but only one was said to be oral. Examples of their anxiety about aggression are taken from first the psychiatric interview and then the psychological evaluation.

> As striking as what she did say was what she did not say. For example, aggression was studiously avoided. Even the children at school were described as helping each other. Furthermore, the control that she spoke of was in the service of preventing aggression on her part, not in protecting her.

> Patient presents an almost classic picture of an overly-socialized, overly-controlled and inhibited child. He is unable to express aggression in any but the most indirect and sublimated ways .... Aggression of any sort is denied and projected outward, but never acknowledged as originating within the self.

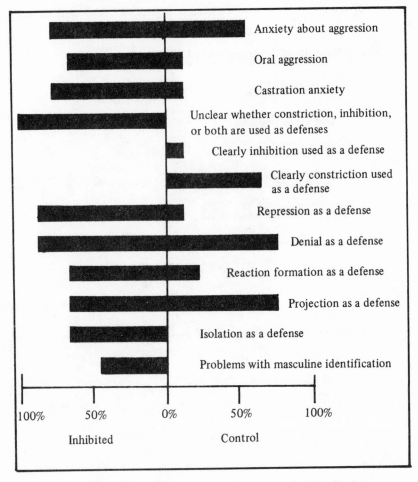

Figure 5. **Boys: Psychological and Psychiatric Evaluations**

An example of oral aggression from the psychologicals reads:

> Her inner life has . . . monster, (who) breathes out smoke which turns into blood or eats people, people are tied up for tigers to eat and witches send all kinds of frightening things out to scare people.

In the remaining boy, an effeminate teenager, the aggression was 'oedipal. Two of the above, one of whom was an effeminate ten-year-old,

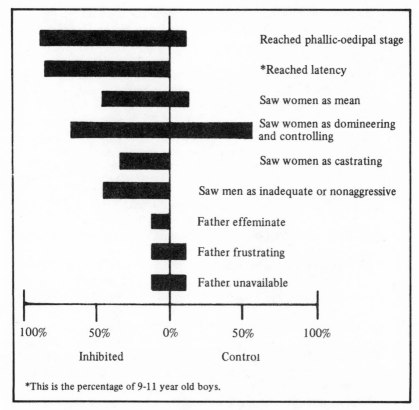

Figure 6. Boys: Psychological and Psychiatric Evaluation

were said to have anxiety about phallic aggression as well as oral aggression. Three of the boys and the girl evidenced anxiety about sexual matters and in seven of the boys castration anxiety was particularly noticed (p.007). This was noticed in one control. Their response to this anxiety was constriction and/or inhibition and it was not possible to tell which defense was being used. All of the boys and the girl were constricted or inhibited or both. One control used inhibition as a defense and six used constriction.

The most prominent defense used by eight of the nine boys was massive repression. Repression, not particularly massive, was used in three controls. Denial was used in as many cases and in seven controls. In six of the boys, not always the same six, there were defenses of reaction-formation, projection, and isolation, this last of which was also used by the girl. Seven controls used projection, none used isolation, and two used reaction-formation. The use of isolation had a p of .005. The repression would seem to be a higher level of defense but many of the defenses were from primitive levels, especially in the girl, and some were from anal levels.

Four of the boys, including two effeminate boys, had problems identifying with males but this was observed in no controls. An example from the chart reads:

> Patient has a lot of confusion about sex; he is unable to clearly separate men from women. Men often appear effeminized and damaged, women stronger and phallic. He drew himself as a little boy with a skirt.

Eight of the boys were functioning in the phallic or oedipal level of development. This was true of one control (p.002). The girl and the remaining boy, a rather isolated child who had difficulty with basic trust, were functioning at the oral and anal stages. Five of the six, nine-to eleven-year-old boys reached latency in their development at some point in time (p.008). Again, the isolated boy had not achieved this and none of the controls had. The six-year-old girl occasionally showed phallic level functioning. The charts did not always contain references to the superego. It was mentioned as being there in six boys and the girl but still to a certain extent externalized in one boy and the girl, and not very prominent in the isolated boy. There was said to be no superego in one control and a largely external superego in three. It was mentioned as present in two more. Four of the boys saw woman as mean and six saw them as domineering and controlling. In controls, one saw women as mean and five saw them as controlling. It is striking that none of the boys in the inhibited or controls saw their mothers as sexually seductive. Three of the boys, including two effeminate ones, saw women as castrating, not seen in controls. Two of the boys saw men as inadequate, and two, including an effeminate boy, saw men as nonaggressive. Therefore, four of the nine boys saw men as either inadequate, or nonaggressive. This was not seen in the controls.

Examples from the charts read:

> Patient is having difficulty in accepting a masculine aggressive competitive identity which he views as leading to failure. At the same time he sees the female role as more successful but dependent . . . she is the recipient of gifts and often it is she who generates the situations in which men fail. He drew a picture of a fifteen-year-old boy and a fifty-six-year-old woman with the only differences being the length of hair.

> Patient is a very angry, depressed youngster with most of his anger being directed toward women. In his TAT stories, women are seen as dom-

ineering, frustrating, mean and punitive. Although he also expresses a fair amount of anger toward men, they are generally seen as being weak and ineffectual, subject to the domination of the women in their lives.

The father of one of the effeminate boys was also effeminate, not seen in controls. One was frustrating and one was unavailable, as was true in controls. Thus we have passive cooperative but anxious children. They are anxious about oral aggression and castration. The boys tend to see their mothers as castrating, domineering and controlling, and their fathers as inadequate and nonaggressive. The girl sees her mother as kind and giving and her father as a helper and a fixer. The effeminate boys, who are more anxious about phallic or oedipal concerns, have an even greater tendency to see their mothers as castrating and their fathers as effeminate. The children are all trying to deal with their anxiety by constriction and/or inhibition. The boys used massive repression, denial and somewhat less reaction-formation, projection and isolation. The effeminate boys do not seem to be identifying with women so much as with effeminate males although two of the three have problems identifying with the male. In spite of the boys' great concern about oral aggression, they are mainly functioning at the phallic or oedipal level, do have superegos and, at times, are age-appropriate in their development. The girl is functioning in the oral/anal level of development.

Although the girl had many of the same characteristics of the other children discussed, there were several additional features which were present in none of the boys. Her approach to the Rorschach was an obsessive compulsive one and was described by the psychologist in the following way: "Her powers of concentration were tremendous and the striving for successful completion she displayed would be unusual even in a much older child." On the last Rorschach card, the psychologist allowed her to continue until she stopped herself. She gave seventeen responses which is about the norm for the entire ten cards. There were also evidences of potential for formal thought disorder shown by inaccuracy over ideation, illogical combinations and contaminations when structure was removed. It appears that the only girl in this diagnostic category is more disturbed than the boys, perhaps cultural expectations play a great part in determining referrals for inhibited behavior. Thus, girls must show more extreme behaviors to cause concern and therefore referral.

Diagnoses

Certain of the characteristics of inhibited children suggest relationships to other diagnoses. The linkage between oral aggressive concerns and phallic oedipal concerns together with massive repression is reminiscent of hysteria. The presence of superego id conflict around oedipal concerns suggests a neurotic disorder. The whole life style with unresolved problems from the oral period and characterological use of defenses makes the diagnosis of personality disorder also appropriate. Although women are seen as domineering and controlling, the issue of control of the external world does not seem to be as important with these children as it is with the obsessive compulsive. Furthermore, they do not have to win the battle of control as the oppositional child does. However, control of intrapsychic forces seems paramount.

Similarities to other diagnostic categories led some to consider labels other than overly inhibited for the boys. The boy with lack of basic trust was almost labeled an isolated personality. Compulsive personality was considered as a diagnosis in another boy. One of the effeminate boys was almost diagnosed as an overly dependent personality. There was some consideration given in other boys to the diagnosis of psychoneurotic disorder with either depressive or oppositional features. Oppositional features were thought to be present when the inhibition and constriction were interpreted as withholding.

Although inhibited personality may be a complete diagnostic category, it is helpful to additionally characterize this diagnosis in specific cases. The effeminate boys seem to be a distinct subgroup. It would probably help to specifically label these boys as overly inhibited with effeminate traits to pinpoint the complex of items that have been mentioned and which seem to go together with the effeminate boy. Another distinct subgroup appears to be children who are more seriously impaired. The boy with some lack of basic trust who, like the girl, had not progressed as far as others in his development, should have his diagnosis qualified to indicate that his prognosis is poor and treatment will be difficult. Along with the girl's low level of psychosexual development, her potential for formal thought disorder should be taken into consideration and be included in the diagnosis.

Treatment

There was a variety of treatment methods recommended for the ten more typical children. Individual therapy alone was recommended for two boys and one girl. Individual treatment with group therapy at a later time was recommended for one boy. Individual therapy with remediation was recommended for two boys; with the isolated boy this was to be done at the same time, whereas, with another boy this was to be done separately. Individual or group therapy was recommended for two boys. Group therapy was recommended for one case and family therapy for another. In controls, individual therapy was recommended in six cases with additional family therapy in one. One was referred elsewhere and one was given no recommendation beyond management advice. Six sets of parents were seen conjointly. The parents of the isolated boy were seen in a parents group. The remaining set of parents were seen sometimes together and sometimes separately, for a while, the family was seen all together. These parents eventually divorced but the mother and the boy continue to be seen.

Treatment was refused by one boy and one girl. Treatment was refused by two controls. Four boys started treatment but terminated before completion. One of these, the isolated boy, dropped out of treatment after six months. Another, the effeminate teenager, was pulled out of his group treatment after six months when his father became more assertive in conjoint therapy and threatened the family balance. The effeminate six-year-old was pulled out of therapy after two years when his parents refused to change therapists. The last of these four, a teenager, was in family therapy for five months; it was felt that this therapy never took hold. Of these four, only the effeminate six-year-old was felt to have benefited from treatment, he became more boyish and less enuretic. One control pulled out of therapy after six months and one control was terminated after 20 weeks for failure to meet appointments. One control child was terminated after a few weeks as the family moved. Three boys are still being seen. The boy who was seen occasionally with his family continues in treatment after several years. Another boy has been in treatment for nine months with rather poor attendance. The last of these three remains in treatment after seven months and some improvement has been noted in his schoolwork One child in the control group continues in treatment after 4 years.

One child successfully terminated after twelve months of treatment. His symptoms were alleviated. He was less dependent, had better peer-relationships, and had been able to deal with his anger in treatment. The parents are continuing in treatment, however, because of another son who was the original identified patient.

Thus, when family treatment and group therapy were tried, they were unsuccessful. The treatment which seemed to work best in this small sample was individual therapy. Regardless of the type of therapy used, treatment of the overly inhibited child has proven to be slow and difficult at best.

Cases that were Misdiagnosed

There are three boys and three girls who were probably misdiagnosed and it is hard to arrive at a totally acceptable diagnosis. Although the two seven-year-old boys presented with learning problems, the main problem of these boys and a nine-year-old girl was aggressive behavior and acting out—including tantrums, stealing, fire setting and negativism. They were not described as shy or fearful although one boy was said to lack friends and the other two were said to be unhappy. One boy was first-born and the other two were second-born. There were marital difficulties in the boys' families. All the mothers were from intact family backgrounds. The mother of one boy and the girl may have been hysterical. Neither of the fathers of the boys had gone past high school and both were anxious but otherwise all fathers were dissimilar. The findings on the psychological evaluations and psychiatric interviews really separated these children from the others. They were all said to be both passive cooperative and oppositional during the evaluation. All were anxious about aggression which was oral and none was anxious about castration or sex, a striking difference from the other group. They were anxious that the world was a threatening place and they dealt with this by constriction.

Examples from the charts read:

> Patient greatly feared loss of control, which led to his severe inhibition of verbal responses and physical movement. He has a lot of difficulty in controlling feelings and attempts to cope with this by being very rigid.

> Patient feels helpless and powerless in a threatening world . . . is constantly trying to inhibit impulses and to conform in order to avoid the threatening consequences.

They were potentially explosive with no middle ground or control, either totally controlled or totally uncontrolled. Although repression was found in one boy, much more primitive defenses of denial, projection and isolation were more frequently present. All had poor basic trust. They were functioning in the oral and anal stages and the anal stage was used as a protection against oral concerns. The anal structures were used so much to protect against oral fears that these fears were not picked up until the psychological protocols were reviewed in one boy's case even though they became prominent in his therapy.

A few phallic strivings were seen in one boy. Women were viewed as domineering and controlling by the boys. The girl exhibited retardation in the area of sexual identification. The superego was either still largely externalized or not even perceived. Thus, these three were in a struggle with the external world to keep control of themselves and were so involved with its primitive roots that they had not progressed to age appropriate stages. It would be tempting to label these two boys as having some kind of oral/anal behavior disorder and leave it open as to whether they were going to turn out to be impulse ridden sociopaths, or isolated or suspicious personalities, or oppositional personalities. An alternative diagnosis for the girl was given as schizoid because beginnings of ego disintegration were seen when her defenses were not organized properly. Another important consideration in diagnosis should be what it is that needs treatment. The main problem in these children was not the constriction but the explosiveness and its origins in poor object relations at the oral level. The differential diagnosis of one of the boys was phobic neurosis because he was so fearful of what he saw in the world. The term neurosis seems to be inappropriate in the absence of superego and oedipal concerns. In other words, we would like to suggest that children without oedipal development or sexual concerns whose main problem is loss of oral/anal aggressive control should not be labeled overly-inhibited though they may be quite fearful and constricted on early interviews.

The ten-year-old boy presented with being unable to cope with his peers and with a dislike of school. He was shy, unhappy and an unplanned first-born child. The mother, although from an intact family, was depressed. The father, a Ph.D was obsessive compulsive and a good provider. There were marital difficulties. On examination, the boy tended to be oppositional and very depressed. He was anxious about relationships and used obsessive compulsive defenses including distancing and isolation; he also used denial. There was some basic trust exhibited at times. He was mainly functioning in the anal stage although there were some phallic striving and occasional oedipal fantasies. His superego was still somewhat externalized. The differential diagnosis for him was obsessive compulsive neurosis with some depression. Prominent in his material were self-deprecating statements and very low self-esteem and a depressed affect. The constriction noted seemed to be more an accompaniment of the depression than a symptom formation of a true inhibited type. What mostly needed treatment was the dysphoria and that, therefore, should be the main diagnosis.

There are two remaining girls to be discussed. One is a three-year-old who was too young to have been labeled with a personality disorder. Her presenting problem was "autistic-like tendencies," in other words, she walked like a robot and lacked expression of feelings except fear. Her parents manifested considerable psychopathology and although an unusual procedure, both were tested at the clinic. The mother was diagnosed as a borderline patient of basically hysterical character disorder type and father was seen as an obsessive compulsive character with borderline psychotic potential. Both the psychiatrist and psychologist agreed that the girl had premature development of ego defenses and that their overuse was causing her to appear constricted; she was not inhibited. When the patient entered treatment, her therapist saw her as active, controlling, manipulative and prone to severe regression and physical acting out. Due to the girl's distortion of reality and her inability to form any meaningful relationship with the therapist, she was considered to be borderline psychotic.

Another eight-year-old girl came in with the chief complaint of not talking in school although she did talk in other places. Because she did not talk here either, there are no psychiatric or psychological data. Other complaints were that she was oppositional, had visual motor problems and had attacks of screaming and crying. The latter should have taken her out of the over-inhibited catagory. When she entered treatment, she was seen as an oppositional child who would talk easily to the secretaries and say, "They think I'm going to talk, but I won't."

Thus, 38 percent of all the cases were probably misdiagnosed. There are obvious reasons why this should not have happened. In three cases, the main problem was aggressive acting-out, in one it was depression and in another, although the chief complaint was elective mutism, there was a problem with aggressive acting out; in the last case, the patient was too young for the diagnosis of a personality disorder. This chapter hopefully attempts to prevent future misdiagnoses by giving examples of case histories and diagnostic data on overly inhibited children. In this attempt, it also discusses the diagnostic criteria, it shows the relationship to other diagnostic categories, and it suggests the need for additional subgroups under the diagnosis.

CHAPTER 13

Psychotherapy of the Inhibited Child

DORIS C. GILPIN, M.D.

The overly inhibited child needs to be understood in depth in order to be treated by psychotherapy. Superficially one might be tempted to prescribe an activity type of group experience (Slavson) for these quiet, apathetic, nonreactive and essentially passive youngsters, especially the boys, so as to mobilize them into some degree of energetic participation, but as one examines the dynamics more closely, it becomes evident that pushing or pulling them from the outside can only reinforce the proclivity to leave interaction and action to someone else. One discovers that every mode of activity can be affected by the inhibitory process.

First, although these children try to shut sexual thoughts out of their minds, they call attention to their sexuality by various parapraxes, such as, inadvertently touching or rubbing their genitals or exhibiting excessive modesty.

The next most obvious behavior they show points to an inhibition of aggression to the point of lacking all self-assertiveness. They seem quite unable to initiate any exchange and when given a task, their extreme passivity interferes with their anxiety to cooperate. Such behavior is only too frequently successful in provoking adults to prod them or perform the task themselves. The unwillingness to try is not related to a low level of self-esteem but to a reluctance to assert themselves especially when assertiveness is equated in their minds with masculinity or destructiveness. In either case they are afraid that action will result in damage to themselves. In the case of boys, women are seen as especially damaging and mother figures as vindictive about any show of aggression in the male and in fantasy, their vengefulness is directed at the phallus. Fathers, on the other hand, are regarded as being like themselves—passive, constricted, and anxious—and therefore also at similar risk and unable to help them. The main identification is with the inadequate, unobtrusive paternal image. The inner controls (the conscience formations) are heavily buttressed by such unconscious thoughts that warn against any sexual or aggressive impulse until gradually the prohibitions conduce to inhibitions of all impulse expression. As a consequence, spontaneity disappears, fantasies become sparse and the arid internal life becomes gradually syntonic with the ego. Such impoverishment of the personality is not conducive to popularity so that these children are very much alone. However, a lonely life is still preferable to one racked by anxiety and guilt, by angry feelings toward the fantasied aggressors, and by fears of retaliation. The increased dependency on the mother makes it even more dangerous to destroy them and lose their main source of supplies. They want to bite and yet, at the same time, cannot risk biting the hand that feeds them.

The Mothers of Inhibited Boys

Like most frigid women, the mothers of these boys are given to double-bind messages in the sexual sphere. Their early history is typical of hysterical individuals who have been grossly overstimulated across incest barriers. Their adult sexual life is unsatisfying. They both invite and repel the male sexual advance and are therefore likely to end up with husbands who are undemanding and unthreatening. Their sons are subjected to the same mixed messages that say, in effect: "I am stimulating you but do not dare to let me know that you notice it or are responding to it." The pre-oedipal history of these cases is less well documented. Many women of this hysterical type have underlying conflicts around nurturance. They respond to the birth of these male babies with ambivalence so that the early feeding experiences are tinged with the same confusing and contradictory message that characterize the sexual interchanges with resulting unresolved frustrations. "I want to feed you for the satisfactions you will give me. You cannot satisfy me but I can satisfy you. I can satisfy you or not satisfy you as I wish. You have no natural right to my breast." One can speculate that in some such early transaction, a fierce aggressiveness is born—but too much to let out. They must at all cost preserve the nutritional one if they are to survive. At the next stage they retain their anger and remain nonthreatening to preserve the integrity of their bodies and bodily parts. The confusing and contradictory messages of the pre-oedipal stage are translated into the language of this later stage and the boy's unconscious response to it is: "I must keep my phallus powerless and hidden if I am to keep it at all." Since the mothers are not only dominant in the family but domineering, there is no way in which her power can be challenged. The only thing for the boys to do is to sit back quietly and passively, let the world go by, and do as little as possible to call attention to themselves.

The Two Critical Aspects of Treatment

How can one treat patients who do not participate or cooperate actively in the treatment process and do their best to remain uninvolved? There are two important considerations to bear in mind: the first is that the therapist should provide a setting for the appearance of assertiveness, should nurture it when it first shows itself, and should not in any way repeat conditions that have in the child's past inhibited his assertiveness. Should the therapist present himself as an assertive model for the patient? Historically, the boys have had an assertive model in their mothers and have preferred to identify with their nonassertive fathers. It is more therapeutic for the child first to understand his choice of identification before providing him with an assertive model. In the earlier stages of treatment he may not be able to identify with an assertive male since his general fear of assertiveness is uppermost. All the therapist can or should do at the beginning is to recognize and appreciate any small show of assertiveness that emanates from the child.

The second main consideration is for the therapist to help the child question his own lack of assertiveness and thereby move to an uncovering of its roots. At the very least he would hope to awaken or support some uneasiness in the child about whether his mode of adjustment to life is either necessary or desirable. He needs to do this without undermining the very sensitive self-esteem of the child and without entering into a battle over it. The exposure of roots is carried out most efficaciously in the context of the therapeutic transference.

The following account of psychotherapy with an eleven-year-old boy with clinical inhibitions will help to clarify and illustrate some of the issues already discussed.

The First Session with the Child and his Parents

I said to the parents that I did not know exactly what the social worker had already said to them about treatment and so I wondered what they knew about it. Mother explained that they had learned about their son after the diagnostic evaluation and now they knew that therapy was to begin and that a therapist had to be selected who would accept the case. I asked Tom if he knew what the word "therapist" meant and he indicated that he did not. I explained that a therapist was someone who would try to help him while they talked or played so that he would not have so much trouble with his thoughts or feelings. He made a little face with a half smile, and I said it looked like he had some feeling about that. I wondered if he could tell me what it was. He did not answer and his mother tried to get him to do so. I said that he probably could not give a full answer yet about how he felt about coming. He would need to get to know what it was like and not just hear the words about what it was like. I said he might have some questions after he got into it and of course I would be glad to answer them.

Thus in this first encounter, one sees the mother trying to force the issue and the therapist merely encouraging the assertiveness that was shown. The father is as usual setting an example of sitting back passively and allowing the mother and the therapist to take the initiative.

It was decided to see the child once a week because this was all that was possible at the time.

The First Session

When I saw the boy alone I explained what the evaluation had told me about him. Tom moved to a chair closer to me at this point. He seemed nervous and restless; I wondered whether he thought I might be aggressive in the way that his mother was aggressive. He did not apparently understand the word "aggressive" so I explained it as "pushy," such as making people do things when they did not really want to do them. I imagined that he found his father easier to deal with and he agreed. I thought that being pushed like this might make him afraid of all grownups. Perhaps he had an idea that they would hurt him in some way and maybe even make him feel less of a boy. I said that of course that was not going to happen. I wondered whether he thought his mother had been a little "pushy" when she had drilled him on our names—as if he were a dummy and he really was not a dummy. I asked whether he had noticed that and he said no. I said I hoped to help him notice these things so that he would not have them just happening to him without him being able to do something about it.

The Second Session

At this second session there was considerable silence as the therapist waited for Tom to initiate the process. He did a good deal of squirming and rubbing of his eyes, and looked down at the floor most of the time. I said that it looked as if he were thinking why he was here today. He smiled but would not look at me. After a while he began to scan the room especially at the corner where the toys were. I said that now it looked as if he were doing some looking. He smiled but again without looking at me. After a while he yawned and I commented that he might be feeling tired of doing nothing and maybe he now wanted to do something. He bagan to look around even more after this with increasing interest. He began to bite at his hand and I said it looked as if he wanted to bite himself and perhaps he was not pleased with himself. He stopped biting his hand and began to bite his nails. I said that it seemed as if he could not stop biting himself and I wondered what this meant. For the first time he looked at me directly and I commented on this to the effect that he was less worried at being with me. He was still far from spontaneous and did not begin anything. The therapeutic focus was on him *as someone who did things*.

The Third Session

The third session found him finally engaging in some kind of action. He sat down and began looking toward the play area. When I remarked that he seemed very interested in looking at things in my room he withdrew his gaze. I pointed this out and wondered if what I had said had caused him to stop looking. He denied this and began once again to look around. I followed the direction of his glance and when he noticed this he turned quickly and smiled self-consciously at me. I said that I had been trying to look at what he was looking at to see what it was. He seemed at a loss, played with his fingers and stared at the carpet. I wondered whether he was thinking about the situation here with me and if he thought I was being a little "pushy" like his mother. I was talking to him with the hope that he would be able to talk back to me so we could talk together. It was not helpful for one person to do the talking. That would make me like his mother and I preferred that we talked together. He stared at the desk and I said that unless he shared his thoughts with me, I could not tell at all what he was thinking. If he chose to do so I might be able to help him with his feelings. Of course he did not have to talk to me in words. He could draw or use clay if he so wished. It was up to him. Whatever he decided to do was all right by me. Quite suddenly he said "clay" and I immediately agreed that this would be fine. For a while he was undecided where to take the clay and I made no effort to help him. Finally he took it to a small table and began to work on it. At first he began building a house. When I asked if it belonged to somebody he looked perplexed. I said I meant did somebody live there and he thought for awhile. At first he said no. Then he changed his mind and said yes. I asked if there was a family or was it just someone living alone, and whether it was a he or a she person. Again he thought for a long time and said finally that he did not know. At this point I felt the "pushinesss" in me and decided not to pursue it further. There was silence while the building progressed. After a while I ventured the observation that it was quite a nice house and wondered again for whom it might be intended. He said "she," and I observed that a "she" might enjoy living in it. I asked him how he felt about his construction, and he said "O.K." I agreed it was O.K. and nice for a "she" to be in. He proceeded to add a very tall cylindrical tower and I thought aloud that the "she" might like that tall firm tower and admire it. He looked pleased.

The therapist was demonstrating her efforts at understanding his activity, her interest in the personal significance of his creation, her acceptance of his decisions as binding, and her neutrality in regard to his responses. Yet at the same time she was providing him with what Mahler has emphasized as being of great importance during the "reproachment phase" of separation-individuation, "an encouraging environment" or in Winnicott's terms "a facilitating environment." She is however, conscious of the counter-transference degrees of "pushiness."

The Sixth Session

He was becoming aware and beginning to acknowledge his passivity regarding his needs, his dislike of intrusion and intrusiveness, and even, more vaguely indicated, his wish to interact more actively. I commented on how he seemed to enjoy building tall things that stood up strongly by themselves. Perhaps he was trying to show her what a big strong boy he could be, and maybe this helped him to have better feelings about himself. I said that it was easier for him at first to show me what he could do than to tell me about it. There was considerable talk about how hard it was for him to verbalize.

The Ninth Session

In a session three weeks later, he verbalized a feeling for the first time. Just as he was negotiating the last piece of roof on his building it collapsed. I asked how he felt about it breaking down and he said "mad!" and looked as if he felt it. I sympathized with him and remarked that I understood how he felt. It must be hard to feel mad and not be able to say or do something about it. I knew quite ordinary kids who would shout and bang about and say angry things when they got mad. Perhaps he felt all these inside him but could not let them come out. He denied this. I said that sometimes angry feelings inside got so strong that it was difficult to keep them in.

He was continuing to build even taller buildings and feeling better about himself. He added a guard with a long sword who would protect the building. If however the guard should faint from tiredness, the long sword would help to hold him up. I commented on the use he made of tall things and long things to hold things up, to keep things safe—it made him feel good.

The Sixteenth Session

The following session showed him becoming more conscious of the fact that his passivity was not absolutely necessary.

I said I wondered how come he didn't bring the rest of the blocks from the drawer with him. He went to the drawer to bring his building blocks and left behind a building that someone else had already constructed. I called his attention to this and asked what had stopped him from bringing the completed building. He went over and brought it to the table and began taking it apart too. I said something had stopped him before and that maybe we could figure it out by thinking about it together. I asked if he noticed how he was feeling when he looked in the drawer, and at first he was blank but then after much hesitation he said "unhappy." It was something done well by someone else. I said that was one way of acting about things that make us unhappy—to walk away from them. Now it looked as if he were doing something else about them—taking them apart. At one point he dropped a lot of blocks on the floor and some of them were very close to me; he got up out of his chair and retrieved them for himself rather than asking me to get them, and I pointed this out to him. When he did not answer I said that sometimes he must feel that I was pretty bossy asking all these questions and trying to get him to answer. I hoped he would tell me when he thought this happened. I wondered whether he might not find his parents bossy at times and found it hard to tell them although he might think it inside. He said that he had never told them such a thing. I said that he might find it less worrying to think and say such thoughts in this special situation with me. But I understood too it might be much easier for me as a grownup to think of his mother as bossy than for him to do so. Also I felt that I had been a little bossy asking him so many questions and I could understand if he sometimes felt mad at me about it.

In the next fifteen sessions his building projects were conducted more actively and vigorously and he began moving around a lot. The static buildings became connected with mobile objects—airplanes, space ships, cars, trucks, etc. As the activity increased he started wishing that he could travel.

The Thirtieth Session

He opened the doors for me and I thanked him on the way to the playroom. He was able to demolish the constructions of the previous sessions and to start anew without waiting for any direction. I commented on the fact that he was now using his own ideas and that these were very interesting. I mentioned that I would have to miss our sessions in the following week and wondered how he felt about that. He said it would be O.K. I said that he seemed now to be so interested in building that he might miss that. He agreed that he would. I said that he might also have some feelings about me and not seeing me. Perhaps he might be kind of glad to get away from talky Dr. G. for a while, and he agreed. I said that I knew there were things that he wished I did not talk about and also things he might like to hear from me. He could ask me questions just as I asked him questions. He looked very comfortable and concentrated on his building. It was a larger structure and I commented on how strong and powerful and important it looked.

Therapeutic Changes

He now began to participate more in the interchanges, to make spontaneous although brief utterances, to indicate negative feeling when he experienced pressure from the therapist and to "act out" in the transference, that is, he unloosed some of the early aggression felt toward his dominant, intrusive mother. He seemed constantly surprised that he could do all this in relative safety and without retaliation. He was now smiling more frequently, at times defiantly and at times seductively. He seemed altogether more alive and lively in the treatment situations.

At school he was also doing much better and coming out with comments more frequently in the classroom. The danger was that his mother would experience the new self as threatening to her way of life and remove him from treatment before the roots of his inhibition in the castration anxiety had been fully uncovered. So far the progress was felt by all parties to be good but far from complete.

Conclusion

It can be seen that even this very inhibited boy had some rudimentary assertiveness that could be encouraged to grow under the aegis of therapeutic patience. Each tiny element of self-expression had to be encouraged and quite often it was two steps forward and one step back. Another element that was also slow to grow was the patient's ability to express his feelings in words. The real treatment could only begin after the general blanket of inhibition had been lifted. The psychotherapy of the inhibited child had, therefore, two phases: (1) the establishment of a nonthreatening therapeutic alliance that conveyed a sense of safety, and (2) the treatment of the neurotic conflict buried under the inhibition. With Tom, the first phase had been more or less completed. What was to follow would take a more usual therapeutic course. Much of the preparatory treatment needed to be passed in comparative silence and whatever interventions there were had to be phrased as nondemandingly and as nonintrusively as possible. An attempt must be made to create a mutual way of working together so that child and therapist can together become curious about the strange phenomenon of inhibition and its origins. Working together is by no means an easy task to set up with the inhibited child. Too often he takes fright with the first interpretation, the first analysis of defense, the first transference manifestation. The treatment requires great tact, consideration, patience and sensitivity from the therapist who must basically respect the child and his style.

It can be tedious work with gains more easily visible over a long time than from moment to moment, but the rewards that come with the lifting of the inhibition can be a very worthwhile compensation. With this particular patient, the extreme inhibition of verbalization made treatment difficult but it was then delightful to see the gradual unfolding of mobile and creative fantasies in such a frozen child.

CHAPTER 14

Summing Up
on
the Inhibited Child

E. JAMES ANTHONY, M.D.

The workshops, discussing these presentations, were unquestionably fascinated, intrigued and perplexed by the different pictures of inhibition manifested by "the rocking horse winner," the child Jerry—followed through his development—and the boy, Tom, treated in psychotherapy. A curious fact emerged from the various discussions: the setting in which the child was described appeared to have a subtle effect in derailing the evaluative process. One child, for example, was seen within the setting of his family, a second in the context of a longitudinal study, and the third in a dyadic treatment situation. It seemed difficult to believe that the picture of inhibition presented could have a similar basis.

Several questions were focused on prevalence: was there, in fact, a steady load of inhibited children within any given population; did they represent extremes of a normative tendency; and were there fluctuations in the level of inhibition over the course of development? Did such children move in and out of clinical states of inhibition?

Constitutional versus environmental factors were also very much in question. The groups wanted to know to what extent similar degrees of inhibition were evinced by the biological as opposed to the acquired parents and siblings? If there is a constitutional predisposition to inhibition or nonengagement, to what extent can it be altered by experience and intervention? Is it possible, in considering predisposition, to separate out constitutional from congenital, intrauterine or traumatic birth influences?

The differentiation of internal from external factors in the genesis of inhibition was clearly hard for the working groups to disentangle. If a particular child is inhibited and his family is not, to what extent is it possible to integrate him into the family group? Was it possible that parental patterns, as assumed in the clinic presentation, were not casually related to them. Would, for example, hysterical or seductive parents automatically produce inhibition? Would punitive or restrictive parents conduce to a similar or different syndrome?

From a diagnostic point of view, many of the working groups had difficulty in differentiating the syndrome of inhibition from incipient psychosis, depression, characterological passivity, or the diagnostic aftermath of excessive traumatization or overstimulation. Many of the clinicians present felt that disengagement was merely a nonclinical euphemism for depression. It was also thought that the three presentations may have been addressing themselves to three different etiological disorders of inhibition, resulting in one case from family pathology, in a second from a constitutionally derived low drive, and in a third from withdrawal in response to sexual overstimulation.

Psychosocial and cultural factors were also brought up. Were Black children more prone to inhibition or was their inhibition an artifact of a White environment? To what extent was diagnostic inhibition a function of the therapist's posture and approach, his ethnicity in relation to the child, and the imposing nature of the environment when the child came from relatively modest surroundings?

Throughout the discussion, there was a subtle and pervasive suggestion that male and female roles could be classified alternatively as active and passive patterns of behavior. Pathology was then considered when a particular individual manifested a countrasexual response. Value judgments, based on such stereotyped sex roles, played an inordinant part in making a diagnosis. Male children, for instance, were easily identified as inhibited because they were passive so that inhibition and passivity were then assumed to be part of the same clinical manifestation. Activity in female parents was often seen as causative in the genesis of inhibition and described negatively as "intrusive," "aggressive," "castrating," etc.

There was also some complaints that the depth of clinical study did not permit the clinicians from tracing the source of inhibition to vicissitudes in the sexual or aggressive drives, to problems of identification, to resolutions of the Oedipus complex and to even such less penetrating factors as the size of the family, the presence or absence of particular parents, the dominance-submissive roles, the ratio of girls to boys and the sibling spacing.

In the Neubauer case, the child was clearly not a patient and his parents, teachers and doctors did not regard him as clinically abnormal or deviant. He was less active that other children and also, over time, less engaged, almost in the Sartrian sense. For this reason, therefore, nobody considered intervention because nobody knows enough about the long-term development of such cases to feel sufficiently confident that they could alter the course of events.

It is true that schizoid, autistic and depressed children behave with insufficient activation and engagement but in the case of Jerry, the picture was one of developmental progression toward a certain style of behavior rather than a clinical deviation or conflict.

In conducting longitudinal studies, one is reminded, over and over again, of the wide range of individual variations some of which certainly encroach on the kinds of diagnostic reactions discussed by the groups such as autistic, schizophrenic and depressive. What one also learns from prospective investigations is the way in which certain children, under certain conditions, with certain contributions from the environment seem inevitably to follow a certain individual pattern of development that is specifically theirs. As mentioned earlier, we still do not comprehend enough to know whether to correct or how to correct such tendencies.

The more experience we have in this matter, the more impressive is the individual variation in progression (from precocity to delay), in thresholds (from high to low), in anxiety tolerance (from marked to slight), in drive endowments (from strong to weak), in autonomic functioning (from responsive to vegetative), and so on.

The important question, as postulated by Neubauer, is therefore not whether individual variations should be modified or whether one human being should be made to respond like the majority of human beings, but, within the givens of the dispositional characteristics, to examine the modifications that can take place within the organismic system under certain conditions of life and environment. The New York study was therefore designed to deliniate the interplay of individual variation with environment rather than to extract evidence of pathology. Over time, the investigator as intervener learns about the limitations of his own omnipotence with respect to effecting change as well as the maturational stability of individuals irrespective of time and circumstance. Because the New York study was of development and not of treatment or parental guidance, the question of modifiability of nonengagement remains a moot one until someone else considers the problem from this angle. There is no doubt that nonengagement acts as a provocation to parents and teachers and therapists as much oppositionality, but we know far less about the modifiability of nonengagement than oppositionality.

The problem is aggravated by the process of fostering or adoption. Here the parents are even more likely to misjudge the situation and feel that the child who is inactive, disinterested and passive is merely showing a covert form of stubbornness and resistance.

As in the general area of inhibition, nonengagement is rarely total. Jerry, for example was able to move forward along certain channels; was able to act under certain circumstances but he seemed to make his own choice and any extra stimulation imposed on him made him distinctly uncomfortable and withdrawing. He was also able to assimilate the environment visually, conceptually, logically, cognitively and thus to constitute some form of universal frame of reference for himself. This implied a certain measure of engagement, involvement and basic interest. Perhaps this is where parental guidance might have helped to increase or improve the channels between the child and the world outside.

As time went on, secondary effects began to accrue as the dispositional factors began to have reciprocal interactions with aggressive discharges, social interchanges, exposures to frustration and developmental conflicts. This would represent what Freud referred to as "the complementary series" between natural endowment and experience. The final picture, whether nonclinical or clinical, represents a complex interplay between the two.

The feeling one gets about this child is that he is becoming someone who maintains his distance in life to an optimal degree for his own comfort and prefers to look at life from a safe distance, rather like a scientist through a microscope. Given such life conditions, it could very well become creative; nevertheless he would never prove a great social success. In terms of invention, what one would have liked to prescribe for him from very early on is a carefully prescribed dosage of contact, communication and relationship—not too much or not too little at any developmental phase but sufficient for his ongoing needs.

Neubauer's main contention was that basic knowledge in this area was still scanty: one was not sure at all about the level of thresholds, about the constitutional strength of impulses, about developing ego constrictions, about undue sensitivities, about tolerance for closeness and proximity: all these ignorances hamper us in our strategy of intervention. When we add to this the secondary effects, the defensive systems that build up around oral, anal and phallic conflicts, the situation becomes even more nebulous and confusing. If to this admixture, one further added variations in activity and sensitivity that mismatched with the activity and sensitivity of the adopting or fostering parents, then we place ourselves therapeutically in a "no man's land."

Many investigators have found, including Neubauer, that only a living-in experience with the family can help to bring out these constitutional differences. It is very hard to discern differences within these normal dimensions by means of films and videotapes. It is also difficult to correlate differences in the cognitive and emotional styles of families and the timetable of emergence of new developmental phenomena such as speech, stranger responses, smiling reactions, phobias, etc., and one gets the impression that maturational sequences and developmental timetables are fairly strongly locked in to each other, although content may vary. So while there are differences with different environmental influences at work, there are also many things surprisingly alike; yet the field is still too complicated and unexplored to make any more than gross predictions with regard to future developments given a certain degree of environmental constancy. Neither nature nor experience make things easy for the would-be investigator.

Whether we will ever be in the ideal position to differentiate very early on in life between the inhibited, the isolated, the conflicted, the depressed, the nonengaging, the constricted and the child with an inadequate autonomous function is still very much for future consideration. At present, we are still very much in the area of speculation.

In this review of the inhibited child, therefore, we have discussed him developmentally, phenomenologically and diagnostically, seeking to find an appropriate niche for him in a schedule of classification. He has been labeled according to his ego functioning in terms of constriction, restriction, nonengagement, noninvolvement and nonappetent; he has been labeled in descriptive terms of muted, passive, unresponsive, nonreactive and nonspontaneous; in popular parlance, he has been called unforthcoming, low-key, shy, subdued, and a loner; and finally it has been claimed that when the developing child at the age of three begins to become a personality, the inhibited child remains a nonperson. This medley of impressions does little more than remind us of the Victorian child of the last century whose childhood duty it was "to be seen but not heard."

In my introduction, I focused on the existence of a hypothetical "constitutional complex" and of a normal inhibitory mechanism that might be amplified through environmental experiences. I pointed out, however, that it still remained a matter of conjecture as to whether a child or his environment was basically nonengaging and whether the detachment was primary or secondary. Often a history could be elicited of traumatic events but an absence of trauma was as frequent.

Nevertheless, I think that we are wiser than when we started because we have looked closely at a phenomenon not only in the way that has developed or the way that it manifests itself within the family, or the way in which it appears diagnostically in the clinic or, finally, in the way that the process of inhibition has revealed itself microanalytically in treatment. We have not been able to investigate the biochemical or psychophysiological aspects of inhibition but there is no doubt that such investigations would help in the clarification of the phenomenon.

The case for family diagnosis and therapy was made with singular clarity by Mandelbaum. It is particularly useful for enmeshed families that have reached a stalemate in the power struggle among themselves and have established chronic coalitions that act somewhat like psychological Maginot Lines. It is useful in families that have a special need to scapegoat a particular member and the victim may be a handicapped, an inhibited or an acting-out child. It is useful in a family that is already inundated with insight that they seem unable to put to use except in destructive ways. When one of the parents is also markedly inhibited, a sympathetic liason is rapidly established and maintained between parent and child and the two may then be treated by the rest of the family as a sick unit. If the mother is active, outgoing, dominant and attacking, and the father is quiet, timid and inhibited, the boy with an inhibitory disposition may find it easier to identify with the aggressed one than with the aggressor.

The family approach used by Mandelbaum is transactional rather than analytic and the emphasis is then on the power struggle than on libidinal conflicts. As one watches the family in action, the reasons for nonengagement become very evident. Two other factors are also evident: the reluctance to examine content as if only the mode of communication mattered, and the excesses of countertransference that emerge. Whether he likes it or not (and he usually seems to like it), the nonanalytic family therapist is inexorably caught up in the same manipulations and machinations as the rest of the family and may sometimes become obnoxiously authoritarian and confronting.

The therapist, Gilpin, is constantly aware of the countertransference pitfall and wonders aloud whether she is being too bossy, too intrusive, too impinging or too castrating. In a sense, the child almost seems to

"ask for it" and the therapist is often torn between becoming passive like the child or sufficiently thrustful to make the treatment move. To the child he or she may appear as an inhibited and therefore unhelpful parent or like a punishing, dominating, pushing and therefore threatening and frightening parent.

One learns a great deal about this dilemma in the dyadic treatment. The family therapy illustrates the process but tells us very little about what is going on inside the inhibition: is the inner space empty or loaded with conflict; is the problem an intrapsychic or an interpersonal one; and can changes occur in the individual inhibition without concomitant changes in the structure of the family; and if one intervenes on the inhibition how can one do it without driving the patient into still deeper inhibition if he experiences the therapeutic process as interfering, intruding, and intimidating?

The only firm comment with which we can end this summing up is that we need to know about the genesis of inhibition before we can do anything to mitigate it.

PART III: *The Depressed Child*

CHAPTER 15

The Genesis of Childhood Depression

E. JAMES ANTHONY, M.D.

As recently expounded in a book by Benedek and Anthony, our guiding concept of depression regarded it as a phenomenon of human life and an integral part of human existence.[2] In this view, therefore, the depressive affect, at all stages of development, was felt to be normal, necessary, ubiquitous and inevitable. Like all other feelings in the general repertoire of human emotions, it could, under certain circumstances, become clinically transformed. There are three overlapping components to this perspective which is essentially a psychobiological one: a basic biological component with neuro-endocrine ramifications throughout the body, a basic psychological component experienced by all human creatures as a prerequisite of human existence, and reactive component related to the human conditions prevailing in the world of the individual at any given time. I would like to review these three components in turn.

About fifty years ago, the biologist, Hoagland, maintained that, in general, animals react in one of two ways to stimuli that tend to influence their behavior: positively, by making appropriate adjustments such as

165

attacking, retreating or manipulating, and negatively, by ceasing all movement and remaining quiet even in the presence of violently disturbing conditions.[8]

About thirty years later, Engel and Schmale at Rochester (1972), also constructed a working model comprising a two-prong response of all living cells or organisms to any changes in the dynamic steady state: one being an active attempt at the restoration of equilibrium through some sort of rearrangement in relation to the environment (and which necessarily required a source of available energy); and the second represented a passive insulation against a possibly noxious environment by encystment or hibernation (when energy sources were depleted or threatened with depletion).[6]

When the second set of circumstances occurred, there resulted a behavioral triad consisting of immobility, quiescence and unresponsiveness that Engel termed conservation-withdrawal meant to designate the underlying somatic homeostatic processes.

Having discussed the arrest of activity in phyllogenetic and ontogenetic terms, they went on to extend the concept psychobiologically and psychologically. The psychological pattern expressive of or deriving from or reacting to conservation-withdrawal is depression. According to them, therefore, what starts as a biological response is gradually transformed during development into psychobiological and psychological equivalents: thus, the first step is termed conservation-withdrawal, the second, the depressive equivalent, and the third, depression. All, however, express the basic withdrawal tendency. Some infants, from the very beginning of life, seem to show a disposition to conservation-withdrawal while others acquire it during the course of early development. These sensitive individuals can be likened to Shakespeare's snail "whose tender horns being hit, shrink backward in his shelly cave with pain."

Engel's pioneering work was based on the case of Monica, (1956) the infant with a gastric fistula, whose gastric secretions were carefully assayed and correlated with events and affects between the fifteenth and twenty-first month of life in the original series of observations.[5]

1. The stranger reaction: instead of showing the usual stranger anxiety, on the approach of someone new, Monica ceased all movement and averted her gaze. Her limbs became motionless, her eyes no longer appeared focused, and she seemed to be staring past or through the stranger. Within ten to fifteen years she would quietly drift off into a sleep-like state. It seemed like a complete disengagement from the environment.

2. The familiar reaction: Monica's reaction to a familiar person was

quite different. She would immediately engage him in activity and respond affectively to him.

3. The mixed reaction: if a stranger and a familiar stood on either side of her crib, half of her body responded in one way and half in the other.

During the withdrawal reaction, not only was her activity completely reduced but there was a cessation of gastric secretion. The components, therefore, of withdrawal included hypotonia, inactivity, diminution of affect, failure to accommodate visually, a sleep-like state and cessation of gastric secretion. Engel referred to this total state as "the depression of infancy."

The Engel phenomenon had some antecedent observations. Ribble (1943), had described an infant whose response to minimal frustration in the feeding situation took the form of a deep sleep from which it could hardly be awakened.[10] It was also found that intense stimulation, such as in the performance of circumcision, may also induce the child to fall into a sleep that is synchronized without rapid eye movements. This would suggest that neural system is organized on a bipartite system with a built-in trophotropic component to protect against overstress. The universality of the response obtains further support from its appearance in child victims of famine and in infant pigtail monkeys removed from their mothers. In addition to being universal, it is also persistent and consistent: for example, Monica today, as a young woman, still displays a low threshold of response that is reminiscent of her infantile conservation-withdrawal reaction. What she has gained in the interim, because of the therapeutic contacts, has been a new skillfulness at rapidly mobilizing assistance from the environment.

According to Engel, therefore, various layers are put together, from the biological to the psychological, to generate the final picture of depression. He regards the conservation-withdrawal mechanism as the core objective experience, weakness, lack of energy, apathy and disinterest as the core subjective experiences, and helplessness and hopelessness as the core affective experiences. He does, however, make a distinction between nonspecific depressive manifestations of "giving up" from clinical syndromes of depression.

The Existential Component

All human beings have to come to terms with the brute facts of "birth, copulation, and death" and the more dynamic therapies, in contrast to the traditional psychologies preoccupied with learning, cognition, perception, judgment, conceptualization and problem solving, have placed emphasis on relationship, falling in love, hating, transgressing and overcoming evil through the medium of such magical devices as prayers and supplications. This world of human existence is haunted by such basic dreads as anxiety, depression, shame and guilt. Investigating depression, therefore, in the laboratory or under experimental conditions may have quite a different connotation from the patient and provoke quite different reactions. The authentic life may be different from the academic one, a difference summarized in Kierkegaard's little joke about the absent-minded professor who was so academic that he hardly knew that he existed until one fine morning he woke up to find himself dead! Depression, therefore, is seen to play an integral part in this "tragic vision of man" in which the human individual painfully struggles with the fate of being human and where human life begins, as Sartre put it, "on the far side of despair."

One would expect on these grounds that both anxiety and depression are ingredients of human existence and that they each have a role to play in the operation of human living. Some children seem more prone from the very beginning to develop anxiety as a consequence of circumstances whereas other children are more depressive-prone. This could be based on a biological propensity toward excessive conservation-withdrawal or a psychological proclivity originating in bereavement, deprivation or humiliation.

In order to discover what depression does to an individual, one needs to compare it etiologically and phenomenologically with anxiety:

1. Anxiety is predominantly an activating agent: it orients the individual toward the environment so that he can react more appropriately to it. It facilitates speech, imagination and perception and in this sense behaves like a stimulant. In fact, as long as it remains below the level of disruption when defenses need to be applied, it seems to promote good mental functioning.

2. Depression is almost the antithesis of this and is predominantly a deactivating agent. It orients the individual inwardly and by withdrawing attention and cathexis from the environment, it conduces to a sense of isolation. Instead of promoting mental processes, it tends to slow them down; in place of stimulating the well-being, it diminishes both self-esteem and self-confidence.

Both affects have signal functions: that of anxiety has been well studied by Freud, but, at a certain point, the appearance of depression may indicate the emergency need for energy supplies that are not forthcoming. If the environment fails to respond, withdrawal then occurs.

Although clinical depression makes a late appearance in childhood, a depressive mood, pervasive, persistent and nonlocalizable, has been observed by Mahler in certain children with certain types of transacting, mainly rejecting mothers.[9] In later childhood, depressive moods tend to show themselves in feelings of homesickness and boredom. Both are inwardly experienced as privations: homesickness or nostalgia is linked to an intense longing for the primary object mother, whereas boredom seems almost to be self-administered. There is less direction and no particular object, but the feelings of emptiness are associated with vague wishes and longings to have someone do something that will re-engage interest. Most children can become bored when physically or emotionally unwell, but the child who is easily bored is on the road to clinical depression, although the relationship of mood to illness is not easy to formulate.

The Component of the "Human Condition"

Depression may be natural, developmental, and existential, but, for the most part, it is brought into being by bad conditions—rejecting parents, systematic cruelties, deprivations, losses, failures and the general inhumanity of man to man. Children, especially, become victims of the human condition.

In a study of the background of children with affective disorders, McKnew and Cytryn, were able to document a number of important conditions associated with the development of childhood depression.[4] These included frequent separations for periods of several months in the first few years of life, indifferent or neglectful surrogation during phases of separation, sudden losses as a result of death, divorce or hospitalization, rejection and depreciation by parents that undermined the child's sense of worth and adequacy, a loss of involvement and interest in the child because of such outside events as birth, illness, death, or remarriage, and perhaps, most perniciously of all, the occurrence of depression in one or both parents. This latter factor has been of special interest since it may come about either by the child's identification with the parent or through the psychic abandonment that depression induces. It would seem that in the early stages the depression in the child is more reactive and may improve with separation from the depressed parent but after a certain time, the process is evidently internalized since the children continue to remain depressed even when the depressive model has been removed.

Depressive-Proneness in Children

There is some evidence already accumulating to suggest that a small percentage of children (10-15 percent perhaps) are at high risk for clinical depression during childhood, adolescence and adult life. These individuals can be identified from fairly early on through a configuration of qualities that include moodiness, self-centeredness, hypersensitivity to small losses or frustrations, a tendency to withdraw when conditions are not perfectly suited to the child, clinging and demanding relationships of a highly ambivalent kind. In the presence of inadequate mothering, early spoiling followed by later rejection, promises frequently made and not kept and frequent preparations for which the child is not at all prepared, coupled with the dispositional characteristics make future clinical depressions almost predictable. In Hartmann's terms, these children never seem to develop a capacity for tolerating and dealing with normal, developmental depression. What Mahler refers to as the two pillars of early infantile well-being and self-esteem—a belief in the child's own omnipotence and a belief in the parents' omnipotence—are prematurely disrupted with the result that the individual fails to develop his own autonomy and the constancy of the object.

One additional introductory factor must be mentioned: the apparently increased tendency to depression in girls as recorded by Mahler in toddlers,[9] in Harrington and Hassan during latency[7] and in adolescents by Anthony.[1] It is difficult to account for this on simply experiential factors but there is as yet no evidence that the conservation-withdrawal reaction, in excess, is commoner in female infants. Mahler has suggested that the depressive mood in girl toddlers may be due to anger and disappointment in the mother not providing them with a penis, with her conscious or unconscious disappointment in not having a boy and with the mother's inability to deal with her own sense of biological and psychological inadequacy with which the little girl identifies. The reason given by Harrington and Hassan is a splitting of the mothering function during the first two years of life with resulting faulty identification and difficulty in the process of separation-individuation. All the little girls were good, clean and clever but so self-depreciatory that their self-esteem was constantly eroded.

References

1. Anthony, E. James. (1970). Two contrasting types of adolescent depression and their treatment. *J. Amer. Psychoanal. Assn.* 18:841-859.
2. Anthony, E. James. (1967). Psychoneurotic Disorders. In Freedman, A.M. and H.I. Kaplan eds., *Comprehensive Textbook of Psychiatry.* Baltimore:Williams & Wilkins.
3. Anthony, E. James. (1975). Childhood Depression. In Anthony, E.J. and T. Benedek eds., *Depression and Human Existence.* Boston:Little, Brown and Co.
4. Cytryn, L., and McKnew, D.H., Jr. Proposed classification of childhood depression. *Am. J. Psychiatry* 129, 1972.
5. Engel, G. and Reichsman, F. Spontaneous and experimentally induced depressions in an infant with a gastric fistula. *J. Am. Psychoanal. Assoc.* 4:428, 1956.
6. Engel, G. and Schmale, A. (1972). Conservation Withdrawal: In *Physiology, Emotion and Psychosomatic Illness.* Ciba Foundation Symposium 8. Amsterdam:Elsevier.
7. Harrington, M. and Hassan J. (1958). Depression in girls during latency, *Br. J. Med. Psychology.* 31:43.
8. Hoagland, H. (1928). The mechanism of tonic immobility. *J. Gen. Psychol.* 1, 426-447.
9. Mahler, M. On sadness and grief in infancy and childhood. *Psychoanalytic Study of the Child.* 16:332, 1961.
10. Ribble, M. (1943). *The Rights of Infants.* New York:Columbia University Press.

CHAPTER 16

The Theoretical Status of Depressions in Childhood

CARL P. MALMQUIST, M.D.

Preliminary Questions

Before proceeding to some of the specific topics related to childhood depression, I am going to raise some questions about the diagnosis that need asking. To begin with, no official diagnosis of childhood depression exists. By "official" I mean what is available to us if we confine ourselves to the official manual of the American Psychiatric Association.[1] While a separate category is provided for "Behavior Disorders of Childhood and Adolescence" no diagnosis exists within this grouping for depressed children. This separate grouping is supposed to include disorders more stable, internalized and resistant to treatment than "Transient Situational Disturbances" but less so than psychoses, neuroses, or personality disorders. For some unknown reason the reactions of children are confined to overactivity, inattentiveness, shyness, feelings of rejection, overaggressiveness, timidity, and group delinquency. True, all of the categories available for adults are supposedly available for children, but then the question must be asked as to why our special set of childhood diagnoses were created at all? With this little resume of the nosological dilemmas attending childhood depressions, let me move on to other selective questions.

Perhaps the greatest differences between the reliance on a static classification system, and a perspective on childhood which sees it in terms of multiple systems in flux, is the omission of developmental thinking in the former. Hence, while we may get into a debate amongst ourselves as to when a true neurotic conflict exists so that a depressive neurosis is present, there would be little debate about depressive affect as a developmental phenomenon which can be experienced quite early in life. Such affect is experienced in response to many situations and in different quantities. All of these responses are not psychopathological, e.g., the need to mourn which occurs as a necessary part of grieving. This can occur in response to specific losses but also in the form of coming to terms with changes that are occurring within the child and his environment. Sad affect itself in a child, like more general moods, do not in themselves mean the child is clinically depressed.

What if we progress a step further where we recognize a conscious conflict exists? An infant deprived of "good enough mothering" is thus observed to become apathetic, sleep poorly, eat fitfully if at all, and in time not thrive. The response to the deprivation, or the misinterpretation of it, seems related to this set of reactive symptoms. Similarly, a depressed parent complains about his latency-age child's performance in school having fallen off, that the child does not appear interested in anything anymore, and seems to lack vitality. In such examples, we are again dealing with depressive affect, but not at the level where they have become a fixed personality pattern or become entwined with unconscious meanings to a degree sufficient for a neurosis.

Given these types of situations it is also possible that over sufficient time, certain mood instabilities gain prominence. At that point they are not removed when the precipitating events are gone. If we prolong the period of insufficient caretaking, reversibility in the child becomes more difficult. Here we become aware of the vista of theoretical problems from the diverse orientations of people who are interested in developmental aspects of depression. As one example, take the studies dealing with deprived animals, especially monkeys. (I personally find these studies fascinating and I envy the type of rigorousness which they can employ, particularly since this is rarely available to the clinician.) To what extent are we permitted to extend their findings to the problem of how children react with depressive affect? Hence, an experiment of rearing isolated monkeys who then show retarded and deviant social behavior in comparison to other monkeys with the former called "depressed." A conclusion is made that reactive symptoms, or even developmental deviations, are not immutable since these depressed monkeys can be "cured" by placing them with younger female monkeys for a 26 week period.[2] We are immediately into not only the question of the reversibility of such depressions, or rather reactive states, but also into questions about the ongoing development of an organism in a maturational sense when confronted with environmental adversities.

A diversity of specific questions can be raised about childhood depressions. Suggestive answers to some of these questions appear in the course of this chapter.

1. What is the actual incidence of different types of depressions in childhood? How frequently do reactive depressive disturbances occur in children in contrast to other types of reactive manifestations?

2. When do we begin to see developmental deviations ensuing therefrom? Or, what are the variety of developmental problems related to depression that are possible?

3. When do we begin to see actual depressive neuroses in children? What is the nature of the debate about this issue in both theoretical and empirical terms?

4. What types of family transitional states are most likely to give rise to childhood depressions? It is presumptuous to say that these must be restricted to one type of event, such as death or divorce of a parent. Many other interpersonal phenomena occur as well as variations in how a child will adapt to situations.

5. What intrapsychic events are most related to a depressive diathesis? We talk of loss, but what makes for the different sensitivities to loss in different children? The variables of a child's ego strength cannot be ignored.

6. Since children, or their parents, rarely come complaining that the child is depressed—in contrast to the adults—we need clarification on a descriptive level of the nature of childhood depression. In that manner, by recording and classifying symptomatology, we will begin to get a more valid baseline regarding the incidence of disturbances in this area.

7. The next step would be to have longitudinal studies dealing with the outcome of childhood depressive phenomena. At this point, apart from

retrospective impressions based on work with adults in therapy, we do not know the diverse pathways by direct follow-up from such a group of children. We actually have more knowledge about socially deprived children who are environmentally neglected.

8. Do depressive disorders in children differ in parts of the country and world? This is simply a variation on the impact of different cultural contexts.

9. What are the kinds of dreams depressed children have? These could be studied by the manifest content if we were going to quantify, or by clinical significance as in therapy.

10. I would also reiterate the position that the very fact of discussion about a particular condition, for whatever reason, increases the frequency of its diagnosis. Hence, one clinic reported that when phenothiazines were reported as alleviating schizophrenic symptomatology, the diagnosis of schizophrenia became more frequent; when lithium received more publicity several years later the diagnosis of affective disorders went up in the same clinic.[3] A prognosis is made that childhood depressions will increase in popularity over the next decade as a diagnosis.

Early Studies

Early manifestations of depression are often lumped together within some vague grouping of "infantile depressions." Part of this vagueness is associated with the old problem in comprehending anything connected with depressive phenomena since all or one of the following may be present: (1) a symptom of sadness present in depressions or with other clinical diagnoses, (2) a mood state, (3) a depressive syndrome with certain signs and symptoms which may then receive a diagnosis. Note that none of these possibilities deal with etiology or the subtypes of diagnoses of depressions.

Reliance on retrospective data from children and adults who manifest some particular part of this spectrum adds to the skepticism about our knowledge of depression. Efforts have been made to extend directly a "deprivation hypothesis" to longitudinal studies of such children. Early reports had the methodological difficulty not only of dealing with children of different ages, but they were also in different settings such as nurseries, foster homes, hospitals, and diverse institutions. Observations were made by different personnel of disruptions in the capacity to form consistent human attachments based on an affectional deprivation.

Another line of approach stressed the associated deficits in cognitive-intellectual functioning. Early childhood was seen as the vulnerable contributing period. Some of these approaches were based on clinical work; others were based on work with the mentally or emotionally retarded. Not until later was the animal model for studying depressions introduced with its own set of methodological problems in transferring conclusions to children. Biochemical models came even later, again utilizing animals for behavioral observations or chance consequences such as reserpine precipitating depressions in humans.

The problems that arise in studying the developmental phenomenon of depressive-proneness are similar to that encountered in investigating many areas of bio-psychosocial development.[4] This work began in the 1920s and 1930s. Although we can find fault with many of their approaches, keep in mind that before that childhood depressions were either ignored as psychological phenomena or seen as unexplained cachexias. Thus, Levy reported on an eight-year-old girl in 1937 who had been in a succession of foster homes and then adopted. The child continued to manifest an incapacity to form attachments described as a lack of emotional responsiveness and having a "hunger" for affect.[5] In 1943, Goldfarb studied 30 children, age 34-35 months, and concluded that 15 of the children brought up in institutions had lower IQs by 28 points than those raised in foster homes since the age of four months.[6] Observations on children placed in the Hampstead nursery during the bombing of London in World War II revealed less serious maternal deprivation repercussions for the older child, but the effects were more serious when occurring at an earlier age.[7] Again, it is interesting to call attention to how such clinical observations receive confirmatory evidence 30 years later from animal workers who found that traumatic separations of monkeys in infancy predisposed later to despair reactions on separation while those 3-4 years at separation only went through protest types of responses.[8]

However, it still remains controversial and unsettled, if greater emotional harm occurs from experiences which occur at a younger age. Clinical impressions based on the greater biological vulnerability of the young organism continue to favor this hypothesis. However, developmentally the younger organism possesses a greater adaptive capacity, such as being able to accept substitute objects, which can work in its favor. In this early work some of the confusion between emotional deprivation, lack of sufficient maternal care, possible organic cerebral impairment, and the syndrome of infantile depression are all present.

The syndrome of "anaclitic depression," elaborated by Spitz, is actually a deprivation reaction.[9] Pediatricians encountering this condition in children called it "marasmus," but the best they could do was view it as some type of degenerative or dystrophic disease. Spitz recognized that after objective recognition at six months, separation led to a grief reaction if the relationship with the maternal object had been previously satisfactory. We now realize that earliest types of perceptual and attachment behaviors occur from the earliest period of contact with maternal object. Infants in such situations become sad, weepy, apathetic, and have immobile faces with a distant look. They react slowly to stimuli, exhibit retarded movements, have anorexia and insomnia, and show little of the motility characteristic of infants. The diagnosis of depression was attached since these behaviors appeared similar to those in adults who were depressed. After three months of such a separation, a full restoration to emotional capacity was believed rare.

Similar symptoms and signs were observed in children institutionalized as infants and kept separated from their mothers without adequate stimulation and fondling. This had more serious overtones since both mental and physical development lagged, repeated infections were common, and in some cachexia and even death occurred. The clinical picture described as "hospitalism" emerged from its frequent association with children maintained in emotionally sterile institutional settings. A similar clinical picture was seen in infants with gastric fistulas.[10,11] Engel and Reichsman hypothesized a "depression-withdrawal" reaction in their fistulic infant. In the presence of a stranger, inactivity, hypotonia, a sad facial expression, decreased gastric secretion, and finally sleep, occurred. Subsequent studies attempted to appraise this work on institutionalized children.

Criticism centered on methodological considerations and questions as to how adequate the physical evaluation procedures employed has been. Infants with nutritional deficiencies may appear indistinguishable in some cases from those subject to prolonged institutionalization. Even more striking is the similarity with nonhuman primates in which signs of distress are witnessed similar to the anaclitic depression in human infants.[12] Brief separation experiences produce symptoms in Rhesus monkey infants similar to those in human infants.[13] Such variables as the age at the time of separation, length of separation, and sex of the infant need consideration since different behavioral consequences are associated with these variables.[14] Most impressive are reports from animal work that the effects of experimental work with subhuman mammals last for months or years even in certain brief separations.

In 1951, *Maternal Care and Mental Health* reviewed previous studies and presented new formulations.[15] There have been subsequent updatings.[16,17] It is most impressive that radically different conclusions have not emerged. There is the consistency of certain hypotheses on one hand, and on the other the usual type of refining of hypotheses by criticism of methodology and the lack of conceptual clarity. One of the major difficulties when appraising these studies is to separate the impact of "maternal deprivation" as one antecedent relating to the genesis of depression from the syndrome of maternal deprivation *per se* which appears like a depression. Different kinds of deprivation—psychological, social, cognitive, and organic—need to be specified. This need for specificity has been the greatest obstacle in attempts to unravel the effects subsumed under maternal deprivation. Not until specific independent variables are tied-up as components of depressive-proneness, will higher correlations in outcome studies of development be possible.

What the critiques have sought to do is select several of the factors frequently mentioned as related to an outcome of depressive-proneness. It was originally felt that prolonged disruptions during the first three years of life have a certain impact on the child's personality, such as appearing emotionally withdrawn and isolated. This was particularly seen with respect to children maintained in nurseries and residential settings with "inadequate mothering." This is now seen as only one of many variables. Other family members may have a significant impact as well as other individuals with whom they are in contact. This is particularly so if these other individuals are conflicted and have depressive problems of their own. In addition, the various types of perceptual and cognizing experiences a child has influence the way he begins to view the world as a place where people are unhappy or a "vale of tears." Nor can the whole panoply of organic and genetic factors as antecedents towards certain lines of development be ignored.[18]

In the early writings about maternal deprivations an unlimited number of outcomes were predicted: psychosis, neurosis, or delinquency. This type of hypothesizing is so broad as not to be refuted, endless confirmations occurred but never the crucial observations to refute. A more specific hypothesis asks if a particular type of deprivation has any specific etiologic role for the later emergence of depressive vulnerability? Further, is this manifest then in childhood, adolescence, or adulthood? Even though details of the specific mechanism as to why some children are fortunate enough to be excluded from later consequences, the hypothesis is possible of testing. Distinctions are now made between disruption of affectionate relationships that have already been established, and which are more conducive to a depressive outcome, and relationships which have failed to form are then more related to psychopathy. There has been criticism of the heavy emphasis in maternal deprivation formulations that outcomes are rigidly proscribed in the earliest months of a child's life. There is a tacit assumption that early mother-child relationships will inevitably have to lead to certain outcomes. It is basically a hope that if we knew all the variables, we could predict a depressive or a psychopathic outcome. Such a degree of specificity has not been established. The concept is weighted in the direction of an overemphasis on early infantile experiences leading to an unalterable outcome without sufficient cognizance of other significant variables in the child's life. Wooton has pointed out that subsequent broader influences in a child's life are also not sufficiently accounted for, such as school associations, vocation, and marriage, which can taper and modify early experiences.[19] The inevitability may not be so, nor the irreversibility. Other specific experiences contribute to depressive-proneness. Death of a friend, pet, or neighbor, contribute as well as that of a parent. Nor is deprivation to be considered literally in terms of losing an attachment to a person since moving to a new neighborhood can elicit similar feelings. It is not so that symbolic losses are less frequently seen as significant than traumatic separations from a loved one.

Early Psychodynamic Formulations

Clinical knowledge concerning depressions in adults began within the framework of descriptive psychiatry. Freud and Abraham extended this work by psychoanalytic theorizing which raised psychological hypotheses about what had occurred during the childhood of the depressed. The earliest formulations saw childhood as significant to the extent that a "trauma" left a child vulnerable to depressive illness. These traumas were viewed primarily as retrospective curiosities. Concepts such as orality, introjection, turning against the self, narcissistic injury, loss of an object, anal-sadism, and ambivalence were introduced as explanatory constructs to account for the development and maintenance of depressed states. In 1911, Abraham emphasized the repression of aggression leading to depression analogous to the postulation of "actual neuroses" being from repression of sexuality leading to anxiety.[20]

The theory of psychosexual stages led to knowledge about fixations and regressions. Introjective processes with their attendant ambivalence, along with regressions to anal-sadistic and oral cannibalistic stages, were the mechanisms postulated intrapsychically. Regression subsequent to loss of a love object was part of the early theorizing.[21] Abraham expanded this to include the mechanism of double introjection.[22] The original love object is introjected as part of the ego-ideal and conscience; it then becomes subject to hostile attacks as well. Developmentally, a crucial step with relevance to depressions is the child treating the internalized object as something over which control is exercised. This is similar to the way in which control over other possessions, such as body parts and contents are perceived. An equation is made between loss of such objects and loss of bodily possessions. The cognitive antithesis is: "losing-destroying" versus "retaining-controlling." Emergence of depressive-proneness in a child reveals an emphasis on control and orderliness—the basic obsessional personality seen in the compensated depressive as maturity occurs.

These early formulations about intrapsychic mechanisms are pointed out since it took 50 years complex and later depressive problems and efforts to validate the hypothesis by empirical means.[23] In an earlier publication I have gone into a detailed explanation of what Abraham's concept of "primal parathymia" entailed for later thinking on the subject of childhood depressions.[24] His points will be summarized here to indicate how seminal his thinking was, but also to illustrate the impact it had on subsequent theorizing which borrowed and expanded from him.

Five independent variables were listed which were all seen as necessary for a depressive line of development to occur.

1. A constitutional element involved the area of a *predisposition* towards oral eroticism. This leaves a diathesis towards excessive needs for contact, touching, etc. Early frustration and poor toleration of it would be a result.

2. As a result, affectionate relationships become tinged with excessive needs for affection or a correlative feeling hurt—that the child was not getting what he or she needed. A possible off-shoot was the emergence of masochistic character trends.

3. Traumatic episodes involving infantile narcissism were seen as leaving psychological scars. Such things as birth of a sibling or premature weaning were originally postulated as the types of traumas, but this laid the groundwork for much more sophisticated inquiries into the role narcissism plays in depression. We now think in terms of the seemingly constant effort to repair or keep intact grandiose images.[25]

4. It was also postulated that the first major blow to narcissism, as an antecedent to depressive development, had to occur prior to the resolu-

tion of the oedipal conflict. The significance of this was that the type of triadic relationship implied by the oedipal was not yet effected, and a mixture of love and hate focused on part objects would leave a residual of ambivalence toward any person later functioning in a maternal role.

5. When subsequent blows to narcissism occur, in the form of disappointments, the old mixture of hate is resurrected. The difficulty ensues from the inability to abandon ambivalent objects which have remained internalized. Later, the "stickiness" of object relationships in the depressive would be seen as an extension of this context.

Subsequent work focused on intrapsychic components for some time. The expansion of theory by way of the structural model allowed the role of the superego to be introduced. When children put themselves in place of one another, they can eliminate others as well as recreate them. Wishfulfilling creations and destructions in response to loves and hates are enacted. One part of the personality is crucial for bestowing esteem—in the form of the superego giving to the ego. Self-esteem in the depressive becomes delicately balanced due to self-esteem being so dependent on approval from others. Depressive responses in the latency-age period are often triggered by minor disappointments and associated with the primitive rage of an infant from hunger like the failure to satiate from sucking. This is what Rado called the failure to have a good "alimentary orgasm."[26]

The paradigm of self-esteem based on the equivalent of "feeding" experiences leads to a heightened dependency on others. Parallel are expiatory efforts of the ego towards the superego. Since part of the hostility and rage is directed against internalized representations, when ego development is sufficient, guilt becomes a prominent part of the picture. Reparative efforts are needed to atone. "splitting of the incorporated object" directs anger against the object or back from it. Depressive character maneuvers are observed in children of elementary school years. Interpersonal ingratiation and cautiousness with respect to expression of aggression are prominent. These are efforts of the ego towards the superego as the controller of self-esteem to reinstate a loving and beloved superego in place of one which is predominantly harsh and primitive.[27] The perpetuation of pressing childhood demands for approval and affection may be associated with conflicts during the oedipal period which lead to anxieties, aggression, and suffering.[28] These thwarted the pursuit of object relations without prominent ambivalence.

From psychotherapy with adult depressives, an interest in how the depressive character structure emerged occurred. Power needs were seen as part of this structure. "The discouraged child who finds that he can tyrannize best by tears will be a cry-baby, and a direct line of development leads from the cry-baby to the adult depressed patient."[29] Early infantile passive-aggressive activities such as pouty, whiny behavior, or feeding disturbances, are early manipulative techniques. The childhood prototype of the potential masochist is saying in essence, "It is giving my love ones what they deserve if I harm myself." By adolescence this theme can get replayed endlessly by all manner of self-defeating behaviors such as drugs, alcohol, learning problems, and some types of delinquent activities. Similarly, the childhood prototype of the manic-depressive is that of beginning everything with great enthusiasm, but then giving it up quickly with crying and protest behavior if brilliant success is not forthcoming. Such a child alternates between pessimistic ruminations in the realm of not having performed well, having few friends, and a feeling of self-righteous superiority.

To keep self-esteem inflated, acute sensitivity to competition arises. Demands on them personally are resented since they feel they are being used unfairly for others' selfish interests. Consequently, such children are unwilling to give gratifications to others unless they feel they can receive themselves. If others do not give to them, they seek to extract as some kind of vengeance. To them this seems like gaining justice.

While Jacobson has written about individuals who need to betray as part of paranoid developments, I would hypothesize that depressive trends are equally conspicuous.[30] This appears connected with their seeking idealized persons or groups, from whom and through whom, they hope to maintain their self-esteem. When they are disappointed, the need to hurt gains momentum. During adolescence this type of sensitivity can lead to antisocial tendencies. If these tendencies are acted upon, they stem from a feeling that the acts are justified from past grievances. These traits are laid to childhood socialization experiences where the needs of a child for sincere, solicitous care were unfulfilled. Manipulative efforts towards peers and authorities are repeat patterns for dealing with extractive and manipulative parental figures. "He has been deprived, and he feels gyped and is angrily determined to get what is rightfully his . . . . In this defiant, stubborn, angry, begrudging battle of something-for-nothing, he loses the enjoyments of adolescence, of young adulthood, and of later adulthood."[31] How valid are these observations of the childhood depressive as manipulator? These character traits are observed in children, and they acquire increasing sophistication in their use. However, theorizing which makes manipulative aspects of personality development the crux of the depressive personality underemphasizes other key elements which are necessary. The "depressive character" is not synonymous with the "neurotic character."

Object Relations and Depressions

Theories with respect to the development and maintenance of "object relations, attachment, bonding, and dependency needs" have implications for the depressive prone child. Opportunity for confirmation or disconfirmation of theories takes place via observations in the naturalistic setting where children develop since that is where depressive affect takes origins. Confusions have emerged from different usages for all these terms.[32] Workers from different disciplines employing different psychological frameworks have accentuated the problem. Some have worked in nurseries, others in nursery schools, and yet others have carried out experimental work. None of these sources derive their theories from clinical work which provides yet another source for ideas about object relations.

"Object relations" is the term most clinicians use in referring to the agents who gratify or deprive an infant. In this context, the infant is seen as dependent. "Instinct theory" conceptualizes the object against whom drives are carried out. Discriminatory and perceptual capacities are diffuse in the young infant with little cognitive appreciation. Rather, an awareness of tensions is experienced psychologically as narcissistic disequilibrium. As more ego functions develop, an increasing capacity to distinguish his "self" and body from others permits distinctions between objects and their types of responses. This is not seen simply as a passive registry but rather an active organization or seeking of stimulation.[33]

"Object constancy" permits images, qualities, and affects associated with objects to be maintained in their absence. Nor is this confined to states of satisfaction or deprivation. It is via this internalization that the pre-object child establishes the permanence of objects. However, this ongoing presence of introjects can be supportive and bestow self-esteem, or they can be critical or punitive.

These formulations have analogues with social learning theory aspects which focus on "dependency" as a secondary (acquired) drive. Primary satisfaction was used along which, incidentally, went the developing awareness of an "object." When an infant satisfied his physiological needs, he learned who it was who gratified him. Social needs were acquired as byproducts. This drive-reduction theory for dependency has been criticized. If behavior attributable to "drives" can be accounted for in terms of "reinforcing stimuli" operating in the environment, behavior is contingent upon environmental reinforcement. The environment becomes primary rather than the organism. These stimuli are events occurring subsequent to behaviors which are operantly emitted and controlled by instrumental conditioning. "Dependency" is viewed neither as a reflection of a drive or a trait but rather simply certain learned behaviors. The "object" is significant only as a particular stimulus object. Dependency is linked to objects, but not restricted to the context of someone who is providing food or reducing tension. Rather than an emphasis on the "rewards" provided by objects in the service of drive reduction, there is a stress on the salience of objects. Salience attaches to an object's "attention-getting" characteristics, or by an increased frequency of exposure. As an example, sheep become attached to television sets when isolated from other animals but in constant propinquity to an operating set.[34] An implication for a theory of depressions is present here. Separation from a salient object should have no more significance than setting in motion a process of re-learning to whatever new object is currently salient.[35] Over time, strength of attachment should thus directly wane, but in practice we do not find this so. It is mentioned to illustrate how some experimental findings can be incongruent with clinical work and also with the experience of continuity in psychological life. It does demonstrate a type of theorizing divorced from a framework where account can be taken of internalized neurophysiological structures as well as cognitive and affective processes.

Besides a secondary drive theory or environmental operants a third alternative for the development of object relations has its roots in biology and ethology. Developing an attachment in itself is seen as *primary*. The infant is seen with a built-in need for an object in its own right apart from drive reduction. Attachment develops apart from feeding experiences but also where "releasing" stimuli of many types activate the process. Internal neurophysiological and neurohumoral states are the "primers" operating on a genetic substate which has the potential to activate attachments. Learning operates to reinforce or lessen certain attachment behaviors. The "attachment process" originating in the organism is distinguished from the various "attachment behaviors" mediating it. Although the latter is overt and hence more easily measurable, it is not the same as the basis for these behaviors. The deceptiveness of relying on external behaviors is seen by assessing a child who clings and weeps as necessarily more depressed than a child who sits forlornly with little animation. Conversely, more demonstrative attachment behaviors do not imply greater attachment. Hidden in these formulations regarding object ties is the possible need to rethink our hypotheses regarding "oral mechanisms" and depressions. The emphasis in attachment theory is that the system underlying attachment, with its crucial significance for social relations, is not a consequence of the original feeding prototype. It is its own discrete and endogenous system.

Bowlby and Klein

Bowlby's ideas about "instinctual response systems" in humans as contributing to attachment should be noted.[36] These maintain the proximity of children to maternal objects. Attachment occurs by way of certain behavioral systems being activated for five response patterns: sucking, clinging, following, crying and smiling. Evolutionary processes elicit these and they interact with principal figures in the environment.[37] Many arguments persist regarding the functions served by attachment behaviors. A prominent criticism is that no postulates about "drives" are needed and reliance on control systems suffices. There is also the criticism that studying "attachment behaviors" in terms of manifest behaviors is not actually studying the internal psychological processes involved in attachment and object relations.[38]

Many clinicians rely on object relations theory for their theory of childhood depressions. Melanie Klein postulated introjective-projective processes occurring from birth onward.[39] This is criticized as telescoping certain psychological processes into the first year, processes which are ordinarily spread out throughout childhood. The "depressive position" is connected with the loss accompanying weaning between three and twelve months. This is seen as a normal and unavoidable developmental situation derived from an earlier "paranoid position." Superego structuralization during the first year is believed to be related to feelings of possessiveness and destructiveness towards a parental object rather than to incestuous wishes which emerge several years later.

The "depressive position" develops in moving from a "part" to a "whole" object relationship. In the pre-depressive position only relations to parts of objects, such as a breast, were believed present. During the depressive position the mother is perceived as a whole object. This permits ambivalence and accompanying anxiety about the loss of the entire love object. The infant experiences a guilty anxiety with a need to preserve this good object which calls forth magical devices. Reparative work is in the service of making amends to undo sadistic attacks on introjective objects; parallel to these intrapsychic maneuvers are actual situations where the excited infant achieves instinctual gratification, such as during feeding. Since the object "attacked" is the same one providing security, there is the potential for despair. The infantile depressive position is related to this potential since later depressions occur over loss of objects with fear of abandonment and loss. The contrast is the security where internalized objects are accepted as bestowing love and security. An individual can build up memories of experiences felt to be good so that they become part of himself and assimilated into the ego. In this way the actual mother gradually becomes less necessary.[40]

Grief and Mourning

Grief and mourning in infancy have been discussed by Bowlby in connection with activation of attachment behaviors when maternal figures continue to be unavailable.[41,42,43,44,45] This work is important regarding the nature of childhood bereavement. It also generates hypotheses regarding the pathogenic potential of mourning processes when reaction to losses can take a pathological turn. Removal of young children from their mothers initiates successive psychological phases: Numbness, Protest, Despair, and Detachment. These each have an accompanying parallel response of separation anxiety, grief and mourning, and defense, although they all operate as part of a unitary process. "Mourning" refers to a psychological process set in motion by loss of a loved object while "grief" is the parallel subjective state in such a loss. "Depression" is the affective state when mourning is occurring as distinguished from the clinical syndrome of melancholia. One of Bowlby's postulates is that the loss of a mother figure between six months and 3 to 4 years has a high degree of pathogenic potential for subsequent personality development due to the occurrence of mourning processes.

Protesting behavior manifests itself in crying, motoric restlessness, and angry efforts to regain the lost object by demands for its return. This sows the seeds for later psychopathology. Subsequent disorganization with painful despair hopefully leads to a reorganization in connection with relinquishing the image of the lost object in which new objects help. Anger is believed essential for efforts to recover the lost object. Yearning is mixed with repeated dissappointments in not recovering the object that is lost. "Grief" is seen connected with an irretrievable loss while "separation anxiety" is a response to a situation where hope persists that the loss is not irretrievable.

Persistence of efforts to regain experienced losses can have four possible types of pathological outcomes: (1) Unconscious yearnings to recover lost objects persist. These seem surprising to clinicians since there is an "absence of grief." (2) Angry reproaches against the self and other objects to attain a reunion. Displacement of reproaches occurs in which inappropriate objects are used or "mourned at a distance." Development to the level where anger can be directed against the self as a psychological process is an index that guilt is experienced. Guilt is generated via reality-based realizations that the child has played a role in the loss, or by way of fantasies that the object was destroyed. Psychopathological displacement is due to prolongation of anger without direct expression. Chronicity itself leads to a waning of affectionate components. (3) Absorption in caring for others who are suffering rather than grieving oneself by way of projective identification and vicarious mourning. This should be raised as a possibility when a child is plagued by "bad luck" or indulges in compulsive pitying of others. (4) Denial of the permanency of object loss operating on a conscious level necessitates a "split in the ego." Acute losses have a greater tendency to result in such denial. Children are particularly prone to react to losses in this manner. Losses predispose the child to character changes which leave the child in a state of readiness to evoke similar reactions when subsequent developmental, psychological, or environmental losses occur. This is a process analagous to being exposed to an allergen.

Bowlby's theories are not automatically accepted. He once held that no qualitative difference existed between mourning in children and adults on the basis that their behavior appeared similar. However, Bowlby's position was later clarified in holding that pathological mourning persists in children because of their failure to engage in normal mourning processes at the time of the loss of the object.[46] A review of the literature concludes that children, in contrast to adults, do not go through a stage of mourning where they gradually go through a painful detachment from the inner representation of the person who has died.[47] Rather, a complex set of defensive phenomena function to deny what has occurred, and this has a high pathogenic potential.

There is a need to consider differences in successive developmental stages and how they affect psychological reactions to object loss.[48] When young children grieve, they experience a "hurt" rather than undergo the same psychological processes as an adult. Some describe this in terms of a lack of developmental readiness to mourn prior to adolescence. "Until he has undergone what we may call the trial mourning of adolescence, he is unable to mourn. Once he has lived through the painful, protracted decathecting of the first love objects, he can repeat the process when circumstances of external loss require a similar renunciation. When such loss occurs, we may picture the individual who has been initiated into mourning through adolescence confronting himself with the preconscious question: 'Can I bear to give up someone I love so much?' The answer follows: 'Yes, I can bear it—I have been through it once before.' Before the trial mourning of adolescence has been undergone, a child making the same tentative beginning of reality testing in regard to a major object loss is threatened with the prospect of overwhelming panic and retreats into defensive denial in the way we have observed."[49]

Extensions of Object Loss into Depessive-Proneness

Object loss as a concept has been expanded far beyond that of a literal loss to include distortions in object relationships. Depressive consequences can be subtle and not show up in the form of gross disturbance but lie in wait until some unspecified future time. Depressed moods in mothers during the first two years after birth create a tendency to similar moods in the children which later become manifest.[50] Fusion with a depressed mother induces the mood disturbance in themselves. This is especially so for children who live an "as if" existence where they perceive themselves as necessary for validation for parental needs. The liability is the threat of abandonment if they are not validating.[51] Serious and chronic preoccupations in the parents leave little room for spontaneous curiosity and interaction with the child in his world. Pessimistic moods in the parents induce feelings of failure in children whereby the child feels he is somehow responsible for the predicament of the parents. A depressed and worried parent interferes with the freedom of children to play and test their environment free from apprehension about their parents. Similarly, parents staving off their depressed moods by extreme and unpredictable activity and periodic overstimulating play with a child contribute to the depressive outlook of the child.[52]

Clinical work reveals that not all children with "narcissistic vulnerabilities" have lost an external object. Relevant are the developmental lines striving to attain object constancy in efforts to achieve separation and individuation. Individuation gives rise to a period of increased psychomotor activity from ten to eighteen months in which the mood is believed to be one of infantile elation. Actively leaving and returning with a maternal readiness for the infant doing this are steps towards acquiring an internal object constancy. "Giving up" the fusion promotes individuation and is a step towards lowering magical maneuverings.[53] Depressive moods are generated by a child's relinquishment of a belief in his omnipotence, and a feeling that the parents are withholding power from him. These moods manifest themselves by separation and grief reactions marked by temper tantrums, continual attempts to woo or coerce the mother, and then giving up in despair for awhile. In some cases there is an impotent resignation and surrender which may have a marked masochistic coloring. On the other hand, discontentment and anger can persist after a short period of grief and sadness.[54] The natural history of these early mood states in the preschool child reveals many of them giving way to premature earnestness ("little adults"). An undue seriousness indicates precocious superego formation. Other signs of failing to attain object constancy with respect to mood are marked ambivalence, precocious overidentification, pseudo-self-sufficiency, and a flattened overt emotional spontaneity.

The evolution of a depreciated self-concept is a major predisposing influence in the formation of a depressive nucleus in a child. Emotional distantness on the part of family members puts children into a nuclear conflict. They are not in a position to understand or appraise the reasons for this treatment of them. Nor do parents comprehend the innumberable ways their reactions to children are manifested. Early self-derogatory cognitions emerge in the form of negative self-cognitions, to wit, "I am no good." Nor are these confined to major areas of failings, for they are carried out with respect to many minor failings initially. Self-evaluations as intrinsically defective or disappointments as a person emerge. Feelings of loneliness and abandonment proceed to states of despair and general incompetence. An adolescent, born with a congenital hair lip, which precipitated a hospitalized depression in her mother described her childhood years as distant from her mother. She had heard her mother telling her aunts how she would never take a chance on another pregnancy which was so. Losing herself in books worked up to a point as did her compulsive study habits. They were not sufficient to contain her depression after mother's death when her regrets centered on verbalizations that she would now never know her mother and her anger about this.

Given how serious these young children view life, anything less than perfection in them raises the possibility of abandonment.[55] The internal threat is far more severe than that from the parents. While parental anger has limits, the superego may not. Unattainable ideals are related to this perfectionism. This manifests itself in a vulnerability to seek out hero-figures who possess the perfect characteristics lacking in the potentially depressed child. In children this is seen in overevaluating others as more competent, more popular, brighter, etc. However, heroes are always subject to disillusionment in which the opposite occurs and all their faults are overevaluated.[56] One of the benefits of an accepting therapist for these children is that they find the therapeutic setting being one where they do not have to earn acceptance. In time the idealizing transference with the therapist will need handling.

Within our expanding knowledge of the developmental role of narcissism in children lies another key to understanding the impact of loss on children. Repeated rebuffs or losses are reacted to as confirmations that a significant person did not value them and that they are therefore unworthy.[57] How they feel becomes more sensitized to transient environmental approvals than other children which leaves them narcissistically vulnerable. When pushed to an extreme this can lead to deficits in reality testing. This is in accord with a principle that an increase in narcissism occurs as the importance of real objects diminishes. Yet, such withdrawal is unsatisfactory to children and leads to "restitutive" attempts to restore real relationships.

In the young child, "losses" are partially met by an increase in narcissism, and also by their capacity for adaptation by acceptance of substitute objects. Loss of self-esteem as a response to loss is not thought to appear until a structural division of mental activity has been accomplished. By then object constancy has been attained so mourning as a process of detachment from inner representations can occur. Only when an object has attained value does its loss lead to self-devaluation. Aggression directed against the self is witnessed in masochistic phenomena as part of a depressive picture. When an object becomes important the child becomes concerned with the question, "Who will love me when I am left?" and the answer, "no one may want you."[58] A child who feels depleted and devalued as an object does not conceptualize himself as worth much.

Mood variations are another accompaniment. Somatic manifestations are the template for similar symptoms as they grow up which appear as hypochondriasis, motor restlessness, sleep upsets, and gastrointestinal complaints. Children's moods have three main characteristics:[59] (1) Affective manifestations are more intense than in adults. This is because of insufficient ego-superego controls; (2) Mood swings are of briefer duration. They change rapidly due to the instability of object relations and the greater readiness of children to accept substitute objects and gratifications. (3) The affective range in children is more limited from the lack of ego differentiation. When a propensity towards pathological mood disturbance develops, there is actually less variety and spontaneity of moods. A more exaggerated quality is presently seen in persistent forlornness and sadness or exaggerated excitement.

Latency Age Depressions

An increasing amount has been written about the depressive responses in young children and animals on one level, and about the more flamboyant behavior of the depressed adolescent on the other. Yet, the child from five years of age to puberty may actually comprise the most hidden group in terms of incidence. Confusion is present as to how thwarted dependency needs. Physical illnesses, and losses induce depressive reactions in this age group.[60] Although internalized conflict creates possibilities for many types of neurotic conflicts, not all feel that the concepts elaborated about depression are applicable to children.[61] Confusion is compounded by the "latent" manifestations of depression at this age in which there is often an absence of the overt symptoms associated with depressions. Hence, crying, verbalized self-condemnations, and overt expressions of guilt are not the primary symptom picture. Parental use of denial regarding one of their children who appears sad or unhappy further masks true incidence.

Clinical and developmental studies confirm that latency is not quiescent. Coupled with this is the emergence of a control system which has the potential for severity. Superego functioning seems particularly prone to upset in view of developmental problems. It is not unusual to observe latency children placing demands on themselves which are quite severe. This may be explained in terms of the immaturity of their superego, or a projection of aggression onto internalized objects which are then used against themselves. This mechanism seems to ensure that transgressions will not occur since the child is not "on his own."

Articles which appear describe children who are clinically depressed. These vary from widely different initial problems and current difficulties exist in attempting the application of a systematic classificatory scheme. For diagnostic purposes at present, perhaps nothing more is needed than a diagnosis of "childhood depression" indicating its presence. However, for purposes of increasing our sophistication and research a more elaborate system is needed to give an awareness of the protean possibilities for children who may have a depressive picture. There is a tentative classificatory scheme which I use to encompass the diverse manifestations of depression in children. It relies in part on age but also at least indicates other dimensions which contribute to the clinical picture: (1) Deprivation syndromes (anaclitic depressions); (2) Associated with organic diseases (primary such as in diabetes or secondary such as in response to a disease); (3) Difficulties with individuation and separation; (4) Object loss types; (5) Overdeveloped ego-ideals; (6) Depressive equivalents; (7) Cyclothymic mood disturbances.

How does the depressed child appear? As with depressions in different age groups, a myriad picture is possible. Although there is a confluence in some children, the signs and symptoms vary widely. Some of these observations are made from children in intensive therapy while others are from children on in-patient units and yet others out-patient departments or court settings. Some of them are from a retrospective awareness of symptom picture in mid-childhood by adolescents or adults who realize in the course of their own therapy how depressed they really were at that time.[62] Drawn from these sources, the following is a composite picture of how a depressed child would appear based on our present state of knowledge.[63,64]

1. A general picture of a sad, depressed, or unhappy looking child may be present. The child does not complain of unhappiness, or even being aware of it, but rather conveys a psychomotor behavioral picture of sadness.

2. Withdrawal and inhibition with little interest in any activities may be most prominent. It is a listlessness which gives an impression of boredom, or physical illness, and often leads an observer to conclude that the child must have some concealed physical illness.

3. Somatizing takes the form of physical pain (headaches, abdominal complaints, dizziness), insomnia, sleeping or eating disturbances—"depressive equivalents."

4. A quality of discontent is prominent. An initial impression is that the child is dissatisfied and experiences little pleasure, and in time the clinician gets the added impression that somehow others—even an examiner who has barely met the child—are somehow responsible for his plight. In other cases there is a casting of blame on others in the sense of easily criticizing other children.

5. A sense of feeling rejected or unloved is present. There is a readiness to turn away from disappointing objects.

6. Negative self-concepts reflecting cognitive patterns of illogically drawing conclusions that they are worthless, etc.[65]

7. Reports are made of observations of low frustration-tolerance and irritability; this is coupled with self-punitive behavior when goals are not attained.

8. Although the child conveys a sense of need or wanting comfort, it is then accepted as his due, or he remains dissatisfied and discontent although he is often in ignorance as to why.

9. Reversal of affect is revealed in clowning and dealing with underlying depressive feelings by foolish or provocative behavior to detract from assets or achievements.

10. Blatant attempts to deny feelings of helplessness and hopelessness are seen in the "Charlie Brown Syndrome" modeled after the cartoon character of a boy from 7 to 9 years who avoids confronting his despair and disillusionment by being self-deprecatory and then springing back with hope.[66] These indicate a hope that self-depreciations, avoidance of rewards, dedicated effort, and other examples of being "good" will lead to rewards that are just—perhaps when one grows up or at least in the hereafter. In childhood, hope manages to avoid the more overt manifestations of depressive pessimism seen in the adult when disillusionment occurs.

11. Provocative behavior which stirs angry responses in others and leads to others utilizing this child as a focus for their own disappointments. Such scapegoating exhibits suffering which leads to descriptions of him as a "born loser." Difficulties in handling aggression may be a frequent initiator of referral.

12. Tendencies to passivity and expecting others to anticipate their needs. Since this is frequently impossible, they may express their anger by passive-aggressive techniques.

13. Sensitivity and high standards with a readiness to condemn themselves for failures. There is a preference to be harsh and self-critical. This appears as an attempt to avoid conflict associated with hostility by in effect saying, "I don't blame you—only myself." In some this extends to the point of feeling they are so bad they should be dead.[67]

14. Obsessive-compulsive behavior in connection with other types of regressive, magical activities.

15. Episodic acting-out behaviors as a defensive maneuver to avoid experiencing painful feelings associated with depression.

The phenomenological experience of the depressive-prone child presents an intriguing picture. In some ways they appear as caricatures of the adult intellectual who intensely worries about the state of mankind. With children, the worry is about their own worthwhileness. They convey an inner hesitancy which shows up as a fear of commitment—be it in peer relationships or activities. This seems to correlate with an uncertainty about others remaining reliable and steadfast. Clinicians sense a cautious seeking for attachments in the course of therapy and in reports of their daily life. In contrast to a schizoid child who prefers his withdrawal, the depressed child hungers for a relationship but he is doubtful about its sustainingness. Although the child is externally forlorn and sad, he is usually unaware of the reasons for his altered moods or why he periodically reacts this way.

Affective states of nostalgia and self-pity do not seem present developmentally until age three to four. At that time children verbalize their feelings when someone leaves them and they are missed. Sensitive observers sense mild depressive affect when a parent, pet, or friend is absent for more than a short period. Displays of narcissistic mortification may amuse adults. Thus, a 4-year-old may refuse to participate in an activity which he enjoys a great deal when something is denied him or he is reprimanded. Miscarried attempts to hurt frustrating and controlling objects by not cooperating in some activity pleasing the other party is a possible outcome. All manner of masochistic phenomena may follow, such as learning problems and putting oneself at a disadvantage with other children. A girl of 12 years turns down a role in a school play because she is afraid her friend, not invited, will not get invited. A boy of 11 holds back in a race for fear of winning. The line between altruism and masochism can get quite thin. When these behaviors are described by the child, and one senses an accompanying affect of self-pity for the sacrifice, we are probably safe in seeing it as masochistic. The subjects of success phobias and those wrecked by success are relevant. Some children can become quite skillful in arranging situations where they can feel offended. For example, a child wants a certain job in school, but manages by reticence and concealing not to have her assets known while a child, with many less qualified abilities but more assertive, obtains the job. She then nurses her wounds in solitude but experiences hurt and mortification.

A frequent pattern that cannot be ignored as an antecedent is the presence in the home of an adult who gets periodically depressed. The emotional tone of sadness, hurt and loneliness in the adult leaves a tone of sadness in the child. This could be based on an identification with a depressed parent, or using depression as a defense to control the degree of rage which has not been handled otherwise.[68]

It is from this background that children with clinical depressions appear as sufferers. Some rely on somatizing processes or endless appearances at physicians' offices for problems which do not yield to a physical explanation. In many ways these are varieties of "masked depressions"[69] which get subsumed under the category of endogenousness for adults. The most frequent somatic symptoms in children are headaches, dizziness, cephalalgias, nausea, abdominal pain, or wandering pains in different parts of the body. In two successive series of 100 children investigated for recurrent abdominal pain ("Little bellyachers"), only 8 percent and 6 percent respectively were found to have an organically explainable etiology.[70] Not only abdominal complaints, but anorexia, pruritus, and migraine headaches have been viewed as depressive equivalents in children.[71]

Severe encopresis has been considered a depressive equivalent in children where there is more open expression of aggression. Similarly, enuresis has been viewed as part of a symptom-complex in a depressed child where genitourinary evaluations and cystoscopy do not reveal organic pathology.[72]

Depressed children can be "loners," not in the sense of schizoidia, but rather because their worries and preoccupation interfere with their engaging with others as they are capable of. Feeling lonely may result in teasing and sadistic behavior. Vicarious pleasure in seeing others commit errors or get injured then become part of the mechanism for diverting self-critical attack on themselves. Abrupt shifts in behavior in a child should raise a question of depression. Thus, a previously alert child who shows signs of withdrawal, apathy or inability to study and lack of interest most often makes people think of a physical source, but I am saying that these symptoms are equally compatible with depression. A previously outgoing and carefree child who grows quiet and preoccupied, or a conforming child with obsessional tendencies who shows more mood variations or episodes of "delinquent" behavior also qualify. A superior student whose achievement reflects high aspirations and ideals is more likely to react with depressive manifestations when rewards for his hard work are not forthcoming or maintenance of earlier overachievements becomes difficult. Their vulnerability lies in their overachievement and overconscientiousness. Obsessional activities in the depressed child represent efforts to compensate for feelings of helplessness. Jarvis noted an association between loneliness and compulsivity in children in which the compulsions served as a defense against sadness and loss.[73] These feelings are evoked in response to a pattern of "withdrawn mothering" where physical needs are met, but the absence of the mother makes her unable to gratify some basic psychological needs of the child.

Hyperactive and restless behavior in the depressed child seem paradoxical. It is interesting that these were the symptoms of depression noted in a 1931 report by Kasanin.[74] Hyperkinesis is seen in a variety of disturbances. These vary from cerebral dysfunction to defensive maneuvers. Hyperkinetic behavior in the depressed child may be similar psychodynamically to hypomanic activity in adults who are warding off depressive feelings. Hyperactive behavior, like antisocial behavior, brings parental condemnation and allows the parent to focus on such behavior while longstanding hostilities are ignored. An increasing amount of clinical work confirms a viewpoint that certain forms of anti-social behavior or acting-out in children are a response to a depressive core. In his original monograph Bowlby felt there was a specific connection between prolonged early deprivation and the development of a personality with shallow relationships with other people, poor impulse control, and the development of an "affectionless, psychopathic character."[75] There is a continued need for clinical documentation of the relationship between depressions and persistent criminality which is so often bypassed in the group statistics on crime.[76]

Depressed Children and Acting-Out

Although it may be unnecessary, there will be an opening caveat. No claim is made that all deficits in object relations give rise to a depressive nucleus which then leads to antisocial behavior. Indeed, if unmitigated hate exists towards an object and its introject, more primitive emotions of hate and rage not tempered by ambivalence occurs.[77] Nor does guilt predominate in this latter type of situation. This type of antisocial development associated with impulsive behavior is not going to be discussed further, and it is mentioned simply for purposes of excluding it before proceeding onward to how neurotically-depressed children resort to acting-out behavior.

Depressed children experience losses as a painful discomfort which makes up part of their depressive core. Their acting-out is related either to anxiety about object loss (separation), or sadness which can progress to despair if they feel the object or part-object will not be recovered. In some of these children, anger related to this predicament can take the form of attacks against people or the environment about the loss of a dependent object or from frustration about their hunger for an object. Neurotically-depressed children behave as though they have already performed in an unacceptable manner. It is as though either some unacceptable impulse has been carried out or they have not come through.[78] The importance of narcissism has been mentioned.

A depressed child with this burden of guilt may also act out in order to secure punishment. This is the model Franz Alexander elaborated some time ago as a concomitant part of the neurotic character.[79] These are the children who tend to be whiny or nagging, or if more deeply guilty they can carry out acts of vandalism or arson and then feel relieved.

> An example is that of a previously well-behaved, but progressively sad, 10-year-old girl. As an only child, there were many mixed unresolved oedipal romance feelings towards her father and guilt feelings towards her mother; she found herself becoming quieter and sadder as latency wore on. In retrospect, her parents agreed with this but this

had occurred so insidiously that they had not done more than comment on it once to each other. On a particular night, their next door neighbor's home, occupied by a childless, newly-married couple, was broken into through an open window. This 10-year-old scratched profane words over the walls with lipstick and then with a knife, slashed the bedding and mattress. While the neighborhood and police at first thought a local "sex maniac" had been on the loose, the mother discovered the used up lipstick tube in the child's bedroom to her horror. The child subsequently felt bad, but this was also accompanied by feeling less sad than over the previous months.

Resistance to a treatment approach which sets limits to acting-out is needed since this requires the child to experience the underlying depression with the therapist. What first appears then is often somatic complaints. Self-destructive behavior often parallels strong guilt and self-hate. Aggressive behavior itself is used to avoid depressed feelings. This is especially so where there is a direct threat to the integrity of the child. Situations when children cannot deny their cravings for affection or when past feelings of worthlessness become overwhelming pose such threats.[80] It is not just that acting-out, and delinquent patterns, represent attempts at coping with some type of depressive nucleus. Further questions arise about the nature of distortions in development that have occurred when the ego permits the aggression to be acted out during a childhood depression.[81,82] To what extent are some of these components in the depressive character structure reversible? How modifiable will they be by therapy, or should we just view these as fixed traits which will characterize an individual as he goes through life?

Acting-out behavior has particular psychodynamic and social meanings. Some believe acting-out is a primary defense in a majority of depressive individuals. As noted, this does not exclude its presence with different diagnostic categories, such as impulse-ridden characters, defective socialization patterns, antisocial personalities, or as part of a schizophrenic process. In part, the problem is a conceptual one since "primary theorists" view depressive affect as crucial to whatever overt diagnostic features are present. By latency, a progressive pattern of hatred and destructive behavior in fantasy, play, and overt behavior is possible. The narcissistic basis and ambivalence in object ties is striking. However, therapeutic work which deals with the personality structure beneath the external aggressive display sees a denigrated self-concept. The child and parent are both mutually identifying with the "bad" parts of each other. This reinforces feelings of worthlessness. Repetitive play themes or fantasies relating to destroying bad things are followed by magically reconstituting them. For some depressed children, the fantasies get acted out and the fascinating question is why this occurs in some of these children.

The formulations of Therese Benedek regarding the "depressive constellation" are relevant here.[83] In situations where oral demands and frustrations of children reactivate similar conflicts in the mother, the transactions between them give rise to an "ambivalent core." Child and mother proceed to interact on a projective and introjective bipolar basis of aggression in an attempt to escape from feelings of being a "bad child" and "bad mother." The model is that of identification of the mother "backward" with her own child who is reenacting the provocative role of the mother as child. The hypothesis is that certain parents have had childhood experiences which heighten this ambivalent core. A pattern of reinforcing hostility is mutually set in motion which gains momentum. The child feels estranged and angry which is superimposed on the disappointment of the parent. In turn, the parent feels justified in condemning the angry, sullen child who develops feelings of shame which lead to increasing distance. Repetitive acting-out then ensues with the original and now concealed depressive nucleus being the impelling motive to these patterns.

This affect of shame is so powerful and painful for a child to deal with that the ego erects a set of defenses to handle it. How does this affect arise in connection with a depressed child? Secondly, what is the relationship of shame to acting-out? Part of the depressive complex is a failure to live up to inflated ego-ideals with a resultant vulnerability to more readily believe one has failed. In such a failure complex, shame is one of the leading affects. The child experiences this failure in interpersonal terms of being criticized, ridiculed, and excluded by others, and in ego terms as one of feeling the pain of humiliation.

But then the question is why some children do not simply rest here and accept their humiliated selves? Some do just that, and they become part of the group of chronic losers. The result is that they accept a picture of inadequacy as their norm. This solution appears related to the threat of greater pain if they do not so acquiesce in that image. On some level this maintains the fascimile of a relationship against the threat of total dissolution.

However, this type of acquiescence may be too painful for some children caught in such a conflict. Projection may be tried where others are blamed for their disappointing performances. This projection can be quite forceful if the parental figures join in with the child. In fact, it may lead to a rare experience of togetherness on an emotional level for the child. Hence, a depreciated and depressed child who blames the poor teaching for his failures to get the "As" his parents want, is joined by his parents in the attack. This is often quite effective since school personnel often take the role of the culprit by accommodating to this type of criticism.

If these measures of getting alleviation for the painful ego state of shame do not work for the child, they may resort to more open aggressive attacks. A child shamed for his deficient academic performance may act out his impulses in a classroom or more brazenly by writing profanity on the lavatory walls for example. A child put down by his gym teacher for a poor performance in a competitive event—as well as by his parents—begins to engage in acts of leaving feces scattered around the school. An 11-year-old girl, subject to disdain by her parents for her not gaining acceptance by the right social group in her school, organizes her own clique. As its leader, she manages in turn to put down many other girls who want to be accepted by her group. These temporary triumphs do little to assuage her nagging sense of shame and inadequacy. While previously seen as a child wanting acceptance quite badly but uncertain about herself, she is now seen as an angry, embittered, and cunning child. "Criminals from a sense of shame" have been pointed out as related to shame just as there are "criminals from a sense of guilt."[84] By adolescence more borderline delinquency, if not criminal acts, are more probable from this depressive framework.

Summary

This paper has surveyed some of the salient problems in depressive phenomena beginning in infancy and proceeding into latency. The multifarious clinical manifestations which occur from infancy onwards up to adolescence are often ignored. They have been dealt with from a critical perspective involving theoretical problems present in evolving a coherent clinical picture. A systematic set of signs and symptoms are necessary if any meaningful assessment of children who are depressed is possible. Developmental aspects of moods, reactive mood swings, and clinical symptom pictures have been differentiated. By the time that a relatively fixed style of responses to losses or disappointments environmentally, or with respect to the child's own ego-ideal, has occurred, the predisposition for clinical depressions has been established. The depressive cycle has then been initiated, and it is a difficult process to dislodge.

References

1. *Diagnostic and Statistical Manual of Mental Disorders* (1968). 2nd ed. Washington, D.C.: American Psychiatric Association.
2. Suomi S.J., Harlow, H.F. (1972) Social rehabilitation of isolate-reared monkeys. *Develop. Psychol.* 6:487-496.
3. Baldesserini, R. (1970) Frequency of diagnosis of schizophrenia and affective disorder from 1944-1968. *Am. J. Psychiat.* 127:759-763.

4. Eisenberg, L. (1971) *Problems for the biopsychology of development, in the biopsychology of development.* Edited by Tobach E., Aronson L.R., Shaw E. New York, Academic Press: 515-529.
5. Levy, D. (1937). Primary affect hunger. *Am. J. Psychiat.* 94:643-652.
6. Goldfarb, W. (1943). Infant rearing and problem behavior. *Am. J. Orthopsychiat.* 13:249-265.
7. Burlingham, D. and Freud A. (1943). *Infants Without Families.* London:Allen and Unwin.
8. Young, L.D., Suomi, S.S., Harlow, H.F., and McKinney, W.T. (1973). Early stress and later response to separation in rhesus monkeys. *Am. J. Psychiat.* 130:400-405.
9. Spitz, R. (1946). Anaclitic depression. *Psa. Study Child* 2:113-117.
10. Engel, G., and Reichsman, F. (1956). Spontaneous and experimentally induced depressions in an infant with a gastric fistula. *J. Am. Psa. Assn.* 4:428-456.
11. Coddington, R.D. (1968). Study of an infant with gastric fistula and her normal twin. *Psychosom. Med.* 30:172-192.
12. Kaufman, I.C., and Rosenblum, L.A. (1967). The reaction to separation in infant monkeys: anaclitic depression and conservation-withdrawal. *Psychosomat. Med.* 29:648-675.
13. Hinde, R.A., Spencer-Booth, Y. (1971). Effects of brief separation from mother on rhesus monkeys. *Science* 173:111-118.
14. *Op. cit.,* Young, Suomi, Harlow, McKinney.
15. Bowlby, J. (1951). Maternal Care and Mental Health, 2nd ed. Geneva, World Health Organization.
16. Perspective on human deprivation. (1968). Washington, D.C., U.S. Dept. Health, Ed., and Welfare.
17. Rutter, M. (1972). *Maternal Deprivation Reassessed.* Baltimore:Penguin Books.
18. Berger, M., and Passingham, R.E. (1973). Early experience and other environmental factors: an overview, in *Handbook of Abnormal Psychology,* 2nd ed. Edited by Eysenck, H.J. London:Pittman.
19. Wooton, B. (1959). *Social Science and Social Pathology.* London:Allen and Unwin.
20. Abraham, K. (1911). Notes on the psycho-analytical investigation and treatment of manic-depressive insanity and allied conditions. *On Character and Libido Development.* New York:W.W. Norton, 1966, 15-34.
21. Freud, S. (1917). Mourning and melancholia. *Standard Edition.* London: Hogarth Press, 1957, 237-260.
22. Abraham, K. (1924). A short study of the development of the libido, viewed in the light of mental disorders. *On Character and Libido Development.* New York:W.W. Norton, 1966, 67-150.
23. Hill, O.W. (1972). Child bereavement and adult psychiatric disturbance. *J. Psychosom. Res.:* 357-360.
24. Malmquist, C.P. (1975). Depression in Childhood. In *Comprehensive Textbook of Depression.* Edited by Flach, F.F., Draghi, S. New York:Wiley.
25. Kohut, H. (1971). The analysis of the self. New York:International University Press.
26. Rado, S. (1928). The problem of melancholia. *Int. J. Psa.* 9:420-438.
27. Schafer, R. (1960). The loving and beloved superego in Freud's structural theory. *Psa. Study Child* 15:163-188.
28. Gero, G. (1936). The construction of depression. *Int. J. Psa.* 17:423-461.

29. Adler, K.A. (1967). Adler's individual psychology. *Psychoanalytic Techniques.* Edited by B.B. Wolman. New York:Basic Books., 229-337.
30. Jacobson, E. (1971). Acting out and the urge to betray in paranoid patients in depression. *Depressions.* New York:International University Press.
31. Bonime, W. (1966). The psychodynamics of neurotic depression. *Am. Handbook of Psychiatry.* Edited by S. Arieti. Vol. III, New York:Basic Books. 239-255.
32. Ainsworth, M.D. (1969). Object relations, dependency and attachment: a theoretical review of the infant-mother relationship. *Child Dev.* 40:969-1025.
33. Gewirtz, J.L. (1973). Attachment and dependence: some strategies and tactics in the selection and use of indices for those concepts, communication and affect. Edited by T. Alloway, L. Krames, P. Pliner. New York:Academic Press.
34. Cairns, R.B. (1966a). Development, maintenance, and extinction of social attachment behavior in sheep. *J. Comp. Physio. Psychol.* 62:298-306.
35. (1966b). Attachment behavior of mammals. *Psychol. Rev.* 23:409-426.
36. Bowlby, J. (1958). The nature of the child's tie to the mother. *Int. J. Psa.* 39:350-373.
37. (1969). Attachment and loss, Vol. I, *Attachment.* New York:Basic Books.
38. Engel, G. (1971). Attachment behavior, object relations and the dynamic-economic points of view. *Int. J. Psa.* 52:183-196.
39. Klein, M. (1948). *Contributions to Psycho-Analysis 1921-1945.* New York: McGraw-Hill, 1964.
40. Winnicott, D.W. (1954). The depressive position in normal emotional development. *Collected Papers.* New York:Basic Books, 1958. 262-277.
41. Bowlby, J. (1960a). Separation anxiety. *Int. J. Psa.* 41:89-113.
42. (1960b). Grief and mourning in infancy and early childhood. *Psa. Study Child* 15:9-52.
43. (1961a). Processes of mourning. *Int. J. Psa.* 42:317-340.
44. (1961b). Childhood mourning and its implication for psychiatry. *Am. J. Psychiat.* 118:481-498.
45. (1973). *Attachment and loss,* Vol. II, *Separation.* New York:Basic Books.
46. (1963). Pathological mourning and childhood mourning. *J. Am. Psa. Assn.* 11:500-541.
47. Miller, J. (1971). Children's reactions to parent's death. *J. Am. Psa. Assn.* 19:697-719.
48. Freud, A. (1960). Discussion of Dr. Bowlby's paper. *Psa. Study Child* 15: 53-62.
49. Wolfenstein, M. (1966). How is mourning possible? *Psa. Study Child* 21:93-126.
50. Freud, A. (1965). Normality and pathology in childhood. New York:International University Press.
51. Brodey, W.M. (1965). On the dynamics of narcissism I. Externalization and early ego development. *Psa. Study Child* 20:165-193.
52. Davidson, J. (1968). Infantile depression in a "normal" child. *J. Am. Acad. Child Psychiat.* 7:522-535.
53. Mahler, M.S. (1961). On sadness and grief in infancy and childhood. *Psa. Study Child* 16-332-354.
54. Mahler, M.S. (1966). Notes on the development of basic moods, Psychoanalysis-

A general Psychology. Edited by R. Loewenstein, L. Newman, M. Schur, A Solnit. New York: International University Press. 152-168.
55. Reich, A. (1960). Pathologic forms of self-esteem regulation. *Psa. Study Child* 15:215-232.
56. Main, A.M. (1971). Idealization and disillusion in adolescence, Sexuality and Aggression in Maturation: New Facets. Edited by H.S. Klein. London: Bailliere, Tindall and Cassell. 14-21.
57. Rochlin, G. (1965). *Loss and restitution, Grief and Its Discontents.* Boston: Little, Brown and Co., 121-164.
58.   (1961). The dread of abandonment. *Psa. Study Child* 16:451-470.
59. Jacobson, E. (1957). On normal and pathological moods. *Psa. Study Child* 12:73-113.
60. Rie, H.E. (1966). Depression in childhood: a survey of some pertinent contributions. *J. Am. Acad. Child Psychiat.* 5:653-685.
61. Koran, L.M. (1975). The Reliability of Clinical Methods, Data and Judgments. *New Eng. J. Med.* 293:642-646.
62. Sandler, J., Joffe, W.G. (1965). Notes on childhood depression. *Int. J. Psa.* 46:88-96.
63. Malmquist, C.P. (1971). Depressions in childhood and adolescence: I. *New Eng. J. Med.* 284:887-893.
64.   (1971). Depressions in childhood and adolescence: II. *New Eng. J. Med.* 284:955-961.
65. Beck, A.T. (1972). Depression causes and treatment. Philadelphia: University of Pennsylvania Press.
66. Symonds, M. (1968). The depressions in childhood and adolescence. *Am. J. Psa.* 28:189-195.
67. McConville B.J., Boag, L.C., and Purohit, A.P. (1973). Three types of childhood depression. *Canad. Psychiat. Assn. J.* 18:133-138.
68. Poznaski, E., and Zrull, J.P. (1970). Childhood depression. *Arch. Gen. Psychiat.* 23:8-15.
69. Lopez Ibor, J.J. (1972). Masked depression. *Brit. J. Psychiat.* 120:245-258.
70. Apley, J. (1959). *The Child With Abdominal Pain.* Springfield, Illinois: Chas. C. Thomas.
71. Sperling, M. (1959). Equivalents of depression in children. *J. Hillside Hosp.* 8:138-148.
72. Frommer, E.A. (1968). Depressive illness in childhood, recent developments in affective disorders. Edited by A. Coppen and A. Walk. *Brit. J. Psychiat.* Special Pub. No. 2.
73. Jarvis, V. (1965). Loneliness and compulsion. *J. Am. Psa. Assn.* 13:122-158.
74. Kasanin, J. (1931). The affective psychoses in children. *Am. J. Psychiat.* 10: 897-924.
75. Bowlby. (1951). *op. cit.*, 1951, p. 34.
76. Cormier, B.M. (1966). Depression and persistent criminality. *Canad. Psychiat. Assn. J. Suppl.* 11:208-220.
77. Berman, S. (1959). Antisocial character disorder: its etiology and relationship to delinquency. *Am. J. Orthopsychiat.* 29:612-621.
78. Brenner, C. (1975). Affects and psychic conflict. *Psa. Quart.* 44:5-28.
79. Alexander, F. (1961). The neurotic character (1930), The Scope of Psycho-

analysis. New York:Basic Books, 56-89.

80. Burks, H.L., and Harrison, S.I. (1962). Aggressive behavior as a means of avoiding depression. *Am. J. Orthopsychiat.* 32:416-422.

81. Kaufman. I. (1955). Three basic sources for pre-delinquent character. *Nerv. Child* 11:12-15.

82. Kaufman I, et al. (1963). Delineation of two diagnostic groups among juvenile delinquents: the schizophrenic and the impulse-ridden character disorder. *J. Am. Acad. Child Psychiat.* 2:292-318.

83. Benedek, T. (1956). Towards the biology of the depressive constellation. *(J. Am. Psa. Assn.* 4:389-427.

84. Levin, S. (1971). The psychoanalysis of shame. *Int. J. Psycho-Anal.* 52:355-362.

CHAPTER 17

Symptomatic Depression as Seen in the Clinic

JUDITH SCHECHTMAN, M.S.W., A.C.S.W.
DORIS C. GILPIN, M.D.
JULIEN WORLAND, PH.D.

Introduction

In the first section of this chapter we will present data from a retrospective study of children at the Washington University Child Guidance and Evaluation Clinic. These are children who, from 1968 to the present, have been given the G.A.P. Diagnosis of Psychoneurotic Disorder Depressive Type. An intensive study of chart material on these children was undertaken in order to determine what similarities and differences we could find in this diagnostic group. Our ultimate goal was to look for trends which might help to differentiate these depressed children from children with other diagnostic labels. For this pilot study we did not use control groups except in select areas. Consequently, this data should not be construed in any way as statistically significant but rather may indicate trends to be more closely examined through rigid research.

Since July, 1968, thirty-three children at our Clinic have been given the diagnosis of Psychoneurotic Disorder Type depression. The composition of this population has some interesting and unusual features in comparison to the general clinic population. (See Figure 1.) Out of 33 children, only 2 were known to be Black; clinic-wide, over a third of our children are Black. There were 22 boys and 11 girls given this diagnosis; again we see a difference from clinic-wide statistics. We have a ratio of 3 to 4 boys to each girl seen. Finally, we were struck by the ages and clustering of these children at the time of their entrance to the clinic. There were no children of either sex with this diagnosis under the age of seven and no girls under the age of nine. Of the eleven girls with a depressive diagnosis, nine of them were twelve or older at the time of clinic entry. On the other hand, the largest proportion of boys, 11 of them were in the nine to eleven range. Our usual peaking for boys is at ages 3 to 4 and 7 to 8; for girls, it is 11 to 12 years of age. As can already be seen, there are apparently some unusual factors operating in this diagnostic group.

We first concentrated on the group of 9 to 11-year-old boys who were diagnosed as depressed. (See Figure 2.) Looking initially at the presenting symptoms, we realized it would not always be easy to predict depression in these children. All of the boys had at least one of the following symptoms: school failure, friendlessness or unmanageable behavior. All but three were either school failures or low achievers at school; in fact, five of them had been referred by the classroom teacher. Presenting complaints that are usually thought to be more directly suggestive of depression such as suicidal threats or complaints of being unloved, occurred in only four cases. By contrast, a symptom list checked by parents indicated that nine of the children were felt to be depressed. Six of the children were said to underestimate themselves, six had problems controlling anger, and five were poor sleepers.

> For Example: The child is described as a picky eater and has trouble getting to sleep, is one who feels he is no good, blames himself and feels he is dumb, is a procrastinator . . . and he is impulsive with poor judgment.

> Or: The parents seem concerned about M's temper outbursts, his sadness and depression and his lack of achievement at school. He is not achieving up to his intellectual potential and is difficult to control in class.

When we began to look at parental histories in these families (See Figure 3.), we immediately became aware of the prevalence of loss and

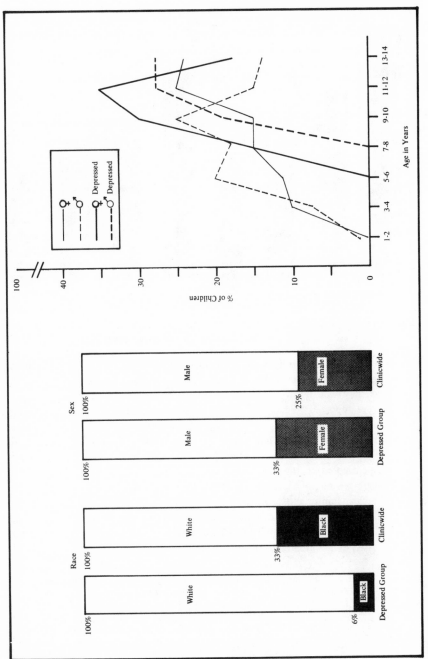

Figure 1.

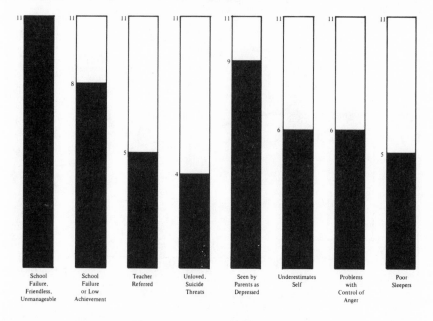

Figure 2. Boys 9-11 Years: Symptoms

depression. Not only were there losses or absent parents in the nuclear family, but the mothers, in particular, had experienced losses themselves as they were growing up, many before the age of twelve. Seven mothers were reported to have been depressed at some time, with five receiving therapy. One of these mothers committed suicide, two were hospitalized before their children had reached the age of five. All but one mother had either suffered an early parent loss, were depressed or both. There were five divorces in these families resulting in five absent fathers. In sum, there were ten out of eleven cases where there was a history of early loss in the nuclear family and/or in the parents' family of origin. Nine out of eleven boys had themselves experienced early loss through divorce of parents, or depression in mothers. Three of the children, in consequence, were partly raised by grandparents and/or sitters.

For Example: Always somewhat of a loner, since her last pregnancy, Mrs. C. has withdrawn from almost all social activities. All her relationships and attitudes are fraught with guilt. Most of her responses to the children are based upon this guilty, anxious attitude, creating much hostile dependency in them. She is almost totally immobilized by both

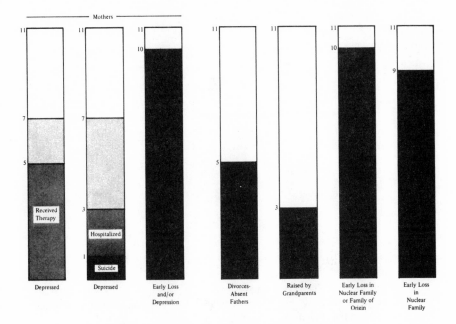

Figure 3. Boys 9-11 Years: Family History

guilt and depression. She has no access to childhood memories prior to age 14 and no access either to feelings. She shows no awareness of anger and defends primarily by denial, withdrawal, constriction, intellectualization, turning against herself. There was a pervasive depression and a generalized loss of energy and withdrawal. She described this as "going into her house and closing the door."

This history of early loss was so striking that we decided to search out all the nine- to eleven-year-old boys seen at the clinic since 1970 who had an early parent loss. (See Figure 4.) We were interested in seeing whether other pathologies were associated with this finding. There were a total of six boys, a surprisingly small number. Two of these did not follow through for an adequate diagnostic. Of the remaining, two were given the diagnosis of sociopath or its G.A.P. classification equivalent—impulse-ridden personality disorder. One child was given a neurotic diagnosis qualified by the statement that it was really a characterological problem. He exhibited typically depressive features—feelings of abandonment, anger turned inward and depression. Apparently, this boy could well have been given the

Diagnoses

Figure 4. Boys 9-11 Years with Early Loss

diagnosis of psychoneurotic disorder type. The remaining child had the depressive diagnosis but was not included in our original sample because of additional diagnosis of oppositional personality and developmental deviation.

Thus all nine- to eleven-year-old boys entering the clinic since 1970 who have experienced the loss of one parent before the age of six *could* have been labeled depressive reaction or impulse-ridden personality disorder.

Going back to our original group of depressed boys, we looked next at the data from the psychologicals. (See Figure 5.) Out of the eleven boys, all but one were tested. Six of these children were described as cooperative, six showed sad or depressed affect and five were seen as lonely. Four were stated as having reached the phallic-oedipal level of development. Six showed evidence of either partly or completely internalized superegos. The major defenses against depression were denial, isolation and displacement.

Turning to the psychiatric evaluations (See Figure 6.)., we had data on nine of the eleven boys. In five out of the six cases where mentioned, basic trust was seen as adequate. Six boys were stated to have poor self-esteem and six to have sad or depressed affect. Seven had reached at least the phallic-oedipal stage and seven showed evidence of partly or completely internalized superego. Thus, all but two children were seen as depressed by either or both the psychiatrist or psychologist. Although one of these

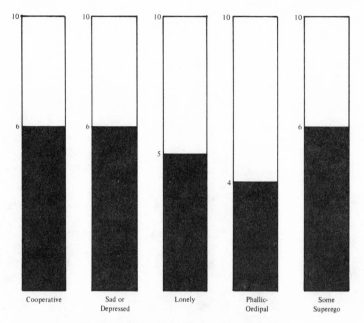

Figure 5. Boys 9-11 Years: Psychologicals

remaining two was seen as depressed by his parents, he may well have deserved the diagnosis of impulse-ridden personality as he was unmanageable, guiltless and without superego. The second of these showed no depression anywhere and he too was unmanageable and aggressive, but was felt to have a partly internalized superego. It is less clear whether he was misdiagnosed.

In sum, from the psychologicals and psychiatrics, we see these boys as depressed, lonely, cooperative, they have basic trust, low self-esteem, some superego development and have reached the phallic-oedipal stage.

> Example: The most prominent feature about M's personality is his depression. This is accompanied by feelings of helplessness and inadequacy, unmet dependency needs and fear of phallic strivings. The oedipal conflict is intense. Superego development is incomplete as is sexual identification with the male.

Finally, we looked at the course of treatment of these boys (See Figure 7.). Of the eleven, two were not treated because of parental refusal and on a third we have no data available. As to the remaining eight, all had individual therapy at some point, and two had additional group therapy.

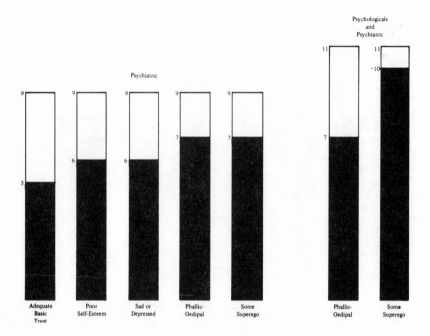

Figure 6. Boys 9-11 Years: Psychologicals and Psychiatric

Seven of the eight had a male therapist for part or all of their course of treatment; five had a female therapist. Duration of therapy ranged from 25 weeks to 130 weeks. As to success of treatment, four were seen as success- ful at termination of therapy. One is still being seen. One boy was term- inated with questionable success and is presently being reevaluated for further therapy. Two boys were terminated unsuccessfully, both because of parents' withdrawal. One of these was then placed in residential treat- ment. Apparently these families are somewhat easier to involve in long- term treatment than those of other diagnostic categories, e.g. oppositional or overly inhibited personalities.

Out of curiosity, we decided to compare nine- to eleven-year-old boys with other diagnoses but with the qualifying label "with depression" attached to the main diagnosis (See Figure 3.). There were six since 1968, of whom five had organic problems, some more or less psychosomatic, e.g. ulcer, obesity, eczema or birth defects and diabetes. Three of the six

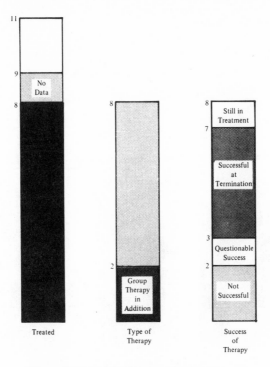

Figure 7. Boys 9-11 Years: Treatment

seemed to have brain damage and in two of these there were other organic problems as well. We then looked back at our main group of depressed boys and discovered that five of them also experienced similar difficulties, e.g. obesity, birth defects, eczema.

Checking further on this new group of boys, we found that three could be labeled oppositional personalities with depression, although one of these was in fact seen as an anxiety neurosis with depression. The only boy without evidence of organicity was labeled an obsessive-compulsive personality with depression. One was diagnosed tension discharge character disorder with depression although there was no mention of superego. He may well have been misdiagnosed and deserved the impulse-ridden diagnosis which we mentioned earlier in relation to the boys with early losses. The last of the six was labeled psychoneurosis with depression and anxiety but had many of the features associated with our major group of depressed boys, loneliness, neediness and depression. Apparently, it is tempting to add the label "with depression" to a group of children who have organic problems as a way of describing the manner in which they cope with their disabilities and probable feelings of loss, damage to self,

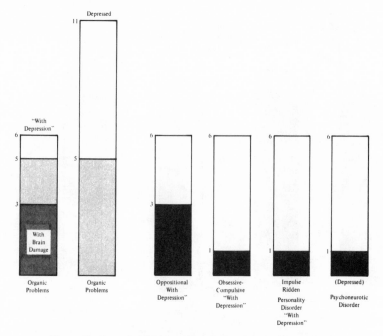

Figure 8. Boys 9-11 Years: Diagnosis "With Depression"

and self-esteem. We are unable to explain why five of our main group had organic difficulties and were seen as pure depressives whereas boys in this smaller group with similar problems were given another primary diagnosis.

Finally we looked at boys ages 7 to 8, and 13 to 15, who were diagnosed as depressed during this same time period—1968 onwards. Presenting problems, physical difficulties and history of losses all showed no remarkable dissimilarities from our major group of 9- to 11-year-olds. Findings from the psychologicals and psychiatrics appeared consistent also.

To summarize our major findings so far:

1. The boys labeled as primarily depressed had mothers who were also depressed, had suffered the loss of one parent, and were not achieving at school. They felt unhappy, unworthy, needy and guilty but tried to cooperate. They had at least reached the phallic-oedipal stage and had some internalized superego.

2. Children labeled primarily something else but who were also noted to be depressed, in general had some physical problem.

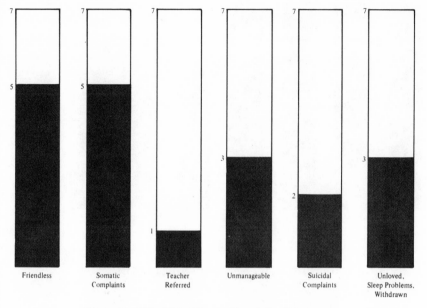

Figure 9. Girls 12-14 Years: Presenting Symptoms

3. Children who suffered a loss of a parent before the age of six were either diagnosed as depressed or impulse-ridden, the major difference being the lack of development of superego and guilt in the latter.

The next group we studied was that of depressed girls (See Figure 9.). As stated earlier, the major cluster came in the age range of 12- to 14-year-olds. There were seven girls in this group, all but one had a diagnostic evaluation. The remaining girl had very little information available for study except in the area of course of treatment.

The most frequent presenting symptoms among these girls were friendlessness (5) and somatic complaints (5). Unlike the boys, only one girl was referred by the teacher and only three were reported to be unmanageable. Two girls had suicidal complaints, three felt unloved, had sleep problems and were withdrawn. In the girls, depression could be inferred more easily from the presenting symptoms.

When we turned to the symptom list checked by the parents, we saw the most consistent results (See Figure 10.). Six girls were reported as having problems with anger control, problems with school achievement, anxieties about school and were seen as depressed. The seventh girl was

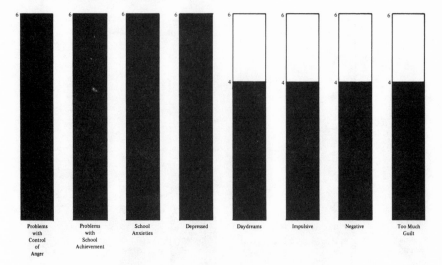

Figure 10. Girls 12-14 Years: Symptom List

the one with no available information. Four of the girls were reported as daydreamers, impulsive, negativistic, and having indications of too much guilt. These symptoms did not necessarily appear together in the same child. As evidenced, there are major areas of similarity between the boys studied earlier and these girls.

> For Example: S. is very moody, is frequently very depressed and blue. She worries about school and how her grades compare to those of siblings: she has never had a close friend. Now at school, she thinks the other kids are talking about her. Recently, she began having nightmares in which someone, usually the parents, were killed. She daydreams this same thing too. At night she will wake up crying. Also, recently, there was an increase in somatic symptoms: parents seem to feel she uses these somatic ills to express resistance and anger. She is afraid of the dark and can't sleep without a night light. Another major problem is her temper. However, she has never threatened or alluded to suicide.

Turning to the families of the girls, we did not see the same pattern of depression in the mothers (See Figure 11.). Only three were reported to have ever experienced depression. But in six of the seven families there have been marital separations and/or divorces when the girls were one-and-a-half through ten years of age. In addition, four of the fathers were

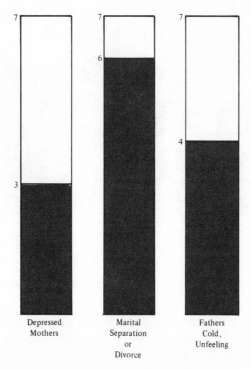

Figure 11. Girls 12-14 Years: Family History

reported to be cold and unfeeling. So again, we were struck by the fact that six of the seven girls had experienced early losses.

The one piece of data which we did not have in any of the girls is that of the onset of menses. We felt this was an important omission because the age of entry to the clinic suggests a possible correlation, and because, as will be seen later, these girls tend to view females and femaleness as a negative.

Looking next at the psychologicals for data (See Figure 12), we found that six of the girls showed poor self-esteem, five of the girls were lonely, showed sad or depressed affect and had reached at least the phallic—oedipal stage. Four of them avoided close relationships and had problems with aggressive feelings. Four of them showed evidence of some superego development. The main defenses used were denial, displacement and intellectualization. In three of the six girls who were tested we saw clear-cut evidence that women are seen as fearful, repulsive, hostile, weak and dam-

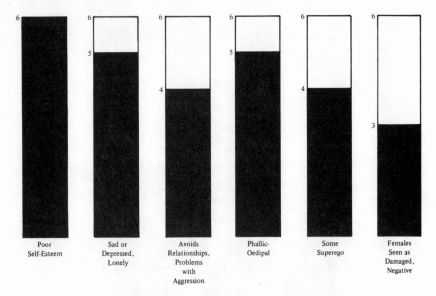

Figure 12. Girls 12-14 Years: Psychologicals

aged creatures. Sexual identification was therefore made extremely difficult for these girls who saw themselves as damaged and generally negative.

The psychiatrists indicated that six girls showed partly or completely internalized superego (See Figure 13). Five of them had poor self-esteem, were depressed and had reached the phallic-oedipal stage of development. One girl had no psychologicals or psychiatric evaluation recorded, so we were without that data. All the remaining girls were judged by the psychologist or psychiatrist or both as being depressed, reaching the phallic-oedipal stage, and having at least partly internalized superegos. Again, we can see the similarities between the boys and girls.

> For Example: C. is struggling with a pronounced case of depressive affect, strong unmet dependency needs, pervasive feelings of being emotionally shut off from her parents and a fear and anxiety about her security. Instead of withdrawal she is using a forced kind of intellectualized productivity to discharge tension and to keep herself from thinking about and experiencing her fears and anger. Her concept of females, including her own self-concept, is one of needfulness, damage, weakness and passive hostility.

Finally, we looked at the course of treatment with this group (See Figure 14.). Five of them had a female therapist at some point in time and

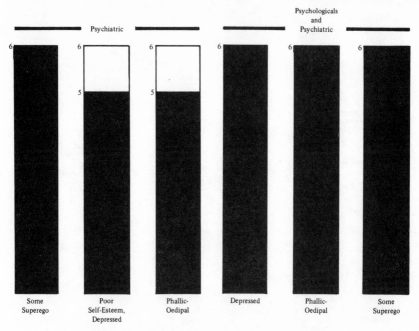

Figure 13. Girls 9-12: Psychologicals and Psychiatric

three had male therapists. Six had individual therapy, one had group therapy alone and one had group therapy in addition to individual. Two had
family therapy as an adjunct to the primary treatment modality. Five
of these girls were treated successfully and one is still in therapy. One girl
was terminated by her family and therapy was not felt to be successful.
The duration of treatment ranged from 20 weeks to 104 weeks. Again, as
with the boys, we see that these families tend to cooperate with long-term
therapy recommendations and do follow through.

For comparison, we looked at the two girls with depressive diagnoses
who were in the 9 to 11 age range. One of these two had a history of birth
defects and some somatic problems as did one of the girls in the 12 to 14
range. Both girls lost their fathers through death or divorce before the age
of six and both mothers then remarried. One girl's step-father is depressed
and the other has separated from his family. Again, we see the striking
history of early losses. The symptom list shows both girls to be depressed,
suspicious, rivalrous, impulsive, negativistic, untruthful and as having
problems with anger control and common sense. One girl had psychologicals which indicated she was depressed but it said nothing about superego
development. The other had no testing. The psychiatrics showed both girls
to be depressed and one girl to have good basic trust, an internalized
superego and to have reached the phallic-oedipal level. None of these

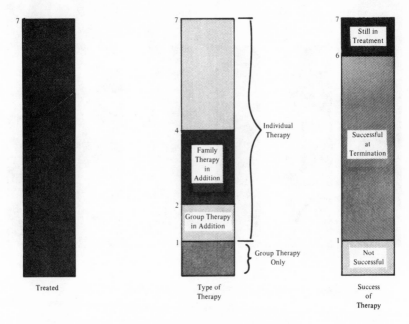

Figure 14. Girls 12-14: Treatment

features were mentioned in the other girl. Clearly these girls show marked similarities both to the other group of girls and to the nine- to eleven-year-old boys.

As to course of treatment, there were differences. Both girls were seen by female therapists in individual therapy. Both were terminated unsuccessfully; one in 6 weeks and one in 12 because their mothers withdrew from treatment.

To summarize our information about the girls: they were friendless, had somatic complaints, problems with anger control and school problems. They too experienced early losses through parents divorce and/or marital separations. They were lonely, depressed and withdrawn. They have some superego and have reached at least the phallic-oedipal stage. In an attempt to study this data from a statistical perspective, we performed a factor analysis. There were difficulties as we were comparing what we considered to be hard data, e.g. the symptom list which was consistent across all families, with softer data from psychologicals and psychiatricals. Nevertheless, the results are certainly suggestive.

Reported first are correlations on hard data from the symptom list, psychosocial history, and presenting problems. In assessing significance, we used stricter criteria than usual because of the problems in using a mix of both hard and soft data. These correlations are significant at the .025 to .01 level:

1. Failing in school and teacher as referral source correlating with mothers being treated for depression.

2. Clinging, restlessness and sleep problems all correlating with each other.

3. Somatic complaints correlating with fathers being out of home.

4. Underestimating oneself correlating with wanting affection and having too much guilt.

5. Anxiety about school correlating with problems with school achievement, impulsiveness and too much guilt.

6. Daydreaming correlating with negativism and untruthfulness.

7. Problems with anger control correlating with problems with school achievement.

Turning next to correlation of hard data with soft data from the psychologicals and psychiatrics, at the same level of significance, we found some theoretically interesting correlations:

1. Guilt over sexual feelings correlating with clinging and restlessness.

2. Displacement as a defense and aggressive or disobedient behavior correlating with partly internalized superego.

3. Underestimating oneself, correlating with internalized superego, punitive superego and shame.

4. Anxiety about school correlating with guilt and internalized superego.

5. Problems with school achievement correlating with guilt.

6. Aggression turned inward correlating with punitive superego, internalized superego correlating with shame, and poor self-esteem.

7. Depression correlating with loneliness, unmet needs, oral dependency—reaching the phallic-oedipal level—correlating negatively with a partly internalized superego.

Finally, we looked at symptoms which clustered together into factors, finding:

Factor 1: Clinging restlessness, sleep problems, low achievement, mother hospitalized for depression, and child raised by grandparent.

Factor 2: Lonely, unmet needs, oral dependency, sad or depressed affect, denial as a defense.

Factor 3: Reached phallic-oedipal level, guilt over losses, friendlessness, and somatic complaints.

Factor 4: Suspiciousness, negativism, untruthfulness, and avoids relationships.

Factor 5: Depressed, wants affection, negativism, punitive superego.

Factor 6: Lying, aggressive behavior, displacement as defense.

In summary, using data from both our major groups—nine- to eleven-year-old boys and twelve- to fourteen-year-old girls—we found the following:

Of a total of 18 cases, there was no consistency or indication of trends in the presenting problems which would lead to a strong prediction of depression. On the symptom list checked by parents, two factors did emerge. Fifteen out of eighteen children were seen as depressed and twelve out of eighteen had problems with anger control.

Family histories showed that 15 out of 18 children experienced some type of early loss, e.g. through marital separations, death, hospitalization of a parent or depression in the mothers.

The psychologicals and psychiatrics showed that 15 out of 18 children were seen as having a sad or depressed affect, 16 out of 18 had some internalized superego formation and 13 out of 18 had reached at least the phallic-oedipal stage of development.

As to the course of treatment, we found that 15 out of 18 families accepted our recommendation for therapy. Two of these 15 families are still being seen; one is presently being reevaluated for further therapy. Three were terminated by the families and were not seen as successful. Nine of the 15 seen in therapy were successfully terminated.

These children are, as the titles suggest, both cross and glum. Yet the chances of successfully facilitating emotional growth through therapy are certainly encouraging.

To quote from the termination summary on one of these children:

"Before termination: B. seems to have her libidinal and aggressive drives under good control, with little or no impulsivity. She no longer needs the secondary gain from illness to fulfill her dependency needs. Her defenses have become more varied and more advanced. Her superego does not appear to be as strict and punitive. She has greater feelings of self-worth and more self-esteem. She also takes more pride in herself as a female." (See Figure 15.).

Following the pilot study on depressed children, we decided to look more closely at the trends we had noticed. Our immediate goal was to determine which, if any, of the variables already identified could reliably and statistically differentiate between our target groups of children with the depressed diagnosis and a group of nondepressed children from the same clinic population.

Methodology

Subjects: In choosing the subjects to be used for the statistical analysis, we focused on the two major groups of depressed children as described

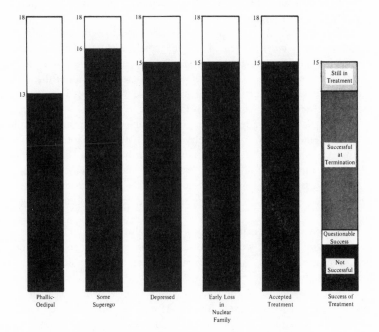

Figure 15. Summary: Boys 9-11, Girls 12-14

in the first part of this chapter. The total N=18 for both the depressed and control group collapsing across sexes. For depressed and control males, N=11, for depressed and control females, N=7.

In choosing the control group we used a random sample of children picked from those cases admitted to the clinic immediately following the admittance of each depressed child. The cases were matched for age and sex, had a diagnosis other than that of depression and had proceeded beyond the Intake interview. Several of the original controls had to be discounted because of insufficient data so we found it necessary to specify that the child had to have proceeded beyond our initial Intake contact.

Data: We evaluated each child on a list of 93 different variables. The variables came from a number of different sources and incorporated both hard and soft data. Hard data included the symptom check list which each of the parent(s) filled out after Intake; the questions and method of presentation were identical across all children. Other data included family history as taken from a psychosocial study, and a list of presenting symptoms which parents give verbally on Intake and during the course of the psychosocial interviews. This latter list was developed by recording each presenting symptom mentioned for the depressed groups and then applying it to the control groups as well.

Soft data include the reports from the psychologist and child psychiatrist who were involved in the diagnostic evaluation of each child. Usually, both the testing and psychiatric interviewing were done in this clinic; nevertheless, there were a few cases where part or all of the evaluation had been done elsewhere. This material was assessed in the same manner with no note being made of the source.

Each variable was rated on its presence or absence in a given child's chart material. The major difficulty in this type of dichotomous rating is that the absence of data does not necessarily mean a "no" response. Report writing is variable across individuals and what one psychologist or psychiatrist deemed important to record may be seen by another as trivial. Consequently, the "no" response is in a "no-don't know" category.

Statistics: The statistics used for data analysis were the chi square to test for significance between depressed and control groups collapsed across sex, and the Fisher's Exact Probabilities Test to determine significance between depressed and controls within like-sex groups. We chose to use the latter test because of the small N within each cell which resulted from our comparison within sexes. Both these tests assume that each variable analyzed will be independently sampled. However, we performed multiple tests all involving the same sample. Consequently, our potential for Type I error was greatly increased. To counteract this, we used more stringent criteria in assigning significance, only discussing results where we have a P value of .01.

Reliability: Reliability and generalizability of results found in this study is very poor, based on the fact that the same investigator rated all the control samples. Consequently, we are even unable to say that the same results would be found again, using an identical control group and the same variables, if the ratings were to be done by other investigators.

Results: As can be seen in Table I, a total of 19 of the 93 variables studied appear to be important in differentiating between depressed and nondepressed children. Of these, sixteen variables differentiated both male and female depressed children from male and female controls. Eight variables differentiated between male depressed and controls and eight differentiated between female depressed and controls. Only one variable, low self-esteem, differentiated in both the male and the female group.

Interestingly, it can be seen that the psychologists' data appears able to differentiate depressed from nondepressed females; psychiatric data differentiates likewise for depressed and nondepressed males. Neither psychiatric or psychological data differentiated for both sexes.

Discussion: In looking at this data, it is interesting first of all to compare our results with those trends we saw in the first section of this chapter. Summarizing across sexes, we saw a high percentage of depressed children having: (a) reached the phallic-oedipal level; (b) showing evidence of some superego; (c) manifesting sad or depressed affect at home and/or during evaluation, (d) experiencing in early loss, and (e) accepting and being successfully treated.

Taking each of these factors separately, we find some differences when we include a control group. Factor *(a)* does not appear as significant in differentiating depressed from nondepressed children. Level of psychosexual development could hypothetically be inferred and even then, one must accept the premise that a child can experience guilt only when he has an internalized superego. This in turn, presupposes that the child has reached the phallic-oedipal level of development.

Factor *(b)* reappears as potentially significant when we look at depressed vs. nondepressed children. It is seen primarily under psychiatric data as a punitive superego. Note should be made of a P=.05, and of the act that it shows significance only across sexes. Again, we can say that there is an apparent trend toward the necessary presence of adequate

TABLE I

Variables Differentiating Depressed From Non-depressed Referred Children

Variables	P Value		
	Males and Females (a)	Males Alone (b)	Females Alone (b)
I. Presenting Symptoms			
failing in school	.02	.02	NS
friendless	.05	NS	.05
sleep problems	.05	.02	NS
II. Parents			
divorced	.05	.02	NS
father cold, unfeeling	.05	NS	.04
III. Symptom List			
*fearful	.01	.01	NS
depressed	.01	NS	NS
problems in school achievement	NS	NS	.05
IV. Psychologicals			
avoids relationships	NS	NS	.02
lonely	.01	NS	.02
sad or depressed affect	NS	NS	.025
displacement as defense	.02	NS	NS
poor self-esteem	.01	NS	.004
V. Psychiatry			
aggression turned inward	.02	.03	NS
punitive superego	.05	NS	NS
guilt	.05	NS	NS
low self-esteem	.02	.05	NS
sad or depressed affect	.02	.05	NS
identification with same sex	.02	.02	NS

*Depressed children were less fearful than nondepressed.
(a) Chi-Square Test of significance
(b) Fisher's Exact Probabilities Test

superego development as a factor in neurotic depression in children, but we cannot state this definitively.

Turning to factor *(c)* in our depressed-nondepressed group, we see sad or depressed affect appearing three times. From the symptom list data, (P=.05) we note that barely more than half the parents of depressed children actually noticed the presence of this affect. In the nondepressed group, exactly half the parents saw their children as having some symptoms of depression. One wonders whether parents of children diagnosed as depressed are themselves struggling with depression and an inability to tune in to their children or whether sadness is simply a common childhood affect present in close to 50% of this clinic's population of boys ages nine to eleven and girls ages twelve to fourteen.

The presence of sad or depressed affect appears again as a trend in the psychologists' data for girls only (P=.025). It arises for the third time in the psychiatrists' data where a trend (P=.02) was seen across sexes and within males alone (P=.05). Apparently, the presence or absence of the affective component of depression is recognizable to a larger degree by professionals who are assessing a child diagnostically than by parents. In general, we can say that the trend found in the first section of this chapter is supported by this later data.

In examining factor *(d)* we note that two pieces of data from the Parental History lend support to the trend that early loss may be a factor in depression. It is interesting to note that it is the fathers' lack of availability which is significant. Additionally, it seems that male children may fare better with a father's presence, no matter to what degree he is emotionally available; female children appear to be less affected by an absent father than by one who is emotionally cold and unfeeling. Perhaps this data supports the theory that successful resolution of the Oedipal Complex is intereferred with by different fathers for males than for females.

In factor *(e)* we see that acceptance of recommendations for, and successful completion of, treatment did not appear to be significantly different between depressed and nondepressed children. On the other hand, it is possible but not demonstrable from this data that other diagnostic groups taken separately might confirm the trend toward a greater success rate with depressed children.

As stated earlier, the only factors we consider to be significant differentiators between depressed and nondepressed children are those of fearfulness, poor self-esteem and lonelinesss (P<.01). It is especially important to note that nondepressed children are seen by parents as having many more fears. It can be speculated that because depressed children turn aggressive feelings inward upon themselves they have less need to project these impulses onto external objects. On the other hand, their use of displacement as a defense (P=.02) could be seen as inconsistent with the above formulation.

Loneliness and poor self-esteem may be viewed as inextricably woven together. If loneliness is a descriptive term for the feeling of emotional distance or isolation from others, we can speculate that at its roots is a feeling a little self-worth stemming from guilt over an ambivalently held object. We have hypothesized that depressed children are unable to cope with their aggressive feelings toward love objects and experience guilt and a feeling of "badness" about themselves because of these aggressive feelings. In other words, guilt and "badness" contribute to their sense of being unworthy to enter into relationships with others and this results in the emotional distance or loneliness described.

In summary, we are able to say that the data we have collected and analyzed thus far indicates that there are trends which confirm the psychoanalytic theory of neurotic depression as it is understood by psychologists and psychiatrists in this clinic. One ultimate goal which evolves from this study is to look for further statistical confirmation of the theory that neurotic depression in children—as differentiated from a more severe type, e.g. anaclitic—has at its roots a real or fantasized loss of love-object, with a component of guilt related to the loss and stemming from an introjection or turning inwards of the anger experienced toward the lost object. A final goal for further research is to eventually be able to predict a diagnosis of Psychoneurotic Disorder Depression Type from a given constellation of factors found in hard data, e.g. presenting symptoms and/or family history. This would be particularly helpful as a contribution toward identifying another population at risk.

CHAPTER 18

Psychotherapy of the Depressed Child

DORIS C. GILPIN, M.D.

It seems clear that depressed children are not all alike so obviously the therapy cannot be stereotyped. Children seem to be labeled "depressed" if they display any kind of unhappiness other than feelings of anxiety or its relatives. We have seen that there are major types of variants on what the depressed affect is really like. Dr. Malmquist pointed out the important fact that in the case of the depressed affect the child feels that something has *already happened* whereas in the case of anxiety there is the apprehension that something *will happen*.

I would like to discuss the two main variants that we saw at the clinic. First is the boy with early losses in his life. Even though the loss may not have been when he was an infant he tends to feel the loss as a deprivation of basic nuturing. He tends to blame his own angers, or assertions, or self for his loss. The angers and assertions are often from a considerably higher level of development whereas assertion in competition with the parent is to be expected. In these children's fantasies their normal impulses are felt as bad, dangerous and need to be punished by uncomfortable guilt at the least. Even though they feel they deserve this guilt and depression, they are also trying to escape their just deserts by using defenses against feelings. They also intellectualize, isolate the feelings, deny or displace them.

Two of these defenses are said to be usually associated with toddler-age origin of problems. There seems to be no particular reason in the history of these children for the toddler age being special except in its meaning of separations and what that might mean in terms of losses. The defenses chosen are particularly socially acceptable ones however, and may say something about the investment these children have in social acceptability. These children feel lonely but they don't deserve loneliness. Presumably, however, they must protect others from their own dangerousness by not cultivating warm relationships; think of the ambivalence they must have about getting into a relationship! If they do develop one, it is liable to be broken by loss and they feel as if they cannot take that again. Nevertheless, they yearn for relationships. Furthermore, they have mothers who, shattered by their own early losses, can provide no help in handling a loss and, in fact, probably have been preoccupied with their own depressed feelings at the age when the child most needed nurturing.

For the boys then, a loss revives the pain of the unnurtured time. These boys in their sadness—possibly hopelessness and helplessness—cannot bother with their school work or bother with all the rules in the ordinary course of their lives. It should be carefully noted that with individual attention they carefully cooperate in doing a task. They do bother to try in a one-to-one situation. How can we understand that? Has there been a temporary replacement for the loss or a symbol of a superego that can be satisfied, at least for a space? Or a corrective emotional experience with someone who is not depressed and gratifying? It is not really clear. In any case, their symptoms do not seem to express fixed personality coping patterns, but express results of a draining, paralyzing affect. They seem to be saying, "I wasn't worth enough to make my mother happy or nurturing, I've gotten rid of my father. I needed them both, but I haven't deserved them because of my pushiness and rage and what I am. Since it is all gone, why try further?"

If we look at the adolescent girls, there is a variation. The girls seem to be understood a little differently. Their loss seems to be a loss of belief in the wholeness of the value of being a woman, which is experienced by them as also a loss of nurturance—of the feeling of not being worth providing for.

The Therapy

All of this suggests some of what is needed in therapy. The child is ambivalently open to a relationship which will give him a feeling of self-worth. He will need a lot of help understanding that termination of the relationship at the end of therapy does not prove his own degradation. Termination is a very crucial part of therapy with this child. He will need help in accepting his own aggressive and assertive wishes without guilt.

Thus, the early phase can be seen as making a relationship, supporting the child, "you are worthwhile." It is important that the child feel accepted just as he is. If he perceives that you do not accept the fact that he feels he is worthwhile then he may not trust you. It is better to say, "Yes, you have had very bad wishes but you are still worthwhile."

The middle phase roughly contains a developing insight such as "You are angry at your mother and you feel that is why she died." For the girls, "You feel that is why you are damaged" or "You feel you have been too much trouble for your parents and that is why they do not seem to want to please you or take care of you."

The final phase is preparation for more healthy acceptance of loss, the loss of the therapist. "You can mourn and rage at me now before I leave you. You deserve to have these feelings and I can endure them. They do not send me away. The only thing that sends me away is your ability now to make it without me."

At the end of the first phase, the children's behavior is often greatly improved and some of the passivity and helplessness about their own future is gone. Often one runs into problems with families who wish to terminate at this point, when it is not yet the proper time.

I will now present a process of a treated case. It was somewhat typical of the boys' group, although this particular boy was a little older.

First Session

He held back and didn't open doors for me or even hold them after me. After I had opened them, he would walk through while I held them. I indicated that he could sit anywhere he liked and he hesitated between a folding chair and a softer chair; finally, he took the softer chair. I talked of how sorry I was about last time when I hadn't been able to see him. I said that I had gotten a message that his aunt was sick today; he said she was.

I asked how he had gotten here. He said that he came by cab. I said, "Boy, you went to a lot of trouble to get here."

I wondered if anybody had explained to him why we felt he needed to come here. He didn't think anybody had. I asked if he had gotten the results of his testing and if people had told him what the tests had shown. He said that no one had. I asked him if he would like to hear about them, and he thought he would. I said that I would try to have the chart and discuss it with him next time.

I asked how he felt about the testing and he said he rather enjoyed it. I said that maybe he would enjoy doing some of the things he had been doing then. I got out paper and a pencil but he said he couldn't draw. I said, "I guess that means you feel that you are not very good at it," and asked if that was what he meant. He said it was. I said that I guessed that was kind of hard to take—to feel that you can't do something very well. He agreed. I asked if he felt that he had done good on the testing and he felt that he had not. I said that *is* hard to take. He was kind of whimpering and making noises. I said that it seemed like he was trying to say something and I wondered if he could. He shook his head no, but eventually he said, "If you haven't got it, you haven't got it." He then said, "Then you try hard and you do good." I said that it sounded like he felt he didn't have it for the things that he would like and I wondered what he would like best to be good at. He thought for a while and said reading. I said that was a real good decision because reading is certainly very important and it is probably more important than the other things that he felt he couldn't do, like the drawing. He was kind of whimpering some more. I talked of how it seemed like it really hurt when he was thinking about this sort of thing. I wondered if anything had helped with the reading. He thought the school had made some efforts and that they did help. He described some remediation that he had had at school. He said something about why he was whimpering that caused me to say that he could really explain things well and that I really had a feeling for what he was experiencing and I thought he was brave to go through this hurting. He then more cheerfully began talking about bikes.

This session illustrates his feeling of not being good enough and shows the therapist trying to find areas to give realistic support.

At the second session, I gave him information about his evaluation which he seemed to try very hard to understand.

Third Session

At the following session, this exchange occurred:
I asked him if he would mind letting me know some of his dreams. He

thought for a while and then told one about when he was a motorcycle jumper. I said, "Oh, like Evel Knievel?" and he agreed. I said, "How did it go?" He jumped the motorcycle, but it didn't make it—the rear wheel hit and so he didn't make it. I said, "My gosh, you're brave to try it right all over again." I asked how it came out that time. He said he still didn't make it. I asked if he was hurt. He said he had gotten a scratch on his arm. I said that was too bad. I asked what happened next, and he said he woke up.

He thought for a while and then he said he had had a dream about being a songwriter. He told this dream a little less clearly, but the idea was that he wrote songs and then he made a lot of money ($50,000 for each night's appearance). He traveled all over the country. I asked if more happened in that dream and he said no. I asked if he woke up and he said no.

I said I guessed he just went on to something else and he agreed. I said it sounded like he not only was a songwriter but he was a singer because he went around and sang his own songs. He agreed. I asked if he could remember what any of the songs were about and he said, "Well, one was called, 'Baby, I Love You.' "

I said that sounded like a pretty good title. It was kind of a song title that would maybe catch people's attention. I asked if he knew how any of the song went and he sang two lines that went, "Everytime I look at you, you make me feel all brand new."

It was actually a pretty good tune. I said that it really seemed pretty good. I asked if when he was a songwriter in the dream if he wrote the song out on paper or if he just invented it in his head and then put it on paper. He said he put it on paper first and then he would try it out and see how it went. I said that's about the hardest way to write music. I asked if he had really written down this song and he said his sister had. He then said he had decided he wouldn't be a songwriter because he needed too much equipment like the amplifiers and all so that probably his real dream was of being a businessman.

I asked what kind of a business and he said he would sell tires. I said, "Well, what would you need for that?" He said he would need some different kinds of trucks and cars and a storage place. He said he would also need a bank account. I asked if he had any of those things and he said he didn't. I said well it sounded like a little bit more than what he needed as the songwriter because he at least had part of one song. I said he had a lot of ideas of things to do—motorcycle jumper, songwriter, businessman.

The time was up and I said that I would like to know if the time had been long enough, or just right, or too short. He felt it was too short. I said it seemed too short for me, too, and I wondered if there was any way to help his mother get them there on time; he couldn't think of any way. I wondered if there was any way Mrs. Allen could help his mother get him here on time. Again he didn't know of any way. I said, well maybe we could think about that and see if we could figure out something that could help her do it. I said since it seems so short today I thought I'd be able to give you a little extra time. I said I do have to see somebody else pretty soon and I had meant to make some phone calls before I saw this other person, but the phone calls aren't all that important. I can postpone them until another time. He said, "Oh, that's okay. You can make your phone calls." I said, "Well, it is very nice of you to say that it is okay, but really they aren't that important and I think it is probably more important for you to have a little bit more time today." He then said he had had another daydream of someday drilling for oil, maybe at the North Pole or Alaska. He wondered if that was where they drilled in the water offshore and I said that I knew that they did do some offshore drilling for oil in some places. He thought that he would rather drill for oil in some warm place in the ocean and he thought there should be some places in the ocean that would be warmer where there would be oil. I said it would certainly be more pleasant to drill for oil where it was warm and comfortable. I said the time was up and I did have to see the next person. We said goodbye.

Fourth Session

Here we saw John sharing some of his compensatory fantasies and not being crushed. He talked about a neighbor who treated him like a son. I said, "He must care about you."

John said, "He likes me." I asked, "How come."

John indicated that he helped the neighbor and I said, "So you take care of them. That would be one thing to like. I imagine there are other things to like about you."

I inquired what he liked about himself and he couldn't think. He did think he liked others who were kind. We see he feels valued only for services rendered, but the therapist is trying to introduce other possibilities.

In the fifth session he told of being in a swim race where he came in last and also where the coach thought he had been cheating.

Sixth Session

He asked me if I had voted, I said I had. He asked if I voted for the schools and I said, "Yes, but they hadn't passed, I noticed."

He said that was right. I asked if his mother voted. He said she didn't.

I asked about that. He said that she had worked until 4:30 and then she had to come home and she had to clean. I said it sounded like she felt she was too busy and he agreed. I asked if she was a pretty busy person. He felt she was. I said I guessed she was busy trying to get some money for the family and he said, "No, what she was busy at was paying the bills." He named some of the bills. I said that she was putting out the money when she was busy, not taking it in. He agreed and he said, "Boy, with five children, whew."

I said it sounded like she thought some things were more important than voting. He thought she usually felt voting was important because sometimes she worked at the polls. He thought that what happened this time was that she just had to get cleaned up for Thanksgiving; that she really felt she had to. I said it sounded like she felt that was more important than voting for the schools.

We see how he is unable to criticize an important maternal figure. The therapist does not force the issue but indicated there may be other possibilities.

Later: I said, "Oh, you have some dogs." He said yes, he had two. I asked their names. He said, "It's Lady and King."

I said, "Those are interesting names. One must be a girl dog and one must be a boy dog."

He said that was right. I had asked if they had ever had puppies and he said that they had. He said that he is supposed to put them in the garage at certain times so that they won't get picked up by the dog catcher and he just talks to them and they go into the garage. He said that if you give them a dog biscuit when they have done something good, they'll do it again. I asked him if he figured that out himself or if someone told him about it. He said that a teacher at school had told him to give the dog biscuits and talk to the dog. He said he used to whack the dog but now he gives him rewards. I said, "And it works when you talk to them and give them rewards?" And he said it did. This introduced the question of the best kind of discipline.

Seventh Session

He talked a great deal about a movie. He had seen *Planet of the Apes*. I asked how he liked it and he liked it real well. In the film, the apes were all working for the humans. He described it at length . . . about how the humans kept the apes working for them by using policemen that had sort of electric prods so that the apes couldn't sit down and some kind of force field to keep them captured and some kind of electric way of doing something to their heads. He said it looked like it really hurt. The apes finally rebelled. I said the hurting seemed pretty awful. I said I knew there were some people who thought that was the way to get others to do things. I said I thought there were better ways than hurting people to get things done. I said most of the time I didn't think it was so important to get something done as to find ways to get along together without hurting. I said I knew that he kind of had the same feeling about not hurting to get things done. I said the way he talked when he really didn't like to spank his dogs. He agreed. He said he really liked it when the apes rebelled and I asked if after they rebelled they had started hurting the humans and he said they had not. I said I bet they were pretty mad and lots of people when they are pretty mad really want to hurt back. He said they did have the humans working for them. He again said how much he liked it when the apes rebelled and took over. I said it sounded like it had a happy ending and he agreed. I asked if he would have liked to have been one of the characters in the movie. He said he would. I asked him which one. He said he would like to be a policeman. I said, "One of the policemen that hurt the apes?" He said no.

At the end there were some ape policeman and they didn't have those electric prods and things. They rode horses. I said, "So they didn't hurt anybody?" He said no they didn't . . . they just looked around and kept watch. They did have swords but he never saw them use them. I said I could see why he would like being a policeman, if he could ride on a horse because I knew he would like that. I hadn't known that he was interested in swords. I said there were some sports with swords. Some of the schools even taught fighting with swords as one of the sports. I asked if his school did and he said no. I asked if he had ever played at sword fighting and he had. I said I didn't know of any place that taught fighting with swords on horseback but they certainly used to do it in the olden days—like in the days of the knights. He said something about swords being better than guns.

Here he does begin to verbalize wishes to rebel against hurting authority which the therapist is supporting.

Eighth Session

I had said that he was pretty close to being on time today. He was not too many minutes late. I asked how he had managed that. He said he had gotten a cab. I asked if he had called the cab himself. He said that he went out and looked for a cab—that it was better that way and he got one quicker. He thought he could look for a cab a little earlier and I said that he had made it pretty good this time. As you see he is taking more responsibility.

He started talking about the fights he gets into. Other boys pick on him and he fights. He is worried about this because his parents have told him that he should just ignore it and walk away. Sometimes he is able to ignore it, and he is fighting less. He gets into fights only about once a year now, he thinks. I asked if his parents got mad when he got into a fight. He explained they don't whip him but they just tell him that when he is older he'll be better able to ignore the others and he won't be in fights. I asked if that was true of his folks and he thought it was. I asked if he would like to be like they are when he grows up and he was uncertain.

Ninth Session

He started looking thoughtful. When he looked up in my eyes I asked him what he had been thinking about and he said that he had been thinking about becoming a daredevil but it was a problem because one part of him wanted to be a daredevil and the other part of him didn't want to get hurt. I said that really was a problem.

He said he wants his children to look up to their father. He wants them to know that he's not just an ordinary, everyday person but that he's a daredevil, really somebody. I said that I could understand him wanting that and that it must partly mean that he himself has wanted to look up to his dad. He thought he had. At this point, he was kind of torn. He was saying his dad was a tire salesman and he did look up to him, but he was also obviously caught by not wanting to say he could look up to him more if he was more of a daredevil. I said that I understood that he did sort of look up to his dad but I thought he was also having some feelings that he would look up to him even more if he had been a daredevil. He still couldn't quite agree to this. He finally did say that his dad had once had a motorcycle and had sold it. I asked what happened. He didn't know. I asked if he could ask his dad and find out. He thought maybe he could. I also had asked if he could tell his dad that he would like to look up to him. He thought he could look up to him as a tire salesman already.

Again, he is ambivalent about authority or identification figures.

Tenth Session

He didn't want to go around and sell candy for his school. I asked about that. He said he would rather watch T.V. than do that. I said that I could understand that and I wondered if there was something about the way people treated him when he knocked on the door to sell candy. He said he had sold candy once before and sold about three boxes. The people were nice to him. He said you only got fifteen pieces of candy for a dollar. I asked if one reason he didn't want to sell it was because he thought maybe people would be mad that they weren't getting enough candy. He thought that might be part of it. I said that I could understand that. I calculated on a piece of paper how much each piece of candy would cost, and I said that wasn't too bad. He wondered if I would like to buy a box and I said yes. Then I gave him a dollar. He thought he might go out and try to sell some more. The time was up and I wished him good fortune if he did go and try to sell.

He is still hanging back from self-assertion.

Eleventh Session

He kind of laughed and said his sister was good at talking for she talked on and on and on and you couldn't get her to shut up. I said he said that she was good at talking and I guessed he meant she was good at being able to talk a long time but it also sounded like he thought there were some things bad about it and he agreed. I said that what one person thinks is being good at something might be seen by somebody else as being bad. It all depended.

Twelfth Session

There was a short silence and I said that I had been thinking about how much talking I did when we were together. I knew how he kind of laughed about his sister talking all the time; you could hardly shut her up and maybe sometimes he had the same feeling about me. I said I hoped that if he did feel that I was talking too much that he would be able to tell me and probably I could shut up. He kind of laughed about this. He is slowly being helped to express negative feelings about authorities.

He then told of being assertive on a field trip and enjoying it.

I said speaking of Christmas we probably ought to talk about the fact that Christmas day falls on Wednesday which is his day to come here and so does New Year's and, of course, we wouldn't meet on Christmas day and New Year's day. He looked very crestfallen about this. He said that he was going to see a James Bond movie on Christmas. I said that I thought he had been going to see the Super Stooges and he said that he called the theater and they said that it wasn't going to be on after all. I said it seemed when he wasn't going to be coming here, he was thinking about that and then he had to think about something that he was going to do; he agreed.

He looked thoughtful and crestfallen again and then looked up and said, "There is something that I don't know even though I have been coming here a long time."

I asked, "What's that?"

He said, "I don't know your name."

Thus he is just beginning to notice the importance of the therapeutic relationship.

Fourteenth Session

At this session he talked of spending his own money to build models of which he is very proud; of earning money in two part-time jobs.

There was a silence and then he noticed my name plate and asked if my first name was Doris and I said that it was. He said that he was probably going to be on time from now on and I said that I had noticed that he had been on time today and I wondered how he managed it. He said that he figured out that he could take a bus. He noticed that a bus went right past the school and came very close to here. It is only a two block walk. I said that was really great. He figured out how to do it and get here on time and also save money. I wondered if it was his money he had been spending on the taxi and he said no; it was his mother's. I said well, whether it was for her or for him, he was still saving money. He pulled the map out of his pocket and showed me how he could find his way around the city and also showed me where the Herbert Hoover Boy's Club was on the map.

He had also gotten into a drum and bugle corp. Thus, this session indicated his taking an active role in his future.

Fifteenth Session

I should say that coming up the stairs I had forgotten and opened the first door and he said loudly, "Thank you." I said, "Oh, dear, I forgot, didn't I." He said I had. At the second door I did stand back and he opened the door and I said, "Thank you."

After a silence I said I had really kind of worried about the sucker he had given me. I knew how he felt about his father not using gifts he gave him and I had worried about how he might feel about me not using the gift of the sucker. He said he was kind of disappointed that I didn't take the sucker and I said that I really was sorry for disappointing him but I felt I really must not. He said he doesn't get fat. At that point, he looked terribly embarrassed, apparently about using the word fat and said that he didn't put on weight when he ate. He could eat anything and maybe put on no more than ten pounds. I said that was really nice that he could.

For the first time, John has allowed himself to criticize the therapist.

Sixteenth Session

I asked if his mother usually understood his worries about things and he thought she did. He felt that he and she tend to worry about the same things. I commented that he sort of took after her then and he agreed. I asked in what way wouldn't he want to take after her and he kind of balked at that. I said you know you can like somebody and not want to be like them in everything. For instance, I know you wouldn't want to be like me being fat. You have a good shape just like you are now and I'm sure you prefer it to having a shape like mine. I asked him if he didn't agree. He very embarrassedly did agree. He said there is one thing about his mother that he wouldn't want to be like. He wouldn't want to be a girl.

He felt that his mother was pretty understanding. She just talked to him. Sometimes she might take T.V. away but usually she just talked and didn't yell or howl. She certainly didn't whip him. I said, was he saying that his father is not as understanding. His father doesn't whip although he used to spank, but now he just talks in kind of a scolding tone. His father says he is not scolding, that he is just trying to teach him so that he won't do the same thing the next time. I said that it sounded as if he felt that it was like scolding and he agreed. I wondered what had made his father stop spanking and he said that father had decided that this made them tougher. I asked if father had figured that out himself or how he had learned that. He said that father said he learned it from his childhood. Father felt that he got tough as a boy when he was whipped, but when he was just talked to then he really learned. I asked what he had done that had brought this on from his folks sometimes. He thought a long time and decided it was when he beat his dogs about a month ago. It seems that they brought trash in the yard and he had to clean it up. He talked to them nicely so they could get close. He said that when his father was spanking the children that they just got worse so spanking hadn't taught them anything. He thinks that is pretty true for dogs, too. I asked how he felt about these talks and he feels kind of guilty when he thinks about hitting the dogs. His mother likes to play with the dogs a lot. I asked if she plays with them more than with him and he didn't think so. I said I hadn't ever heard him talk about playing with her. He said, oh, they would tease her about saying, "Good-night, mom" and then they would say, "Good-night, mom" again and she would tell them to go on. I said, I had meant things like checkers or monopoly. He said that they didn't have a checker set but they did have a monopoly set and she did play that with them. His sister always wants to be the banker. I said she does play with you then and he agreed. She also bakes delicious cakes and delicious cookies. He indicated that they could have cakes and cookies anytime they asked. I said, "Anytime?" and he said, "Well, sometimes she is nervous."

I asked, "What happens when she is nervous?"

There was a lot of hemming and hawing and I had to go after it a little bit. But he did say she gets a headache or gets sick. The times that she gets mad, she gets nervous and then she gets a headache and goes to her room. They try very hard not to get her mad. I said that the time was up, but I could tell that this was a worry to him about his mother getting nervous and maybe we could talk about it some more next time.

He has at last been able to be a bit critical of his mother.

Seventeenth Session

Again I apologized. I said that last time, right at the end, we had been discussing some things that were important and that we really hadn't had a chance to finish talking about them. I said we had been talking about his mother and when she got mad and nervous and then got headaches or sick. I asked if he'd like to talk about it further and he said he would. Then there was a long silence while it was obvious he was trying to think how to begin. I finally said it really seemed hard to get started. He said he just didn't know how to get started. I asked if that meant that there are many ways to get started. He said yes.

He then said he would start by talking about the kids that do something they know they shouldn't do. Then his mother talks to them but she gets mad and upset and then she goes to bed. He said that she has high blood pressure and she gets shots and the doctor says it is under control now. I asked what would happen if it weren't under control. He said she would probably have to go to the hospital. He repeated a couple of times that it's under control now. I said it seemed like it was sort of a worry to him anyway.

He said another thing that upsets his mother is death. There was a neighbor across the street who died and his mother was so upset that she couldn't talk about it and she couldn't go to the funeral. His father gets pretty upset about death too. His father didn't go to the funeral either. I said it really seemed like it bothered him a lot and he said it did. He said that his mother dreams of death. I asked him if his mother told him about these dreams and he said she did. I wondered aloud why she told him. He said she wants to prepare the children for the way life really is when they grow up. He said one dream that she had was that his brother died because of lack of vitamins. I said that was quite a scary dream. He said that then his mother made him take a lot of vitamins and eat what he was supposed to eat; he forgets to take his vitamins before a meal. I said that he certainly looked healthy enough and I didn't see any signs of not having enough vitamins. I said it sounded as if his mother felt that the dreams might come true.

He seemed to be getting more uncomfortable and he suddenly changed the subject by asking if I knew where he could get a second-hand mini-bike. I said maybe he could look at the want ads and maybe somebody would have one for sale second-hand. I asked if he knew what the want ads were and he knew because his mother sometimes marked them. I said they have different headings. I didn't know exactly what heading would be for mini-bikes and bikes. It might be for other things. He said that if a mini-bike cost about $125.00, then he might be able to get a second-hand one for $80.00 which he would have pretty soon. He said he called Sears and they had one for $125.00 but they also had a few more that were more like $200.00. I said that was really good that he called Sears and found out what he needed to know. He said his bike's alright but he sometimes gets tired of pedaling and would like to get on a mini-bike and go "zoom, zoom, zoom." I said that seemed like the way he felt about what we were talking about. He was getting pretty tired of talking about his mother and wanted to start talking about mini-bikes and going "zoom, zoom." He kind of laughed at this.

How frightening this boy's death wishes to a maternal figure are! But he's beginning to face them.

Eighteenth Session

He was right on time. He asked if we had changed for a new time. I said yes we had. It was now 2:00 instead of 1:00. I said we had talked about it last week and maybe there was some misunderstanding. He said that he thought it was just for that one time because of a meeting. I said it was because of a meeting but it is for every time because the meeting is for every week. I asked if it was inconvenient for him and he said no. I said he must have had some worries if he thought the time was supposed to be 1:00 and here he was arriving at 2:00. He said he was worried. I asked if he had told his mother his worries and he said no.

He said that he knew her appointment was at 2:00 with Mrs. Allen. I said it sounded like he didn't want to worry her with his worries and he agreed. I said that I knew we had talked about that when he didn't want her to get mad or sick or have high blood pressure. I said sometimes I got the feeling he treated me that way too. I said it seemed to me that he tried not to worry me as if it were inconvenient for him. He kind of agreed that he wouldn't like to worry me. I said that I really was quite healthy; that he didn't need to worry about sickness or high blood pressure. I said as far as getting mad, I didn't intend on getting mad, but even when I did I thought he could count on me not doing anything too bad. I said certainly the way he tried to keep worries away from his mother showed how very important she was to him and he agreed. I said I knew he had had bad luck in his life about losing people who were important to him so I could understand why he would feel like taking care of somebody important to him. I wondered if it would bother him too much to talk about how it was before he came to live with his mother. He thought for a while and then said that his cousin had a new bicycle and he didn't. I said that I expected he had a lot of feelings about that. He must have been mad and maybe wondered why nobody cared enough about him to get him a new bicycle. I asked if he cried and he said he kicked the furniture. I told him he was really mad and he agreed he was.

I asked if people let him be mad or did they try to keep him from feeling that. He said they kind of let him be mad. He talked in a rather angry voice of how his cousin wouldn't even let him ride the bike. It was a three-speed racer. It turned out his cousin was only a year older than he. He said he didn't see his cousin very often and I said probably he doesn't have good feelings about him. He said when he doesn't think about the bicycle then he doesn't feel mad at his cousin. he said now he has a bicycle. It isn't three-speed, but is is a bicycle. I said he was soon going to have enough money for a mini-bike and he grinned. I said I saw why it seemed better with the mother he was with now than with other people. He was then helped to talk of his rejection by another aunt and his mother's death.

I said he must be awfully mad not to have his real mother just like he was mad about not having a bike. He didn't think mad was how he felt; he just felt very sad when he thought about it. I said I could see that, but it seemed he wasn't letting himself feel how mad he must be. I asked if he still cried about it and he said he does maybe once a year. I said one way not to feel things is not to think about them. I said I supposed it wasn't a very comfortable session today having to talk about things like that. He looked thoughtful for a long time and then began looking at things on my desk.

The therapist is trying to help him get in touch with his anger about losses.

Nineteenth Session

He started talking about how his dogs had been bad but he had kind of a grin as he talked about it. They dug holes in the lawn looking for bones and they chased dogs around the yard. I said none of that seemed too bad. It all seemed sort of natural for dogs to do that.

Twentieth Session

He was five minutes late. He strode boldly to open the doors which I thanked him for.

There was a silence and then he said that there was something else he had been thinking about; he had been thinking about energy. He thought about the men who were sent to the moon . . . whether they had just picked up some rocks and stuff. He thought it would have been more useful to send a spaceship to Mars because there was once life there which must mean that it was an energy source. He thought that they ought to work out how to get to Mars and how to bring back energy. He couldn't understand why people didn't plan ahead about energy long ago. He said it looked like there ought to be energy for a few more years but in 100 years there wouldn't. I said it looked like he was concerned not only about himself but about people after himself and he said he was. He thought that people should plan ahead and I said that sometimes people weren't very good about planning ahead. He said something about just spending your money the minute you get it and I said it didn't sound like he had been that way because of the way he had been saving up his money from earnings. He said that last year he really spent his money as soon as he got it but that he has been saving since then. He wants to save and pay for his own bus fares and things like that. He doesn't want to bother his parents. He said he used to just ask them for a dollar or a dollar and a half and they would just give it to him but he doesn't want to do that anymore. I said that it really was still their responsibility to take care of him but it looked like he kind of wanted to help in that and he said that he did. He then launched into some discussion about all the bills that his parents had to pay—$50 for this and $50 for that. I asked if they were worried about having to pay the bills and he thought they were not. I said that it sounded like he was kind of worrying about being in there and helping and he said he wasn't really worried. I had also asked him what had made him change from a year ago and he really didn't know. He is being overly responsible.

As is evidenced, initial support of his self-esteem eventually enabled John to become better able to criticize the therapist and from that to tentatively say some negative things about the other adults in his life. At the same time, he has become much more active in seeking accomplishments and successes. This case is still in treatment and therefore the important aspect of termination does not yet come into the therapy. Needless to say, this boy will need lots of work and preparation in order to be able to terminate without a recurrence of depression.

CHAPTER 19

Summing Up
on
the Depressed Child

E. JAMES ANTHONY, M.D.

In recalling Freud's definition of depression,

> A profoundly painful dejection, cessation of interest in the outside world, loss of capacity to love, inhibition of anxiety, and lowering of self-regard feelings to a degree that finds utterance in self-reproach and self-reviling culminates in a delusional expectation of punishment.[3]

One thing is clear: that depression during childhood in general displays the adult picture only sporadically and partially.

If one reviews classical psychoanalytic theory, as propounded by Freud and Abraham, depression is explicated as superego phenomenon containing within itself:

1. Aggression turned against itself (with superego attacks on the ego, self-reproachfulness, self-punishment and a trend toward masochism),

2. Excessive orality (with oral fixation, oral sadism, oral introjection and devouring, cannibalistic fantasies),

3. Heightened narcissism (with an increased need for narcissistic gratification, a poorly regulated self-esteem system, a disposition to narcissistic shock, insults and injury, a tendency to narcissistic breakdown because of the inability to live up to the ego ideal, a resulting sense of helplessness and impotence and inflated narcissistic aspirations and identifications),

4. Object loss (with increased ambivalence to lost object, destructive impulses toward the object, sense of guilt and wish to make restitution and reparation),

5. Regression (as a constant concomitant of severe depression with a return to pregenital levels of libidinal organization).

Viewed in this context, childhood depression, in its theoretical form, once again only shows itself sporadically and partially in terms of adult depression. Rochlin denied that depression as a superego phenomenon can occur in childhood because of the immaturity and weakness of the superego and the child's need for immediate substitution and restitution.[4] He sees the child's superego as wound up in an identification with the parents' superego and would therefore expect it to disappear with the loss of the parent. He would prefer to define the total reaction of the child as a "loss complex" based on the dread of abandonment. To a lesser extent, Mahler agrees with this point of view, feeling that systematized affective disorders are unknown in childhood due to the immature personality structure. Beres has reported on transitional states when the child's aggression is sometimes turned against himself but more frequently turned against objects in the outside world. He feels that it is important to differentiate between the child's attack on the body and on the self: the former is not infrequent whereas the latter is relatively rare.

Bibring[2] has suggested an ego psychological approach to due depression (in which orality, aggression turned against the self and secondary delusional phenomena are not essential features) that would both theoretically and phenomenologically fit the clinical picture of childhood depression and this is what Anthony has suggested as a framework for further clinical consideration and work.[1]

Departing from the individual context, one should not forget the importance of the family in the genesis and maintenance of depression in childhood. In such families, there is not only a high incidence of parental depression, a familial impotence in handling depression, a tendency to neglect, reject and depreciate the children, but also a curious interplay between outgoing aggressive reactions and ingoing depressive reactions. Each member of the family, in some way, appears to be struggling with this basic ratio of aggression to depression. As childhood progressed, both components of the ratio could be seen as part of a developing characterological disturbance.

The relationship of aggression to depression appears to be a complicated one. Sometimes a depression is seen as a defense against aggression and sometimes vice versa; sometimes a depression is seen as an identification with the depressed parent and with the aggressive aspects of the parental depression, and in the depressions of latency, children may act out antisocially for a while and then have a short period of depression. It would almost seem as if at this age the tolerance for sustained depression is extremely limited.

The criteria for making a clinical diagnosis of depression during childhood is based on the clinical appearance of the child (his sad, unhappy physiognomy), presenting symptoms (that include feelings of inferiority, of badness, of worthlessness), and on his general reactions of withdrawal, boredom, disinterest, apathy, discontentment and anhedonia. He looks and feels and is a miserable child. He feels rejected and unloved and yet is unwilling to accept comfort. He turns to his own body rather than to others for pleasure (autoeroticism) and those who deal with him have difficulty in establishing and maintaining a relationship. There is an air of immaturity about him due to the regression to oral passivity and the amount of undischarged and unneutralized aggression makes him a difficult and mixed-up customer in any emotional relationship. He is chronically ambivalent. He seems perpetually tired which is not surprising since one of his complaints is that of poor or disturbed sleep.

His main problem is dealing with the dread of depression against which he institutes a wide variety of defenses that includes obsessional controls, manic reversals, progressions, psychosomatic equivalents, denial and antisocial acting out.

The clinician, in an ongoing contact with the patient, may sometimes be confronted with normal transient sadnesses, sometimes with acute reactions to loss and failure with evidence of grief and mourning, sometimes to depressions resulting from vicissitudes of the separation-individuation process, sometimes to continuation of infantile privation of an anaclitic, affectionless character, sometimes to neurotic reactions to conflict that might be intermittent, subacute or chronic, sometimes to chronic rejections and neglect and psychopathic reactions oscillate with depression, sometimes to borderline depressions that are difficult to explain etiologically, and frequently to depressive equivalents reflected in inhibitions, somatic disorders and conduct problems.

Have we described childhood depression once and for all? Let me say, that in spite of this magic torrent of words, we are still only at the beginning of our clinical understanding. But it is not a bad beginning.

References

1. Anthony, E.J. (1975). Childhood Depression. *Depression and Human Existence.* Boston:Little, Brown, 231-278. (Eds. Anthony, E.J. & Benedek, T.).
2. Bibring, E. (1953). The mechanism of depression. *Affective Disorders.* (Ed. Greenacre, P.) New York:I.U.P.
3. Freud, S. (1957). Mourning and Melancholia (1917). *Standard Edition, Vol. 14,* p. 237.
4. Rochlin, G. (1965). *Griefs and Discontents.* Boston:Little, Brown.

Epilogue

January 23, 1974
Box 203, U C.M.C
4200 East 9th Avenue
Denver, Colorado 80220

To:
E. James Anthony, M.D.
President, International Association
 of Child Psychiatry and Allied
 Professions

Dear James:

Of course I can understand your "falling in love" with children at high
risk for future disturbances. You have always, like me I think, suffered from
Spinoza's "intellectual passion" for big unknowables. It is what drives us on.

Thank you for inviting me "to share my accumulated wisdom and experience" with the participants of the 8th International Congress. There is nothing I would like to do better for two reasons:

1. I want to know why some children seem so much more likely
   to become disturbed than other children,
2. I want to know why some children select one sort of disturbance
   to manifest rather than another.

It seems to me that I have been chasing these questions all my life. I would
not be so presumptuous as to claim that I had the answer, but perhaps I

251

have the beginnings of an answer—and this may be the best we can do at this time. You will not be surprised to learn of my belief that the secret is locked away in the early years about which we still know so little. I have oh so many films still unanalysed that present some aspect of the two vital problems being dealt with at the Congress, and I see at least twenty-years of hard work ahead of me* deciphering the many meanings. I wish I could come and share a little of this with all of you but although the spirit is willing, the flesh at the moment is very weak. I must leave it to you and others.

With warmest greetings as always to my old friend.

Prof. Dr. Med. René A. Spitz
University of Colorado Medical
  Center
Denver, Colorado

*Professor René Spitz died on the 29th of July, 1974.

During the preparation of this book, I wrote to Dr. David Levy for advice and although his health, too, was failing rapidly, he was ever ready to offer whatever he could to clarify aspects of his pioneering work on oppositionalism. An effort to write a preface, however, proved too much for him.

These two giant figures of our time have opened up new approaches to these three clinical problems of oppositionalism, inhibition and depression. It is up to us to carry the investigation further.

E. James Anthony, M.D

Subject Index